Gender inequalities in the risks of poverty and social exclusion for disadvantaged groups in thirty European countries

WITHDRAWN

Expert Group on Gender, Social Inclusion and Employment
The national experts and co-authors

Danièle Meulders and Jérôme de Henau (BE)
Iskra Beleva (BG)
Alena Křížková (CZ)
Ruth Emerek (DK)
Friederike Maier (DE)
Anu Laas (EE)
Ursula Barry and Sarah Murphy (IE)
Maria Karamessini (EL)
María Luisa Moltó and María Paszos Morán (ES)
Rachel Silvera (FR)
Paola Villa (IT)
Alexia Panayiotou (CY)
Ilze Trapenciere (LV)
Vida Kanopiene (LT)
Robert Plasman and Salimata Sissoko (LU)
Beáta Nagy (HU)

Roselyn Borg (MT)
Janneke Plantenga, Petra Helming and Chantal Remery (NL)
Ingrid Mairhuber (AT)
Ania Plomien (PL)
Virgínia Ferreira (PT)
Elena Zamfir (RO)
Aleksandra Kanjuo Mrčela (SI)
Magdalena Piscova (SK)
Anna-Maija Lehto (FI)
Anita Nyberg (SE)
Colette Fagan, Jill Rubery, Peter Urwin and Rory Donnelly (UK)
Lilja Mósesdóttir (IS)
Ulrike Papouschek (LI)
Anne Lise Ellingsæter (NO)

Colette Fagan, Peter Urwin and Kathryn Melling

European Commission
Directorate-General for Employment, Social Affairs and Equal Opportunities
Unit G.1

Manuscript completed in July 2006

This report was financed by and prepared for the use of the European Commission, Directorate-General for Employment, Social Affairs and Equal Opportunities. It does not necessarily represent the Commission's official position. Neither the Commission nor any person acting on its behalf is responsible for the use that might be made of the information contained in this publication.

If you are interested in receiving the 'ESmail' electronic newsletter from the European Commission's Directorate-General for Employment, Social Affairs and Equal Opportunities, please send an e-mail to empl-esmail@ec.europa.eu. The newsletter is published on a regular basis in English, French and German.

1	4	1: © Carl Cordonnier/Dailylife
2		2: © Carl Cordonnier/Dailylife
2	3	3: © Carl Cordonnier/Dailylife
		4: © Carl Cordonnier/Dailylife

Europe Direct is a service to help you find answers
to your questions about the European Union

Freephone number (*):
00 800 6 7 8 9 10 11

(*) Certain mobile telephone operators do not allow access to 00 800 numbers or these calls may be billed.

A great deal of additional information on the European Union is available on the Internet.
It can be accessed through the Europa server (http://europa.eu).

Cataloguing data can be found at the end of this publication.

Luxembourg: Office for Official Publications of the European Communities, 2006

ISBN 92-79-02572-4

Table of contents

Country abbreviations

BE	Belgium
BG	Bulgaria
CZ	Czech Republic
DK	Denmark
DE	Germany
IE	Ireland
EE	Estonia
EL	Greece
ES	Spain
FR	France
IT	Italy
CY	Cyprus
LV	Latvia
LT	Lithuania
LU	Luxembourg
HU	Hungary
MT	Malta
NL	The Netherlands
AT	Austria
PL	Poland
PT	Portugal
RO	Romania
SI	Slovenia
SK	Slovakia
FI	Finland
SE	Sweden
UK	United Kingdom
HR	Croatia
IS	Iceland
LI	Liechtenstein
NO	Norway
TR	Turkey

Executive summary

1.   Introduction

Gender mainstreaming is specified as a key requirement in the Social Inclusion Process; however, this
approach to policy design and monitoring is still
under-developed and often absent from National
Action Plans. The aim of this report is to inform and
help develop the gender mainstreaming of the Social
Inclusion Process, drawing on national reports for 30
European countries. It reviews gender differences and
inequalities in the risks of poverty and social exclusion, followed by chapters which focus on selected
examples of disadvantaged groups to illustrate the
relevance of gender mainstreaming for social inclusion policy.

2.   Gender differences and inequalities in the risks of social exclusion and poverty – a brief review

Gender differences and inequalities are a fundamental feature of social exclusion and poverty. Women are
less likely to secure a decent individual income
through employment. This is revealed by women's
lower employment rate, greater exposure to low pay
and more broadly by their lower average earnings.
These average gender gaps in employment are more
pronounced for particular subgroups, such as employment rates for older workers. Women accumulate
lower pension and other benefits where eligibility is
earnings-related or based on individual records of
employment history because of their lower average
earnings, greater likelihood of interrupting their
employment or working reduced hours to attend to
family care responsibilities, and the higher unemployment rates they experience in many countries. Social
welfare systems in most countries still rest on an
implicit and outdated policy assumption that women
have or should have access to the income of a male
'breadwinner' partner or derived benefits as his
dependent spouse. Gender inequalities in employment combined with design inadequacies in social
welfare systems produce a situation whereby poverty
is disproportionately borne by women or is 'feminised'. However, this gender perspective is often
absent from policy debates.

The common statistical indicators adopted for the
Social Inclusion Process provide some hints of the
gender inequalities in poverty and social exclusion.
The at-risk-of-poverty rate is higher for women than
men in 21 of 27 countries, there is a gender equal risk
in six countries and only in Poland is the average at-
risk rate higher for men than women (no data are
available for IS, LI, NO). However, this indicator may
underestimate the magnitude of women's greater risk
of poverty because it assumes household resources
are pooled and shared equally. Research has demonstrated resource inequalities between individual
members of households. In low-income households it
is common practice for women to have to manage the
domestic budget and to reduce their own consumption (food, clothes, heating when alone, leisure, etc.)
to protect the living standards of their male partners
and children.

Living on low income for a sustained period causes
stress and has negative impacts on housing quality,
health and social isolation. In addition to women's
greater exposure to poverty and low income, there
are gender differences in how men and women experience the stresses and social isolation of life on a low
income, as well as gender differences in health and
life expectancy, the experience of crime, and homelessness.

Clear gender differences are also apparent in many of
the other common indicators of poverty and social
exclusion. While these indicators often show that
women face the greater risk, in some the risks are
greater for men. Furthermore, the magnitude of the
gender gap varies according to which dimension of
social exclusion is being analysed within a country, as
well as across countries.

A gender-based analysis is essential for understanding the extent and form of social exclusion among disadvantaged groups within the population for three
distinct reasons.

- Some disadvantaged groups are numerically
  dominated by one sex. Many are female dominated, for example lone parents, older persons in
  low-income households, and victims of domestic
  violence and sex trafficking. Others are male

dominated, and include ex-prisoners, some types of homeless people (e.g. those sleeping rough), and early school leavers or drug abusers in some countries.

- A gender perspective is also relevant where the group membership is more evenly split by sex, for example among the Roma, migrants or disabled persons. This is so that salient differences in the causes, extent and form of social exclusion experienced by women and men can be identified

- Gender relations – or more precisely men's behaviour – are centrally implicated in a number of social problems: domestic violence, trafficking and prostitution, and most other forms of crime.

The concept of 'intersectionality' provides a more nuanced tool than that of 'double disadvantage' for understanding gender-based differences in exposure to various forms of discrimination and social exclusion. For example, how racism and gender discrimination combine to structure the experiences of women from ethnic minority groups. The premise of intersectionality is that gender discrimination, racism, class inequalities and other systems of discrimination interact to structure the relative position of women and men; pushing some to the extreme margins of society while others are more included. Hence women from an ethnic minority group have a substantively distinct experience to that of both men from the same minority group, and from women of the ethnic majority group. This approach also acknowledges that an individual can experience both oppression and privilege in society; for example a woman may occupy a high-status professional position yet still be exposed to racism or domestic violence. By applying the concept of intersectionality it is possible both to develop a gender mainstreaming perspective on social inclusion policy and to inject a greater awareness of inequalities among women into analysis which focuses on exposing the disadvantaged position of women vis-à-vis men in society.

3. The intersection of gender and age in risks of social exclusion – young and older people

The intersection of gender and age in risks of social exclusion is complex and changing. For example, among the younger generations women now achieve qualification levels which match or exceed those of their male peers. Yet other gender inequalities remain which disadvantage young women. Pronounced gender segregation by specialism in education and training means young women are often over-represented in areas which feed into lower-paid occupations; and women's greater propensity to become economically inactive in connection with family responsibilities also starts to open up in the early years of labour market participation. Processes of labour market discrimination mean women still secure lower labour market returns (earnings, career development) than men with similar qualifications and activity patterns.

The lower lifetime earnings of women impacts on their pensions in schemes built on individual earnings and employment records, thus increasing their risks of poverty in old age. In addition, while women benefit from a greater life expectancy compared with men, this also means that they predominate among the elderly, who are more disadvantaged than the younger retired (material assets, health, social isolation). Hence, not only do women predominate among the older age groups, but there are also gender-related differences in the extent and causes of social exclusion for older persons.

Gender gaps in age-related poverty and social exclusion risks

The risk of poverty varies by age group in most countries, and typically the young (16 to 24 years) and older (65+ years) age groups are the most vulnerable. Women are more at risk of poverty in both of these age groups, and the gender gap is particularly pronounced for older people. Gender disparities in poverty risks are also found for the intervening age groups. Summary indicators of common tendencies and difference across countries in the intersection of age and gender gaps are presented in Box 1.

The national differences in the size or direction of gender gaps in poverty and social exclusion for different age groups result from different labour market conditions and social welfare systems. For example, in the six countries where it is young men who face the greater risk of poverty the reasons are likely to lie in patterns of school leaving, industrial restructuring and gender-segregated employment opportunities (CY, DE, LU, PL, PT, SK). Similarly, gender gaps in the risk of poverty in old age are likely to be smallest where the pension system is largely based on citizenship rather than past employment and earnings; or where countries have achieved gender equality in lifetime earnings and labour market participation profiles. Other specific examples of the gender impact of different national policies for young or older people are also discussed, drawing on four national reports which chose to focus on age issues (CZ, EE, ES, IS).

4. Gender differences in rates of long-term unemployment and inactivity, rural poverty and the exclusion of disabled people

Women have a lower employment rate than men in all Member States and the gap is particularly pronounced in some countries. This is a key factor contributing to women's greater exposure to poverty and social exclusion, making them reliant on whatever individual benefit entitlements they have plus intra-household transfers (e.g. the earnings of a spouse or parent). Six national reports provided a detailed focus upon either the long-term unemployed, the hidden unemployed or 'returning mothers' following a period of parental leave or labour market absence (BG, CZ, HU, MT, PL, SK); three identified particular issues of inactivity and under-employment of women in rural areas (IT, PL, SI) and two focused on gender differences among people with disabilities (IE, SI). These national examples are drawn on in this chapter.

Gender gaps in long-term unemployment and inactivity rates and associated poverty risks

Rates of unemployment, long-term unemployment and inactivity vary significantly between countries, but in most cases the rates are higher for women (Box 2). The pattern and size of gender gaps vary between countries, as was the case for age-related comparisons, again demonstrating the relevance of monitoring at a national level for policy purposes.

Gender gaps in unemployment rates cannot be properly assessed without attention to inactivity rates. For example, the female long-term unemployment rate in

---

Box 1: Examples of statistical indicators of gender gaps in age-related risks of poverty and social exclusion, and national differences in the intersection of age and gender gaps

Young people

- Among young people, the **at-risk-of-poverty rate** is higher for women in 19 of the 25 EU countries shown (the exceptions are CY, DE, LU, PL, PT, SK).

- In most countries the **employment rate** for young women is notably lower than that for young men. This gender gap exceeds 10 percentage points in Estonia, Greece, Latvia, Slovenia and Spain. In contrast, the gender gap is small or non-existent in Denmark, the Netherlands and the United Kingdom, while in Sweden the employment rate for young women exceeds that of young men.

- **Early school leaving** heightens the risk of poverty and social exclusion. Overall rates vary across countries, but in 25 of the 29 countries shown (no data for LI) early school leaving is much more prevalent for young men. In another three the rate is slightly higher for boys (DE, IS, UK). The Czech Republic is somewhat exceptional with young women being more exposed to early school leaving.

- The average **youth unemployment rate** in the EU is slightly higher for young men than young women but there are important national differences in the size and direction of the gender gap. For example, recorded unemployment rates are higher for young women than young men in five countries (EL, ES, LU, PT, SI), while in six countries the unemployment rate is at least two percentage points higher for young men (CZ, DE, EE, LT, SK, UK).

- **Economic inactivity connected with motherhood** is also a factor for some young women, and inactivity due to family responsibilities can also mask some hidden unemployment. This is discussed in Chapter 4.

Older people

- The **at-risk-of-poverty rate** in old age is much higher for women in every country except the Netherlands.

- The gender gap in the **employment rate** is more pronounced than for young age groups and among those aged 55 to 64 years the rate is lower for women than for men in every country. The gender gap is smallest in Finland, Sweden, France and Estonia and reaches 40 percentage points in Cyprus and Malta.

- The *average exit age* is lower for women than men (the exceptions are BE, IE, HU, IT, NO, RO).

Box 2: Gender gaps in rates of unemployment, long-term unemployment and inactivity, and examples of national differences in the size of the gender gap

- **Unemployment rates** are higher for women than men in most European countries: in 2003 this applied in 19 of the 25 current Member States; with the reverse situation found in six countries (DE, FI, HU, IE, SE, UK).

- Women also have higher **inactivity rates** attributed to domestic responsibilities in every country. The size of the gender gap varies nationally and is smallest in the Nordic and Baltic states.

- Rates of **hidden unemployment** among the inactive are higher for women than for men in 24 of the 25 Member States (SE is the exception).

- The **long-term unemployment rate** is higher for women than men in 18 of the 25 EU countries shown (the exceptions are EE, IE, FI, HU, MT, SE, UK) although in four of the 18 countries (DK, LV, NL, SI) the gender discrepancy is slight.

- The **at-risk-of-poverty rates** are high for the economically inactive and unemployed, and the size and direction of the gender gap varies between different groups and across countries.

Malta is lower than that for men and is also relatively low by international standards, but this coexists with the highest female inactivity rate in the EU. Similarly, in Bulgaria the gender imbalance emerges in relation to inactivity but not long-term unemployment rates. Likewise, it is important to analyse the gender risks of poverty for specific categories of the non-employed with reference to the gender disparities found on other dimensions in order to interpret the overall gender impact of policies. For example, in Slovakia among the unemployed the at-risk-of-poverty rate is higher for men, but proportionally more women are long-term unemployed or inactive and live in a jobless household.

The policy objective of raising women's employment rates as one source of protection against poverty is congruent with the objectives of the European Employment Strategy and requires gender mainstreaming of active labour market programmes and enhanced reconciliation measures (childcare, working-time policies, etc.). It also raises broader issues for social inclusion policy, given that women (and men) who reduce their employment to fulfil care responsibilities increase their personal risks of poverty; which is rarely addressed explicitly or adequately in social protection systems.

Gender mainstreaming two other examples: rural populations and people with disabilities

Women in rural areas are particularly vulnerable to social exclusion, displacement and poverty in some Member States. The pattern and causes of rural poverty vary between countries, which is illustrated by the examples of Poland, Ireland, Italy and Slovenia. Typically, in rural areas, women have lower earnings from agriculture and are more exposed to unemployment and under-employment associated with agricultural restructuring. Among farm workers, women are more likely to be defined as 'family workers' rather than self-employed or employees – which can mean they have limited social protection cover. If women are in charge of a farm it is more likely to be small and generating low economic returns. Rural areas can include affluent households as well as impoverished ones, for example in Slovenia 'farm women' are more disadvantaged than non-agricultural 'rural women'. Other aspects of rural life also impact on the living conditions of women. Health, education and transport services are often more limited than in urban areas; farm work involves long hours and physically arduous work, and rural isolation can contribute to social problems.

A gender mainstreaming perspective is also important for exposing inequalities and differences in the experiences of people with disabilities. In some countries, including Ireland, rates of disability are higher for women, and among the disabled population women have higher rates of poverty. Among the disabled population of working-age, women have lower employment rates and lower earnings; among the economically inactive, they are more likely to be defined as 'engaged in home duties' while non-employed disabled men are more likely to be defined as 'unemployed' or to be in receipt of disability welfare payments.

5. Lone parents – a female-dominated category

Rates of lone parenthood vary across European countries and are mostly rising. In all countries the majority are female-headed households; accounting for 80 to 95% of all lone parents in most countries. The main entry route into lone parenthood is relationship breakdown for married or cohabiting couples; sole parenting (single women who become mothers without marrying or cohabiting) is much less common.

Previous international comparative research[1] has demonstrated that employment alone cannot ensure the economic well-being of lone mothers. Social welfare systems which provide a high 'social wage' for families in the form of benefits directed at children and their carers in conjunction with childcare services reduce the risks of poverty and stigmatisation for low parents. This is explored further in this chapter drawing on the 13 national reports which included a focus on the situation of lone parents (BG, EE, ES, FI, HU, IE, LI, LT, LU, MT, NO, SE, UK).

The risks of social exclusion and poverty faced by lone parents

Lone-parent households are vulnerable to poverty for several reasons. There are additional financial disadvantages and work–family reconciliation pressures when raising children single-handedly compared with the resources available in dual-parent households. The pressures of being the sole breadwinner are compounded for women because the wages they can obtain in the labour market are lower on average than those of men. Lone fathers are also disadvantaged; for example data from the United Kingdom, Spain and Ireland show that lone fathers have higher employment rates than lone mothers, but lower employment rates than other men. The minority of lone parents who are fathers may be disadvantaged in specific ways in some countries; for example in Ireland poverty rates are even higher for lone fathers.

The EU's statistical common indicators reveal that in each Member State the risk of poverty is much higher for lone parents than other women and men. The discrepancy is smallest in the EU Scandinavian countries (DK, FI, SE; comparable data not available for NO), demonstrating that the social democratic welfare state and employment systems in these countries

provide more social integration for lone parents than occurs in other national policy settings. However, lone parents in the Scandinavian countries are still economically disadvantaged compared with the situation of couple parent households.

Employment alone is insufficient to protect lone parents from poverty. In many countries the high poverty rates experienced by lone mothers coexist with an employment rate which matches or exceeds those of mothers in couple households yet still leaves lone mothers exposed to greater poverty risks. In a few countries, employment rates are lower for lone mothers compared with those for partnered mothers. This is a recent development in Sweden and Finland, following the economic recession of the 1990s, and appears to be partly because many of the job openings are low paid or require flexible working and so make it more difficult for lone parents to secure a viable income and work–family reconciliation. The disparity in employment rates (and poverty rates) is particularly great in the United Kingdom; here, lone mothers' employment rates have risen through targeted active labour market programmes ('New deal for lone parents') but nearly one in three of those who enter employment through the programme are not employed 12 months later, suggesting problems with the quality of job or childcare which they were able to secure.

In recent years the general direction of lone-parent policy in European countries has been targeted at promoting their employment; the so-called 'adult worker' model of integration. This has involved reform to social welfare benefits to increase financial inducements and 'make work pay' in conjunction with active labour market programmes and childcare support. The design and impact of these reforms varies nationally. While this policy approach can help to integrate lone mothers into employment, in itself employment may not reduce their poverty if the jobs available are low paid or insecure or if they are unable to access good quality childcare services and working-time arrangements. Hence the policy impact of the 'adult worker' model in particular national settings requires monitoring. Certainly, problems of childcare availability and cost remain in many countries, despite the Barcelona targets.

In some countries there have been recent reforms designed to increase the financial contribution of absent fathers. However, these initiatives have not always been successful, as demonstrated by the examples from Lithuania, Bulgaria and the United Kingdom.

(1)   Lewis, J. and Hobson, B. (1997), 'Introduction', in J. Lewis (ed.), *Lone mothers in European welfare regimes – Shifting policy logics*, Jessica Kingsley, London.

6. The intersection of gender and ethnicity in social exclusion – the Roma

There are possibly over 10 million Roma in Europe as a whole, and around one and a half million Roma joined the EU when the 10 new Member States acceded to the Union in May 2004. The Roma population is larger than the national population of some Member States and constitutes the largest ethnic minority group within the EU.

Systematic statistical data are lacking in most countries, but the various studies available show that the Roma community faces some of the most extreme forms of social exclusion and poverty in relation to all dimensions of life: political participation and civil rights; health; housing; education; labour market disadvantage; income and social welfare. Discrimination, racism and exclusionary treatment by the majority population are widespread and reduce the access of the Roma to public services. In some countries there are additional problems, such as language barriers, lack of documentation including statelessness, or high rates of enforced institutionalised care of Roma children. The prevailing pattern of economic survival is a marginalised existence of informal and subsistence work combined with social welfare dependency, often in segregated communities in remote or economically deprived areas.

The severely disadvantaged situation of the Roma is rooted in a history of persecution, racism and imposed assimilation programmes. Conditions deteriorated further during the economic and political disruption of the transition period in many of the post-communist countries, accompanied by renewed problems of persecution and statelessness across EU and non-EU countries.

The information on gender inequalities within the Roma is even scarcer; the evidence available indicates that Roma women have additional disadvantages to contend with. We develop this focus, drawing on information provided by eight national reports (BG, CY, CZ, EL, HU, SI, SK, RO).

The particular issues facing Roma women

Gender-based differences in family and economic roles mean that Roma women and men face different forms and degrees of poverty and exclusion. The particular problems faced by women are the following.

- *Traditional Roma culture prescribes family roles for women which limit their engagement in public and political life*
Women's main responsibility is family care work, and engagement in employment, civic or political life is discouraged. Marriages and first pregnancies occur at young ages (14 to 16 years is not uncommon for girls), and women bear a large number of children. These traditional family roles mean that Roma women are even more excluded from the political and civic life of the mainstream society; and one result is that they have more limited access than non-Roma women to legal services and other policy measures promoting gender equality.

- *Roma women have additional health risks connected to early and repeated pregnancies*
The health risks are compounded by their poverty and poor access to health and family planning services.

- *The legacy of forced sterilisation programmes which operated until recently in some countries*
There has been no compensation or public apology yet for the women who experienced forced sterilisation under government programmes which were still running in the early 1990s in some countries (e.g. the Czech Republic and Slovakia).

- *Poor housing conditions, a heavy domestic workload and exclusion from local services*
The domestic roles and workload of Roma women is more arduous than that for many non-Roma women: they have more children to look after; they contend with poor housing conditions and settlements which lack basic amenities (running water, heating); and they have poor access to local services (health, education, etc.), which makes it difficult for them to look after the needs of themselves and their families.

- *The educational disadvantage of the Roma – high rates of illiteracy and low qualification levels – is even more pronounced for Roma women*

- *High rates of unemployment and labour market disadvantage*
Roma women are even more constrained than Roma men to a limited range of low-paid and insecure work, often in the informal economy (street vendors, domestic work, farm work). This is because of the traditional cultural emphasis on their family roles and their lower educational opportunities. These jobs lack social protection and place the women in situations where they are vulnerable to low pay and exploitation.

Dependency on social welfare benefits

Many Roma depend on social welfare, but they often face discrimination or negative treatment from officials, and additional difficulties are faced by those who are nomadic. Women may face additional hurdles because they are even less likely to have accumulated an individual entitlement to insurance-based benefits through labour market participation; and traditional Roma marriages are rarely recognised in official law and this can cause major disadvantages for spouse-based eligibility for benefits, spouse visiting rights in prisons and hospitals, etc.

Prostitution and trafficking

In some countries Roma women are one of the groups who are vulnerable to being caught in prostitution and trafficking, due to extreme and deteriorating economic conditions; but this is not a generalised phenomenon across Europe, for traditional Roma culture forbids prostitution.

Domestic violence

For the Roma communities, several aspects of their living conditions can combine to heighten the risk of domestic violence. These include the material and psychological hardship of living in conditions of poverty and social exclusion, the additional pressures of economic turbulence and disruption, the stress of teenage marriage and parenthood, and a family system which has traditionally bestowed authority and higher social status upon men. Leaving a situation of domestic violence is difficult for all women, but Roma women face additional barriers if the only support services available are located outside the Roma community.

7. Immigrants and migrants

In this chapter, we bring a gender mainstreaming perspective to the risks of social exclusion of immigrants and recent migrants drawing on information provided by the national experts for 12 countries (AT, BE, CY, DE, DK, FR, IS, IT, LV, NL, NO, PT). Immigrant/migrant women account for between 5% and 9% of the female population in most of the 12 country case studies, rising to 19% in the Netherlands. The size of the migrant population is increasing in most of these countries, fuelled by cross-border inequalities in economic and political conditions. In some countries, such as France, Portugal and the Netherlands, there are new policy initiatives which aim to improve the particular situations of female immigrant and migrant workers. In some of the other countries, such as Austria or Latvia, gender mainstreaming is less well developed or missing from policy.

Not all migrants are disadvantaged; those who originate from countries with similar or higher living standards to those of the destination country face little disadvantage (particularly if they share the same colour skin and cultural background). Thus, in general, within the EU it is migrants from Africa, Asia and Latin America, Turkey and more recently from the central European countries (non-EU as well as EU members) who are the most disadvantaged. They migrate to more affluent countries, attracted by the prospect of higher living standards and compelled by political and economic problems in their home countries. They often have limited labour market opportunities on arrival. Typically they are recruited to fill vacancies in low-paid and unskilled jobs, some of which are in the informal economy. They are disadvantaged by a combination of economic and socio-cultural factors: language barriers, poor education or qualifications which are not recognised; race discrimination and xenophobia; and limited legal or economic rights. The undocumented workers who are illegal migrants have an even more precarious position. The extent and form of exclusion is shaped by the national policies in their host country (anti-discrimination legislation, training systems, eligibility in welfare systems, etc.).

The particular issues facing immigrant/migrant women

Migrants who are women can face additional disadvantages. Some enter as economically dependent spouses and this route may limit their independent rights to take employment or to secure social welfare. They may come from a cultural background where women have limited educational opportunities and where it is less acceptable for women to be in employment compared with the values and practices of the host population. They have to contend with sex discrimination as well as other discriminatory treatment and racism faced by migrants.

Documentation and status

National policies can operate in ways that make it more difficult for female immigrant/migrant workers to gain the greater legal security of being a 'documented' rather than 'undocumented' worker. For example, the 'key worker' permit in Austria does not cover domestic work, so much of this work is carried out informally and unregulated.

The status assigned to married women who arrive to join spouses under immigration provisions for family unification can be such that women are defined as economic dependents with no rights to seek employment; which has the effect of enforcing their economic dependence on a spouse.

Employment and unemployment rates
Male migrants typically have higher activity rates, including higher unemployment rates, than non-migrant males. Migrant women often have lower economic activity rates than non-migrant women, but not always. For women, the dynamics of the country of origin play an influential role: cultural factors, such as those concerning women's traditional economic roles, their qualification levels and whether women arrive as dependent family members (wives, daughters) or as independent (single) economic migrants, and the economic period in which the migrants arrive. All of these have influences which shape the labour market integration of migrant women also shape the experiences of second and subsequent generations of women. All of these have influences which shape the labour market integration of migrant women and shape the experiences of second and subsequent generations of women, as can be seen, for example, in the labour market patterns according to ethnic origin of women in the United Kingdom.

Job quality and working conditions of migrants
Labour markets are heavily segregated by race and migrant/non-migrant status as well as by gender. Migrants who secure employment are disproportionately concentrated in precarious and low-paid jobs and in the informal economy. Some work alongside non-migrant labour in better paid parts of the economy, but here the disadvantage is in the form of inferior terms of employment and greater vulnerability to job loss during recession.

Immigrant/migrant women are even more segregated into a narrow range of low-paid and largely female-dominated jobs than non-migrant women. They are largely concentrated in personal services and sales and particularly in cleaning and domestic service. One reason is that many migrant women have lower education levels. Others are highly qualified and their skills are under-used and diminish over time due to processes of discrimination, marginalisation and exclusion.

A growing number of migrant women are employed in private households as domestic workers (care services for children and elders, housework). Many are employed informally with limited social protection or employment rights. This form of employment has mushroomed in Italy where a large informal economy

is a general structural feature of the economy and where limited welfare state services have generated a demand in families for domestic workers to assist with the care of elderly relatives.

The working conditions of migrant women may compare favourably with the poor alternatives on offer in their origin country. However, this does not justify the poor working conditions under which they work in more affluent countries. Furthermore, their vulnerability is exacerbated by labour market marginalisation, which erodes their skills and where poor pay and long hours exclude them from full participation in society and makes it difficult to form or care for their own families.

Education and training (including language proficiency) and active labour market programmes
Poor qualification levels are common for many migrant women, and some have the additional obstacle of language barriers. However, some groups are highly educated and working below their qualification levels, for example many domestic workers who have migrated from central and eastern Europe.

Welfare and social protection systems
The inferior labour market position of women among migrant/immigrant groups means they are even less able to accumulate full entitlements under the social protection system, particularly if their employment is largely in the informal sector. Pension rights are often minimal even for those who have spent a large part of their working life in the host country. The problems are particularly severe in some countries, for example Austria. Even in welfare systems which are more inclusive, such as the Dutch system, the structure of eligibility presents potential problems for migrant women; particularly those with a limited work history or those who enter as a dependent partner through family reunion.

Government reforms, such as recent reforms in Denmark to 'make work pay', may impact more harshly on migrant recipients than on non-migrant claimants if they have inferior labour market prospects.

Access to childcare is also an important aspect of labour market integration for migrant women who are mothers. This can be a problem for migrant women even in countries with relatively good overall provision, for example in Norway.

French policy has a strong focus on promoting the social inclusion of immigrant and ethnic minority groups, in contrast to the low profile accorded this issue in many of the National Action Plans in other countries. A number of the reforms are positive, but although previous National Action Plans (NAPs) have identified the problem of the 'twofold discrimination' of migrant and ethnic minority women, gender mainstreaming analysis of the intersection of gender and origin has yet to be developed in social inclusion policy.

8. Violence and sexual abuse against women – domestic violence; human trafficking and prostitution

This chapter focuses upon women's exposure to violence and sexual abuse in two domains (domestic violence, and human trafficking and prostitution), drawing mainly on national reports from eight countries (BG, CY, EL, LT, MT, NO, PL, RO).

Men constitute the majority of the assailants and customers, and the majority of victims are women; although domestic violence also reaches young boys and some adult males, and disadvantaged young men are at risk of being drawn into prostitution (largely same-sex) through homelessness or drug addiction.

The scale of domestic violence, trafficking and prostitution is often underestimated, particularly when the estimates are based on statistics from reported crime. But, even on these underestimates, the problem is widespread. For example, the UK government estimates that 15.4 million incidents of domestic violence were committed in 2000–01 (of which 84% were against women) and that each week two women die as a result of domestic violence. Between a quarter of a million and half a million women and children are trafficked each year in Europe according to one study; and the problem is growing rapidly across the world, with central and eastern Europe, Africa and Latin America being the major origin regions for trafficking.

Women's exposure to domestic violence

Domestic violence occurs in rich as well as poor families. Women can be more exposed to this risk when relationships are put under additional strains, such as deteriorating or uncertain economic conditions for particular households or society more widely. In Romania, for example, the rapid social change and political uncertainties of the transition period appear to have been accompanied by an increase in violence against women, including domestic violence.

The problems faced by women who experience domestic violence are various and cumulative: victims suffer psychological as well as physical damage which produces an erosion of self-esteem and confidence. This psychological damage limits their ability to seek help, often compounded by their social isolation. It also impacts negatively on concentration and performance in employment, which can lead to job loss or exits. Many stay because they see no alternative – they lack the economic means to escape, divorce is difficult to secure or expensive, or they fear that their assailant will pursue and find them. Additional institutional obstacles exist where public policy does not provide means of support and escape because the problem is not recognised in legislation or police procedures, and where support services (e.g. counselling, refuges and resettlement) are lacking or inadequate. For example, marital rape is not a crime in Greece; while infrastructure to support victims (telephone helplines, emergency housing, counselling and legal services) is inadequate in Greece and Malta and entirely lacking in Romania.

Human trafficking and prostitution of women

Trafficking and prostitution is fuelled by poor social and economic conditions in societies. Poverty and unemployment combined with inadequate legal, police and social services create conditions in which traffickers can effectively target disadvantaged groups of young women and children. The most vulnerable are the poorly educated living in areas of high unemployment and poverty, particularly those with problems of debt or drug dependency, or those who were abused as a child or raised in institutional care.

Economic inequalities between countries create migrant flows of prostitutes, including those who are trafficked: most originate from poor transitional and developing countries, destined for more affluent countries. The collapse of communism has stimulated an increase in prostitution and trafficking across Europe, due to economic and political upheaval (reduced border controls and policy budgets, war zones), adding to trafficking from many other parts of the world. Trafficking flows have increased into and within the EU. Some countries are both countries of origin and destination; for example women are trafficked into Poland from poorer non-EU countries while Polish women are trafficked elsewhere in the EU. The most affluent EU Member States are mainly destination countries for trafficked women. Data for Lithuania give some indication of the profit to be made from trafficking. In the mid-1990s women were sold abroad for the average price of USD 5 000 to USD 7 000, which is very profitable in relation to income levels in Lithuania.

Women caught in prostitution and trafficking are trapped by similar factors to those experienced by victims of domestic violence (see above) plus additional aspects: being forcibly held against their will, sex slavery, sexually transmitted health risks, widespread drug dependency and psychological problems, and fear of prosecution, including deportation. The pattern of entrapment, control and human rights abuse from traffickers is similar, regardless of the country in which it happens. Many women are lured by deceptive offers of jobs as domestic workers, looking after children or working in hotels. Most are unaware that they will be working as prostitutes. A minority of them are sold into prostitution by their parents or husbands, or are kidnapped by trafficking rings. Their traffickers control them by withholding passports and identity documents, imprisonment, violence and drugs. Obviously they have little access to the social protection system, and their problems are confounded in many countries because they are committing a crime by working as a prostitute (the exceptions in our case studies are NO and PT).

9. Conclusions – gender mainstreaming policy directions and priorities for disadvantaged groups

This report has demonstrated that a gender-based analysis is essential for understanding the extent and form of social exclusion among disadvantaged groups in order to design and monitor policy.

Gender gaps in age-based risks of poverty among younger and older people, in unemployment and inactivity rates, and in rural poverty; gender disparities in patterns of social exclusion among disabled people

Women face higher poverty risks when young in many countries and when old in all countries (the Netherlands is an exception). The scale of gender disparities varies between age groups and across countries, demonstrating the relevance of monitoring trends at national level. Furthermore, the analysis for young people shows that, in some indicators, the situation is worse for men (rates of early school

leaving in most countries) while, in others, young women are in the worst position (at-risk-of-poverty rates).

Women's disadvantaged labour market position means they accumulate fewer individual rights to pensions and other social welfare payments in systems where entitlement is closely based on an individual record of employment contributions or earnings. Systems which provide contribution credits for periods of part-time employment or economic inactivity connected with family responsibilities provide some partial compensation; but this does not fully address the negative impact of gender inequalities in care responsibilities on women's individual earnings and pensions. Consequently many women are dependent upon derived benefits as spouses or upon means-tested social assistance; and currently both are inadequate forms of social protection as the example of women's high poverty rates in old age demonstrates. Hence, as long as there are gender inequalities in the labour market, the levels of guaranteed minimum income provided under social welfare systems will remain a key factor in improving the social protection of women from poverty.

Hence, a gender perspective is relevant for the design and evaluation of a range of policies including education, training and lifelong learning; unemployment benefits and labour market programmes; work–family reconciliation measures; active ageing, pensions and retirement; and elderly care services. It also exposes the relevance of gender impact analysis for a wider range of polices, such as rural economic policy.

To achieve coordinated supply and demand side policies which tackle gender inequalities thus requires a gender mainstreaming approach which is applied consistently across the parallel policy tools of the Social Inclusion Process and the European Employment Strategy.

Lone parents are mostly women

Poverty rates are high for lone parents. Their disadvantage is minimised under the welfare state and employment systems of Scandinavian countries, which provide a high 'social wage' to all parents via child-related benefits and extensive childcare services. Policies are required across a range of areas – to increase lone parents' employment rates in countries where rates are low, to increase the rates of pay they can command in employment (such as training programmes for low-qualified lone parents), better childcare services and child-related income benefits.

Roma women

The recent racism and race discrimination directives have extended the legal protection afforded to the Roma. There is also a new Community Action Programme as well as various other policy initiatives by national governments and international agencies (e.g. 'Decade of Roma inclusion 2005–15'). However, a recent evaluation for the European Commission concluded that the disadvantage of the Roma population will only be effectively tackled with a more coordinated, comprehensive policy programme that addresses the various domains of exclusion together (health, housing, education, employment, legal services, racism) and that extensive consultation and involvement of the Roma in the policy design and delivery is a key ingredient for the success of programmes.

Many of these policy initiatives are silent on the problem of gender inequality; yet the intersection of ethnicity and gender compounds the disadvantages that Roma women face. Currently, when measures are targeted at women they usually focus on their role as mothers as a conduit for improving the situation of their children. A wider and gender mainstreamed focus of all programmes is needed which incorporates targeted provisions for Roma women.

Efforts to increase the education and employment of Roma women can come into conflict with traditional values concerning appropriate gender roles in some parts of the Roma communities. Hence, policy consultation and involvement has to be designed to reach the different interest groups and the voices of Roma women as well as men. This can be resource intensive, but productive, as illustrated by the example of a programme introduced in Slovenia ('Roma women can do it' – E Romane Džuvlja Ŝaj).

Statistical indicators are important for identifying and monitoring gender inequalities within ethnic groups, yet currently this is lacking or at best limited in many European countries. Extending statistical monitoring of the Roma and some other ethnic groups is politically sensitive in many countries; but this lack of information is double-edged. It can offer some protection from surveillance and persecution, but it also means evidence is lacking for policy evaluation or for information campaigns to counter racism and discrimina-

tion. The key point here is that a gender-based breakdown must be built into any extension of statistical monitoring.

Migrant and immigrant women

Migrant and immigrant women – particularly those from non-western countries – are poorly integrated into the labour market. Usually they have lower employment rates and higher unemployment rates than non-migrant women in the host country, and poorer employment conditions because they are concentrated in particularly low-paid and unregulated parts of the economy. Some economic sectors are quite dependent on their labour such as sales, catering, cleaning and other low-paid service jobs. More and more migrant women are employed, often informally, in private households to look after children or elderly relatives and to do housework. Their labour market disadvantage is compounded by poor social protection coverage, thus exposing them to greater risks of poverty. Some government reforms to social assistance systems, for example in Denmark, may increase the risk of impoverishment for immigrant households.

Some countries have introduced policies which aim to improve the situation of migrant workers, but if gender differences in needs and skills are not identified then the programmes may be less successful at reaching women. Some countries have introduced new or stronger anti-discrimination legislation which increases the protection that migrants may acquire; but where issues of race and sex discrimination are dealt with by separate legislation and agencies there is a risk that the specific problems migrant women face from the combination of sex and race discrimination may not be adequately addressed because of an institutional division of responsibilities.

In order to generate a better understanding of the specific needs and disadvantages faced by migrant/immigrant women from different countries of origin and in different destination countries, more research is needed as a basis for gender mainstreaming social inclusion policy.

Violence against women – the examples of domestic violence and of trafficking and prostitution

Violence and sexual abuse of women is widespread, yet the scale of the problem is often underestimated in public policy and is rarely a priority objective accompanied by a comprehensive action programme and adequate budget.

The gender dimension is rarely acknowledged explicitly and tackled directly – the fundamental problem is that much of the violence and sexual abuse in society is committed by men against women and children.

Across countries, the causes and effects of these types of violence and abuse are similar, but national differences in policy can be seen in the strength and breadth of the legal framework, support services and preventative measures. The scale of the problem is also different, depending on whether it is a country of origin or destination for trafficking. There may also be national differences in the prevalence of domestic violence, but the information is not available to make this assessment.

In most of the countries discussed in this chapter there have been new policy initiatives in recent years to tackle the problems of domestic violence and trafficking; including legal reform, public awareness campaigns and new resources for services to tackle domestic violence; and extended and more coordinated national and cross-border programmes to tackle trafficking and help women who are trafficked. However, persistent problems include weak legal provisions; vastly inadequate resource levels; poor coordination across the police, the judiciary and support agencies; lack of transnational collaboration on the problem of trafficking; lack of research, services and longer-term social inclusion policies to identify and protect high-risk groups.

What is missing in most countries is a systematic policy approach to address men's behaviour and to reduce the scale of the problem – initiatives targeted at men to stop violent and aggressive behaviour and to regulate and reduce the male-dominated consumer demand for the sex industry. The focus is largely on legal measures to prosecute men who are caught trafficking, running prostitution or committing domestic violence. Norway is one exception where there have been some efforts to reduce the demand for prostitution by forbidding state employees and the armed forces from purchasing sex; however, the policy has been criticised for failing to take a wider approach, such as criminalising the purchase of sex. More broadly, the linkage between these specific policy areas and reducing gender inequalities are not always made in official policy statements. They need to be, for increasing women's independent economic means and social status is a prerequisite for helping women to avoid or escape abusive situations.

Finally, three general points ...

Firstly, the Social Inclusion Process needs to develop systematic monitoring of gender disparities within disadvantaged groups to support gender impact analysis and gender mainstreaming within the National Action Plans. Monitoring average gender differences is ineffective for pinpointing the precise causes and identifying where progress in closing gender gaps is and is not being made.

Secondly, gender mainstreaming emphasises the relevance of a lifecourse perspective for social integration policy; for example the lone parents who are living in poverty today may become the older women who are particularly at risk of poverty in their old age.

Thirdly, some problems which women face cannot be fully appreciated and addressed without a transnational focus, such as migrant labour, trafficking or the size of the Roma population when assessed from a European rather than national vantage point.

Sommaire

1. Introduction

Si l'intégration du genre figure comme élément essentiel dans le Processus d'Inclusion Sociale, cette approche reste sous-utilisée dans l'élaboration et le contrôle des politiques et est souvent absente des Plans d'Action Nationaux (PAN). L'objectif de ce rapport, basé sur les études nationales de trente pays européens, est de contribuer au développement de l'approche intégrée de genre dans le Processus d'Inclusion Sociale. Il examine les disparités et inégalités hommes-femmes face aux risques de pauvreté et d'exclusion sociale et se focalise sur des exemples de groupes défavorisés afin d'illustrer la pertinence de l'intégration du genre dans les politiques d'inclusion sociale.

2. Disparités et inégalités hommes-femmes face aux risques d'exclusion sociale et de pauvreté – Rappel

Les disparités et les inégalités entre les sexes sont au cœur de l'exclusion sociale et de la pauvreté. L'emploi ne suffit pas à assurer un revenu individuel acceptable pour les femmes, comme en témoigne le fait que leur taux d'emploi est plus faible, qu'elles sont plus exposées au risque de bas salaires et, plus généralement, qu'elles perçoivent en moyenne des rémunérations inférieures. Ces disparités moyennes sont particulièrement prononcées pour certaines sous-catégories, par exemple les taux d'emploi des travailleurs plus âgés. Lorsque l'éligibilité est liée au parcours professionnel individuel, le niveau des pensions ou des autres allocations dont les femmes bénéficient est souvent inférieur étant donné que leurs salaires moyens sont moins élevés, que les possibilités d'interruption de leur activité professionnelle ou de réduction de leur temps de travail pour se consacrer à leurs responsabilités familiales sont plus importantes et que le taux de chômage féminin est plus élevé dans de nombreux pays. Les systèmes de protection sociale restent, dans la plupart des pays, basés sur le modèle implicite et dépassé de l'homme représentant le principal facteur de revenu et sur l'octroi de droits dérivés. Les inégalités hommes-femmes face à l'emploi, liées à l'inadéquation des systèmes de protection sociale, créent fréquemment une situation de dénuement chez les femmes: leur risque de pauvreté est plus élevé. Cette dimension reste cependant souvent absente des débats politiques.

Les indicateurs statistiques communs adoptés dans le cadre du Processus d'Inclusion Sociale laissent entrevoir les inégalités hommes-femmes en ce qui concerne la pauvreté et l'exclusion sociale. Le taux de «risque de pauvreté» est plus élevé pour les femmes dans vingt et un pays sur vingt-sept, identique à celui des hommes dans six pays, et ce n'est qu'en Pologne que le taux de risque moyen est plus élevé pour les hommes que pour les femmes (pas de chiffres pour l'Islande, le Liechtenstein et la Norvège). Il se peut cependant que cet indicateur sous-estime l'ampleur du risque de pauvreté des femmes puisqu'il part du principe que les ressources du ménage sont mises en commun et également partagées. Des études ont démontré que les ressources du ménage peuvent être inégalement partagées. Dans les ménages à faibles revenus, il est courant que la femme ait à gérer le budget familial et réduise sa propre consommation (alimentation, habillement, chauffage lorsqu'elle est seule, loisirs, etc.) afin de protéger le niveau de vie de son conjoint et des enfants.

Vivre avec de faibles revenus sur une longue période est un facteur de stress et a un effet négatif sur la qualité du logement, la santé et l'isolement social. Outre le risque plus élevé de pauvreté et de bas revenus pour les femmes, le stress et l'isolement social qu'entraînent de faibles revenus sont vécus différemment par les hommes que par les femmes. Ces différences sont également vraies en matière de santé et d'espérance de vie, d'expérience de la criminalité ou de situation de privation de domicile fixe.

Ces disparités hommes-femmes sont évidentes à la lecture de nombreux autres indicateurs de pauvreté et d'exclusion sociale. Si elles s'observent généralement au désavantage des femmes, dans certains cas, les risques de pauvreté ou d'exclusion sont plus élevés pour les hommes. Les écarts de genre varient également selon la dimension de la pauvreté et de l'exclusion qui est considérée, que ce soit à l'intérieur du pays ou à un niveau international.

Une analyse fondée sur le sexe s'impose pour comprendre l'ampleur et la forme de l'exclusion sociale des groupes défavorisés, pour trois raisons bien distinctes:

- selon les groupes défavorisés, les hommes ou les femmes peuvent y être majoritaires. Les femmes prédominent dans de nombreux groupes, comme les parents isolés, les personnes âgées dans des ménages à faibles revenus, les victimes de violence domestique et de traite d'individus. Les hommes prédominent dans d'autres: c'est le cas des anciens détenus et de certains groupes de sans-abri, de jeunes en rupture scolaire ou de toxicomanes dans certains pays;

- la prise en compte du genre est également pertinente lorsque la répartition hommes-femmes est plus égale au sein d'un groupe, par exemple parmi les Roms, les migrants ou les invalides. Elle permet de mettre en évidence les disparités hommes-femmes les plus prononcées en ce qui concerne les causes, l'ampleur et la forme de l'exclusion sociale vécue;

- les rapports entre les sexes – et plus particulièrement les comportements masculins – sont au cœur de nombreux problèmes sociaux: violence domestique, traite d'êtres humains et prostitution et la plupart des formes de criminalité.

La notion de croisement, ou de recoupement, fournit un instrument plus précis que celle de «double handicap» pour comprendre les disparités face aux risques de discrimination et d'exclusion sociale. Par exemple, comment le racisme et la discrimination hommes-femmes se combinent dans le vécu des femmes appartenant aux groupes ethniques minoritaires. La notion de recoupement ou de croisement repose sur le principe que la discrimination entre les sexes, le racisme, les inégalités sociales et autres systèmes discriminatoires se combinent pour déterminer la situation relative des femmes et des hommes, certains se retrouvant particulièrement marginalisés alors que d'autres sont mieux inclus. C'est ainsi que l'expérience vécue par les femmes des groupes ethniques minoritaires diffère sensiblement de celle des hommes appartenant au même groupe, comme de celle des femmes du groupe ethnique majoritaire. Cette approche tient compte également du fait qu'un individu peut connaître simultanément oppression et privilèges au sein de la société: une femme peut ainsi avoir un statut professionnel élevé tout en étant exposée au racisme ou à la violence domestique. Appliquer la notion de croisement permet d'élaborer une perspective sexuée des politiques d'inclusion sociale tout en introduisant une plus grande prise de conscience

des inégalités parmi les femmes dans une analyse qui vise à mettre en évidence la position défavorisée des femmes dans la société.

3. Croisement du sexe et de l'âge dans les risques d'exclusion sociale – Les jeunes et les personnes plus âgées

Le croisement du sexe et de l'âge dans les risques d'exclusion sociale est un phénomène complexe et évolutif. Les jeunes femmes sont au moins aussi qualifiées, sinon plus, que leurs homologues masculins. Mais, malgré cela, des inégalités sexuelles persistantes défavorisent les femmes jeunes. La ségrégation marquée dans les filières d'enseignement et de formation entraîne une surreprésentation des jeunes femmes dans des emplois faiblement rémunérés; en outre, leur probabilité d'inactivité économique, du fait de responsabilités familiales, est plus élevée dans les premières années de participation au marché du travail. À niveau égal de qualification et pour des modalités similaires de participation au marché du travail, les discriminations de genre induisent toujours une rémunération inférieure (salaires, progression de carrière) pour les femmes.

Les plus faibles rémunérations cumulées des femmes affectent négativement leurs pensions de retraite lorsque les régimes sont axés sur le salaire individuel et le parcours professionnel, et les exposent donc davantage au risque de pauvreté lorsqu'elles sont âgées. En outre, comme les femmes jouissent d'une plus grande longévité que les hommes, elles prédominent parmi les retraités les plus vieux, dont les conditions de vie et de santé sont plus problématiques que celles des retraités plus jeunes (biens matériels, santé, isolement social). Les différences de genre dans le degré et les causes d'exclusion sociale des personnes âgées se combinent donc avec la surreprésentation féminine parmi les seniors les plus vieux.

Écarts hommes-femmes en matière de pauvreté et de risques d'exclusion sociale liés à l'âge

Le risque de pauvreté varie selon le groupe d'âge dans la majorité des pays: les jeunes (16-24 ans) et les personnes âgées (65 ans et plus) y sont le plus exposés, et parmi eux surtout les femmes; l'écart hommes-femmes est particulièrement prononcé parmi les personnes plus âgées. On observe également ces écarts fondés sur le sexe dans les groupes d'âge intermédiaires. Dans l'encadré 1, le croisement entre groupe d'âge et indicateurs d'écarts de genre selon plusieurs dimensions indique à la fois des tendances communes et des particularités nationales.

Les disparités nationales relatives à l'ampleur et à la tendance des écarts fondés sur le sexe face à la pauvreté et à l'exclusion sociale pour les groupes d'âge différents s'expliquent par la disparité des conditions du marché de l'emploi et des systèmes de protection sociale. C'est ainsi que, dans les six pays où les jeunes hommes sont le plus exposés au risque de pauvreté, l'explication réside probablement dans les modalités de déscolarisation, de restructuration industrielle et de ségrégation fondée sur le sexe des possibilités de participation au marché du travail (Allemagne, Chypre, Luxembourg, Pologne, Portugal et Slovaquie). De même, les écarts fondés sur le sexe du risque de pauvreté des personnes âgées ont tendance à baisser lorsque les régimes de retraite sont fonction de la citoyenneté plutôt que du parcours professionnel et du salaire cumulé ou dans les pays ayant mis en place l'égalité hommes-femmes en matière de salaires cumulés et de profils de participation. D'autres exemples précis de l'impact sexué des politiques nationales sur les jeunes et les personnes âgées sont examinés à partir de quatre rapports nationaux qui se sont focalisés sur les questions liées à l'âge (Espagne, Estonie, Islande et République tchèque).

4. Disparités hommes-femmes dans les taux de chômage et d'inactivité à long terme, de pauvreté rurale et d'exclusion des personnes invalides

Les taux d'emploi féminins sont inférieurs aux taux masculins dans tous les pays membres et l'écart est

---

Encadré 1: Exemples d'indicateurs statistiques des écarts fondés sur le sexe dans les risques de pauvreté et d'exclusion sociale liés à l'âge, et des disparités nationales en croisant écarts d'âge et différence de sexe

Les jeunes

- Parmi les jeunes, le **taux de «risque de pauvreté»** est plus élevé pour les femmes dans 19 des 25 pays membres représentés (la situation est différente pour l'Allemagne, Chypre, le Luxembourg, la Pologne, le Portugal et la Slovaquie).

- Dans la plupart des pays, le **taux d'emploi** des femmes est sensiblement inférieur à celui des hommes parmi les jeunes. Cet écart fondé sur le sexe dépasse les dix points de pourcentage en Estonie, en Grèce, en Lettonie et en Slovénie. En revanche, l'écart est faible ou non existant au Danemark, aux Pays-Bas et au Royaume-Uni, tandis que le taux d'emploi des jeunes femmes est plus élevé en Suède.

- La **déscolarisation** accentue les risques de pauvreté et d'exclusion sociale. Les taux globaux varient d'un pays à l'autre mais dans vingt-cinq pays (vingt-neuf pays représentés, pas de chiffres pour le Lichtenstein) le décrochage scolaire affecte beaucoup plus les garçons. Dans trois autres pays, le taux de décrochage est légèrement supérieur pour les jeunes hommes (Allemagne, Islande et Royaume-Uni). La République tchèque représente une exception, les filles y présentant un plus grand risque de déscolarisation que les garçons.

- Le **taux de chômage juvénile** moyen dans l'Union européenne (UE) est légèrement supérieur pour les hommes, mais des disparités nationales importantes sont observées quant à la magnitude et à la tendance de l'écart. C'est ainsi que dans cinq pays (Grèce, Espagne, Luxembourg, Portugal et Slovénie) les taux de chômage constatés sont plus élevés pour les jeunes femmes que pour les jeunes hommes, tandis que dans six autres pays (République tchèque, Allemagne, Estonie, Lituanie, Slovaquie et Royaume-Uni) le taux de chômage masculin est supérieur de deux points au moins.

- **L'inactivité économique liée à la maternité** intervient pour certaines jeunes femmes. L'inactivité due aux responsabilités familiales peut cacher une forme de chômage, comme l'examine le chapitre 4.

Les personnes âgées

- **Le taux de «risque de pauvreté»** pour les personnes âgées est bien plus élevé pour les femmes, dans tous les pays, à l'exception des Pays-Bas.

- L'écart hommes-femmes en ce qui concerne le **taux d'emploi** est plus marqué que pour les plus jeunes. Pour les 55-64 ans ce taux est plus faible pour les femmes que pour les hommes dans tous les pays. L'écart est le plus faible en Estonie, en France, en Finlande et en Suède mais atteint quarante points de pourcentage à Chypre et à Malte.

- L'âge moyen **de sortie du marché de l'emploi** est plus bas pour les femmes (les exceptions étant la Belgique, l'Irlande, l'Italie, la Hongrie, la Norvège et la Roumanie).

particulièrement prononcé dans certains pays. Il s'agit là d'un facteur clé qui contribue à la plus grande vulnérabilité des femmes en matière de pauvreté et d'exclusion sociale et les rend dépendantes des droits individuels aux prestations ainsi que des transferts possibles à l'intérieur du ménage (comme le salaire d'un conjoint ou d'un parent). Six rapports nationaux se sont focalisés sur les chômeurs de longue durée, le chômage caché, ou les mères «en reprise d'activité» à la suite d'un congé parental ou d'une absence du marché de l'emploi (Bulgarie, Hongrie, Malte, Pologne, République tchèque et Slovaquie); trois rapports ont mis en évidence les questions d'inactivité et de sous-emploi des femmes dans les zones rurales (Italie, Pologne et Slovénie) tandis que deux rapports ont porté sur les disparités hommes-femmes chez les invalides (Irlande et Slovénie). Ce chapitre développe ces situations nationales.

Écarts fondés sur le sexe dans le chômage de longue durée, taux d'inactivité et risques de pauvreté induits

Les taux de chômage, de chômage de longue durée et d'inactivité varient considérablement d'un pays à un autre mais, dans la plupart des cas, ces taux sont plus élevés pour les femmes (encadré 2). La tendance et l'ampleur des écarts hommes-femmes enregistrent des disparités nationales, comme c'était le cas pour les comparaisons basées sur les groupes d'âge, ce qui atteste une fois de plus de la pertinence des suivis nationaux en matière de politiques.

Il est impossible d'évaluer correctement les écarts fondés sur le sexe des taux de chômage si l'on ne prend pas en compte les taux d'inactivité. C'est ainsi que le taux de chômage féminin à long terme pour Malte, qui est inférieur au taux masculin et est relativement bas par rapport aux normes internationales, va de pair avec le taux d'inactivité féminine le plus élevé de l'Union. Pareillement, un déséquilibre hommes-femmes est enregistré en Bulgarie en termes d'inactivité mais pas pour les taux de chômage à long terme. Il importe également d'analyser les risques sexués de la pauvreté pour des catégories spécifiques de personnes non-occupées en se référant aux écarts fondés sur le sexe observés dans d'autres domaines, afin de pouvoir interpréter l'impact fondé sur le sexe global des politiques suivies. En Slovaquie, par exemple, le taux de «risque de pauvreté» est plus fort pour les hommes parmi les chômeurs mais une proportion plus importante de femmes sont chômeuses de longue durée, inactives ou vivent dans un ménage sans emploi.

L'accroissement des taux d'emploi féminins comme protection contre la pauvreté est un objectif conforme à ceux de la stratégie européenne pour l'emploi; il nécessite l'intégration du genre dans les mesures actives de l'emploi en même temps que des mesures renforçant l'articulation entre vie professionnelle et vie privée (garde des enfants, temps de travail). Il fait également intervenir des questions plus générales d'inclusion sociale étant donné que les femmes (et les hommes) qui réduisent leur activité pour assurer la garde des enfants accroissent leur risque de pauvreté, un phénomène qui est rarement traité explicitement ou adéquatement dans les systèmes de protection sociale.

Deux autres exemples d'intégration du genre: les populations rurales et les invalides

Dans les zones rurales de certains pays membres, les femmes sont particulièrement soumises au risque d'exclusion sociale, de déplacement et de pauvreté. Les modalités et les causes de pauvreté rurale varient entre pays, comme l'illustrent les cas de l'Irlande, de l'Italie, de la Pologne et de la Slovénie. Dans les zones rurales, les femmes occupées dans le secteur agricole perçoivent généralement des rémunérations plus faibles et sont plus exposées aux risques de chômage et de sous-emploi associés au processus de restructuration du secteur agricole. Parmi les travailleurs agricoles, les femmes sont plus susceptibles d'être considérées comme des «aides familiales» que comme des travailleuses indépendantes ou des salariées, ce qui peut réduire leur protection sociale. Lorsque les femmes dirigent une exploitation agricole, il s'agit le plus souvent d'une petite exploitation à faible rendement économique. Les zones rurales peuvent inclure des ménages à revenus élevés ainsi que des ménages pauvres; en Slovénie les «agricultrices» sont plus défavorisées que les «femmes rurales» en dehors du secteur agricole. D'autres aspects de la vie rurale affectent les conditions de vie des femmes. Les services de la santé, de l'éducation et des transports sont souvent plus limités qu'en milieu urbain. Le travail agricole entraîne de longs horaires et un travail physique pénible. En outre, l'isolement rural peut entraîner des problèmes d'ordre social.

Une perspective d'intégration du genre s'impose également pour mettre en évidence inégalités et disparités de l'expérience des personnes invalides. Dans certains pays, dont l'Irlande, les taux d'invalidité sont plus élevés pour les femmes, et parmi les

---

Encadré 2: Écarts fondés sur le sexe des taux de chômage, de chômage à long terme et d'inactivité et disparités nationales dans l'ampleur des écarts

- **Les taux de chômage** sont plus élevés pour les femmes que pour les hommes dans la plupart des pays européens. C'était le cas en 2003 pour dix-neuf pays sur vingt-cinq des pays membres, une situation inverse étant constatée dans six pays (Allemagne, Irlande, Hongrie, Finlande, Suède et Royaume-Uni).

- Les femmes connaissent des **taux d'inactivité** plus élevés qui sont attribués aux responsabilités familiales dans tous les pays. L'ampleur de l'écart hommes-femmes varie d'un pays à l'autre et est moins importante dans les pays nordiques et baltes.

- Les taux de **chômage caché** parmi les inactifs sont plus forts pour les femmes dans vingt-quatre pays sur vingt-cinq des pays membres (la Suède étant l'exception).

- Le **taux de chômage de longue durée** est plus élevé pour les femmes que pour les hommes dans dix-huit pays sur vingt-cinq des pays membres (les exceptions étant l'Estonie, l'Irlande, la Hongrie, Malte, la Finlande, la Suède et le Royaume-Uni) bien que quatre des dix-huit pays (Danemark, Lettonie, Pays-Bas et Slovénie) enregistrent de faibles disparités hommes-femmes.

- Les **taux de risque de pauvreté** sont élevés pour les inactifs et les chômeurs, et l'ampleur et la tendance de l'écart hommes-femmes varient entre groupes et pays.

---

invalides les femmes enregistrent des taux de pauvreté plus importants. Dans la population invalide en âge de travailler, les femmes ont des taux d'emploi et des revenus plus faibles; parmi les inactifs, les femmes sont plus susceptibles d'être classées comme «se consacrant à d'autres responsabilités» tandis que les hommes en incapacité et non occupés sont plus souvent considérés comme «chômeurs» ou perçoivent des allocations d'invalidité.

5. Parents isolés – Un groupe à prédominance féminine

La proportion de parents isolés varie d'un pays européen à un autre et est généralement en hausse. Dans tous les pays, il s'agit principalement de ménages dirigés par une femme, ce qui représente de 80 à 95 % de tous les parents isolés dans la majorité des pays. Dans la plupart des cas, l'isolement parental se produit à la suite d'une rupture de couples mariés ou en cohabitation; la monoparentalité (des femmes seules qui ont des enfants sans se marier ou sans cohabiter) est bien moins courante.

Des études comparatives internationales[1] ont montré que l'emploi ne suffisait pas à garantir la sécurité économique des mères isolées. Les régimes de protection sociale qui prévoient un «salaire social» élevé pour les familles, sous la forme d'allocations visant les enfants et les personnes qui en ont la charge, et qui s'accompagnent de services d'accueil, réduisent le risque de pau-

vreté et de stigmatisation des parents isolés. Ce principe est examiné plus en détail dans ce chapitre qui se fonde sur les treize études nationales ayant pris en compte la situation des parents isolés (Bulgarie, Espagne, Estonie, Finlande, Hongrie, Irlande, Liechtenstein, Lituanie, Luxembourg, Malte, Norvège, Royaume-Uni et Suède).

Risques d'exclusion sociale et de pauvreté auxquels sont confrontés les parents isolés

Les familles monoparentales sont plus exposées au risque de pauvreté pour nombre de raisons. Élever seul(e) des enfants entraîne des désavantages financiers supplémentaires et des problèmes d'harmonisation entre la vie professionnelle et la vie privée. Le problème est d'autant plus aigu pour les mères isolées qui sont soutiens de famille que les rémunérations qu'elles perçoivent sont en moyenne inférieures à celles des hommes. Les pères isolés sont eux aussi défavorisés: les données relatives à l'Espagne, à l'Irlande et au Royaume-Uni indiquent que si les pères isolés enregistrent des taux d'emploi supérieurs à ceux des mères isolées, ces taux demeurent en deçà des taux observés pour les autres hommes. Une minorité de pères isolés peut être spécifiquement défavorisée dans certains pays: en Irlande, les taux de pauvreté sont encore plus élevés pour les pères isolés.

Les indicateurs statistiques communs de l'UE révèlent que le risque de pauvreté est bien plus élevé pour les

---

(1) Lewis, J., et Hobson, B. (1997), «Introduction» in Lewis, J. (dir.), *Lone Mothers in European Welfare Regimes: Shifting Policy Logics*, London, Jessica Kingsley.

parents isolés que pour les autres catégories d'hommes et de femmes dans chacun des pays membres. C'est dans les pays scandinaves (Danemark, Finlande et Suède, pas de statistiques comparables pour la Norvège) que l'écart est le plus réduit, ce qui montre que l'État-providence social-démocrate et les systèmes d'emploi de ces pays offrent une plus grande intégration sociale aux parents isolés que dans d'autres contextes nationaux. Il n'en demeure pas moins que les parents isolés dans ces pays sont défavorisés, sur le plan économique, par rapport aux ménages en couple.

L'emploi ne suffit pas à mettre les parents isolés à l'abri de la pauvreté. Dans de nombreux pays, les taux de pauvreté élevés observés pour les mères isolées vont de pair avec un taux d'activité qui correspond à celui des mères vivant en couple ou les dépassent même. Dans quelques pays, les taux de participation sont inférieurs pour les mères isolées par rapport aux mères vivant en couple. Il s'agit là d'un phénomène récent en Finlande et en Suède, à la suite de la récession des années 90, qui s'expliquerait en partie par les faibles rémunérations ou les conditions de travail flexible imposées dans les emplois disponibles qui rendent difficile, pour les parents isolés, de s'assurer un revenu viable et de concilier travail et vie familiale. La disparité des taux d'emploi (et des taux de pauvreté) est particulièrement manifeste au Royaume-Uni où les taux de participation des mères isolées ont augmenté sous l'effet de programmes d'emploi ciblés (le «New Deal» pour les familles monoparentales). Mais près d'une personne sur trois qui accèdent à un emploi dans le cadre de ce programme ne travaille plus au bout de douze mois, ce qui remet en question la qualité des emplois ou l'adéquation des dispositifs de garde assurés.

Au cours des dernières années, les politiques relatives aux familles monoparentales dans les pays européens ont visé à promouvoir leur emploi, le modèle d'intégration de l'«adulte-travailleur». Des mesures ont été prises pour réformer les prestations sociales visant à accroître les incitants financiers et à «rendre le travail rémunérateur», en parallèle avec des programmes pour l'emploi et une aide pour la garde des enfants. La conception et l'impact de ces réformes varient sur le plan national. Alors que cette approche peut aider à intégrer les mères isolées dans l'emploi, leur participation ne suffit pas à réduire la pauvreté si les emplois disponibles sont sous-rémunérés ou précaires ou si ces femmes ne sont pas en mesure d'accéder à des dispositifs de garde de qualité et à un aménagement de leur temps de travail. C'est pour cette raison que l'impact des mesures prises dans le cadre du modèle de l'«adulte-travailleur» dans des contextes nationaux spécifiques doit faire l'objet d'un suivi. Il est certain que des problèmes persistent en matière de disponibilité des services d'accueil et de coûts dans de nombreux pays, malgré les objectifs de Barcelone.

Certains pays ont engagé des réformes récentes visant à accroître la contribution financière du père absent. Mais ces initiatives n'ont pas toujours réussi, comme le démontrent les exemples fournis par la Bulgarie, la Lituanie et le Royaume-Uni.

6. Croisement du genre et de l'origine ethnique dans l'exclusion sociale – Le cas des Roms

L'Europe compte environ dix millions de Roms, dont un million et demi est entré dans l'UE avec l'adhésion des dix nouveaux pays membres en mai 2004. La population rom est plus importante que la population de certains pays de l'Union et elle constitue le groupe minoritaire le plus large au sein de l'UE.

On enregistre un manque de statistiques systématiques dans la plupart des pays mais les études réalisées montrent que cette communauté est confrontée aux formes les plus extrêmes d'exclusion sociale et de pauvreté dans tous les aspects de la vie: participation politique et droits civils, santé, logement, éducation, marché du travail, revenus et couverture sociale. Les Roms subissent discrimination, racisme et exclusion de la part des populations majoritaires, ce qui limite leur accès aux services publics. Des problèmes supplémentaires se posent dans certains pays, à savoir les obstacles linguistiques, le manque de papiers et l'apatridie ou de forts taux d'institutionnalisation forcée des enfants roms. Leur modèle de survie économique repose le plus souvent sur une existence marginalisée résultant d'emplois de subsistance ou informels, liée aux prestations sociales, dans des communautés touchées par la ségrégation dans des zones inaccessibles ou économiquement désavantagées.

Cette situation fortement défavorisée des populations roms a pour origine des siècles de persécution, de racisme et d'assimilation forcée. Les conditions se sont encore aggravées avec les bouleversements politico-économiques de la période de transition dans les ex-pays communistes, qui se sont accompagnés d'une reprise de la persécution et de l'apatridie dans l'Union et ailleurs.

On dispose de peu de données sur les inégalités hommes-femmes dans les populations roms. Les chiffres disponibles indiquent que les femmes roms sont particulièrement défavorisées. Cette perspective sera développée sur la base de huit rapports nationaux (Bulgarie, Chypre, Grèce, Hongrie, République tchèque, Roumanie, Slovaquie et Slovénie).

Problèmes particuliers touchant les femmes roms

Les disparités hommes-femmes en matière de rôle familial et économique entraînent des disparités dans les taux de pauvreté et d'exclusion. Les femmes roms sont confrontées aux problèmes suivants:

- **La culture rom traditionnelle impose des rôles familiaux aux femmes qui restreignent leur participation publique et politique**

Les responsabilités familiales des femmes sont prioritaires et on les décourage de participer à la vie civique ou politique. Les femmes se marient et ont leur première maternité très tôt (14-16 ans) et ont plusieurs enfants. Leur rôle traditionnel les exclut encore plus que les hommes de la vie politique et civique de la communauté majoritaire, ce qui fait que leur accès aux services juridiques et autres dispositions qui promeuvent l'égalité hommes-femmes est plus limité que pour les autres femmes.

- **Les femmes roms sont plus à risque du fait de maternités précoces et répétées**

Les risques médicaux sont amplifiés par la pauvreté et le manque d'accès aux services de planning familial et de santé.

- **Effets des programmes de stérilisation forcée qui existaient encore dans certains pays**

Les femmes auxquelles a été imposée une stérilisation forcée dans le cadre de programmes publics encore en vigueur dans les années 90 (dans certains pays comme la République tchèque et la Slovaquie) n'ont pas été indemnisées et n'ont pas reçu d'excuses.

- **Conditions de logement défavorables, lourdes tâches ménagères et exclusion des services sociaux**

Les rôles et tâches domestiques pèsent plus lourdement sur les femmes roms que sur de nombreuses autres femmes. Elles ont plus d'enfants à garder, leurs conditions de logement sont mauvaises dans des regroupements qui manquent de services de base (eau courante, chauffage) et leur accès aux services (santé, éducation) est limité, ce qui complique leurs responsabilités.

- **Les handicaps des Roms en matière d'éducation – taux élevés d'analphabétisme et faibles niveaux de qualification – sont particulièrement marqués pour les femmes**

- **Taux de chômage élevés et situation défavorisée sur le marché du travail**

Les femmes roms sont encore plus cantonnées que les hommes de leur communauté dans des emplois peu rémunérés et précaires, souvent dans l'économie informelle (vendeurs à la sauvette, ménages, travail agricole). Cette situation s'explique par l'importance du rôle familial dans la culture rom et par les faibles possibilités de formation. Les emplois qu'elles occupent ne bénéficient pas de la protection sociale et les exposent aux risques de bas salaires et d'exploitation.

- **Dépendance par rapport aux prestations sociales**

De nombreux Roms dépendent de prestations sociales mais ils sont souvent confrontés à un traitement discriminatoire ou défavorable de la part de l'administration; la situation est encore plus difficile pour les gens du voyage. Les femmes peuvent être encore plus défavorisées car elles sont encore moins susceptibles d'avoir acquis des droits individuels à une couverture sociale par le biais d'une participation au marché du travail. Par ailleurs les mariages roms traditionnels sont rarement reconnus sur le plan juridique, ce qui entraîne des difficultés majeures par rapport à l'éligibilité liée au conjoint, aux droits de visite dans les prisons et les hôpitaux, etc.

- **Prostitution et trafic humain**

Dans certains pays, les femmes roms comptent parmi les groupes exposés au risque de prostitution et de trafic humain du fait de la grande détérioration des conditions économiques. Ce phénomène n'est toutefois pas généralisé en Europe, la culture traditionnelle des Roms interdisant la prostitution.

- **Violence domestique**

Les conditions de vie des communautés roms peuvent accroître le risque de violence domestique, du fait des difficultés matérielles et psychologiques nées de la pauvreté et de l'exclusion sociale, des pressions additionnelles des bouleversements économiques, du stress lié aux mariages et maternités précoces et d'une structure familiale traditionnelle qui confère autorité et statut aux hommes. Il est difficile, pour n'importe quelle femme, de quitter un milieu de violence domestique, mais les femmes roms sont confrontées à encore plus d'obstacles lorsque les seuls services d'aide disponibles sont situés en dehors de leur communauté.

7. Immigrés et migrants

Ce chapitre se propose d'intégrer une perspective de genre à l'étude des risques d'exclusion sociale des immigrés et des migrants récents en se fondant sur les données fournies par les experts de douze pays (Allemagne, Autriche, Belgique, Chypre, Danemark, France, Islande, Italie, Lettonie, Norvège, Pays-Bas et Portugal). Les femmes immigrées/migrantes représentent entre 5 et 9 % des femmes dans la majorité des douze pays étudiés et cette part passe à 19 % aux Pays-Bas. La taille de la population migrante augmente dans la majorité de ces pays, du fait des inégalités transnationales sur les plans économiques et politiques. Dans certains pays, de nouvelles initiatives visent à améliorer la situation des immigrées et des travailleuses migrantes (France, Pays-Bas et Portugal). Dans d'autres, l'intégration du genre est moindre ou ne figure pas dans les programmes de mesures, comme en Autriche ou en Lettonie.

Les migrants ne sont pas tous défavorisés. Ceux qui viennent de pays où le niveau de vie est semblable ou plus élevé que celui du pays de destination ne rencontrent pas de problèmes particuliers (notamment en l'absence de différences quant à la culture et à la couleur de peau). À l'intérieur de l'UE ce sont en général les migrants venus d'Afrique, d'Amérique latine, d'Asie et de Turquie, et plus récemment de pays d'Europe centrale (membres de l'UE ou non) qui sont les plus défavorisés. Ils se dirigent vers des pays plus riches, attirés par l'espoir d'un niveau de vie plus élevé et à cause des problèmes politiques et économiques qu'ils rencontrent dans leur pays. À l'arrivée, leurs opportunités d'emploi sont souvent limitées. Ils sont généralement recrutés pour combler des vacances d'emplois peu rémunérés et non qualifiés, parfois dans l'économie informelle. Ils sont handicapés par nombre de facteurs économiques et socioculturels: langue, faible niveau de formation ou non-reconnaissance de leurs qualifications, discrimination raciale et xénophobie et limitation de leurs droits juridiques ou économiques. Les travailleurs sans documents qui sont des migrants illégaux sont dans une situation encore plus précaire. L'ampleur et la forme d'exclusion dépendent des politiques nationales du pays d'accueil (législation antidiscriminatoire, systèmes de formation, droits à la couverture sociale, etc.).

Problèmes particuliers auxquels sont confrontées les immigrées/migrantes

Les migrantes font face à des difficultés supplémentaires par rapport aux migrants. Si elles entrent dans le pays en tant que conjointes à charge, leurs droits à l'emploi et à la protection sociale indépendante risquent d'être limités. Elles peuvent également venir d'un milieu culturel où les femmes ont peu d'opportunités d'éducation et où il est moins accepté qu'une femme ait une activité que ce n'est le cas dans le pays hôte. Elles font l'objet de discrimination sexuelle ainsi que d'autres formes de discrimination et de racisme dirigées contre les migrants.

- **Documents et statut**

Les politiques nationales peuvent entraver l'accès des travailleuses immigrées/migrantes à la sécurité juridique des travailleurs pourvus de documents. C'est ainsi que le permis de «travailleur clé» établi en Autriche ne prend pas en compte les emplois domestiques, ce qui fait que ces emplois sont souvent informels et non réglementés.

Le statut attribué aux femmes mariées qui viennent rejoindre leur époux dans le cadre des modalités du regroupement familial peut être celui de personne à charge n'ayant pas le droit de chercher un emploi, ce qui renforce leur dépendance économique.

- **Taux d'emploi et de chômage**

Parmi les migrants, les hommes ont généralement des taux d'activité et de chômage plus élevés. Les migrantes enregistrent des taux de participation généralement plus bas que ceux des autres femmes, mais ce n'est pas toujours le cas. Pour les femmes, la période d'arrivée ainsi que la dynamique du pays d'origine (facteurs culturels relatifs au rôle traditionnel de la femme, niveaux de formation et statut possible de personne à charge à l'arrivée en tant que mère ou qu'épouse ou de migrante économiquement indépendante) jouent un rôle clé. Tous ces facteurs déterminent le degré d'intégration des migrantes dans l'emploi et définissent l'expérience vécue par les générations suivantes de femmes, comme l'illustrent les modalités de participation des femmes au Royaume-Uni qui sont fonction de leur origine ethnique.

- **Qualité de l'emploi et conditions de travail des immigrés**

Les marchés de l'emploi sont caractérisés par une ségrégation marquée qui relève de l'origine ethnique, du statut de migrant/non migrant et du genre. Les migrants qui accèdent à l'emploi sont surreprésentés dans les emplois précaires et peu rémunérés et dans l'économie informelle. Lorsqu'ils se retrouvent avec des travailleurs non migrants dans des secteurs plus favorables, leur statut de défavorisé prend alors la forme de contrats de travail à durée limitée ou plus courte et de plus grand risque de licenciement en période de récession.

Les femmes migrantes et immigrées subissent une ségrégation encore plus forte que les autres femmes, qui les cantonne dans des emplois peu rémunérés à prédominance féminine. Elles se retrouvent surtout dans le secteur des services aux particuliers, des ventes, et notamment dans les services de nettoyage et à domicile. Cela s'explique en partie par le faible niveau de qualification des migrantes en général. Certaines migrantes sont très qualifiées mais leurs compétences sont sous-utilisées et se réduisent au fil du temps sous l'effet des processus discriminatoires, de la marginalisation et de l'exclusion.

Un nombre croissant de migrantes sont employées chez des particuliers comme employées de maison (garde des enfants et des personnes âgées, travaux ménagers). Elles occupent souvent des emplois informels qui ne leur offrent qu'une protection sociale et des droits réduits. Cette forme d'emploi s'est beaucoup développée en Italie où le secteur informel représente une caractéristique structurelle de l'économie et où l'inadéquation des services d'aide sociale a entraîné une forte demande de services à domicile pour la garde de parents âgés.

Ces conditions de travail des migrantes sont certes plus favorables que les possibilités offertes dans leur pays d'origine, mais cela ne suffit pas à les justifier. La vulnérabilité de ces femmes est exacerbée par la marginalisation qu'elles rencontrent sur le marché du travail et qui réduit progressivement leurs compétences. Par ailleurs, le faible niveau de rémunération et les longs horaires les empêchent de participer pleinement à la vie sociale et de fonder leur propre famille ou de s'en occuper.

● *Éducation et formation (compétences linguistiques incluses) et mesures actives pour l'emploi*
De nombreuses migrantes sont sous-qualifiées et la langue représente un obstacle additionnel. Certains groupes sont cependant fortement qualifiés et sont employés en deçà de leurs qualifications. C'est le cas de nombreuses migrantes des pays d'Europe centrale occupées dans les services à domicile.

● *Systèmes de couverture et de protection sociales*
La position désavantageuse des femmes migrantes et immigrées dans l'emploi réduit leur possibilité d'accumuler des droits en matière de protection sociale, notamment dans le secteur informel. Les droits aux pensions de retraite sont souvent minimes, même pour les personnes ayant passé une grande partie de leur vie active dans le pays d'accueil. Ces problèmes sont particulièrement prononcés dans un pays comme l'Autriche. Même dans les régimes de protection plus inclusifs, comme aux Pays-Bas, la manière dont l'éligibilité est structurée peut se révéler problématique pour les migrantes, en particulier lorsque leur parcours professionnel est réduit ou lorsqu'elles entrent dans le pays comme personnes à charge dans le cadre du regroupement des familles.

Les réformes publiques visant à «rendre le travail rémunérateur» peuvent affecter plus durement les allocataires migrants que les autres allocataires lorsque leurs perspectives d'emploi sont moins bonnes, comme le montrent les réformes introduites récemment au Danemark.

L'accès aux dispositifs de garde joue lui aussi un rôle majeur pour l'intégration dans le marché du travail des mères migrantes et peut représenter un problème pour les migrantes même dans des pays comme la Norvège, où l'offre globale est relativement bonne.

En France, les politiques suivies se sont focalisées sur l'inclusion sociale des immigrés et des groupes ethniques minoritaires, ce qui les distingue de nombreux plans d'action nationaux dans d'autres pays membres. Un certain nombre de réformes sont positives, bien que les PAN antérieurs aient mis en évidence le problème de la «double discrimination» pour les femmes migrantes et de groupes ethniques minoritaires; il reste à élaborer une analyse fondée sur le sexe du croisement du genre et de l'origine dans les politiques d'inclusion sociale.

8. Violence et abus sexuels subis par les femmes – Violence domestique; trafic humain et prostitution

Ce chapitre porte sur le risque de violence et d'abus sexuels rencontré par les femmes dans deux domaines: la violence domestique et le trafic humain/la prostitution, et se fonde principalement sur huit rapports nationaux (Bulgarie, Chypre, Grèce, Lituanie, Malte, Norvège, Pologne et Roumanie).

Les hommes représentent la majorité des agresseurs et des clients, et la majorité des victimes sont des femmes. Cependant la violence domestique affecte également les jeunes garçons et certains hommes adultes, et les jeunes garçons des groupes défavorisés risquent de tomber dans la prostitution (généralement avec des clients du même sexe) s'ils sont sans abri ou toxicomanes.

L'ampleur de la violence domestique, du trafic humain et de la prostitution est souvent sous-évaluée, notamment lorsque les estimations se fondent sur les statistiques des crimes enregistrés. Ces chiffres suffisent cependant à montrer combien le problème est généralisé. Au Royaume-Uni, selon les statistiques officielles, 15,4 millions d'incidents de violence domestique ont eu lieu en 2000-2001, 84 % de ces incidents ayant les femmes comme victimes, et deux femmes par semaine meurent à la suite de violences domestiques. Selon une étude, entre un quart et un demi-million de femmes et d'enfants sont victimes de la traite des personnes en Europe. Le problème s'étend rapidement partout dans le monde, l'Afrique, l'Amérique latine et l'Europe centrale et de l'Est représentant des zones d'origine majeures.

Risques de violence domestique auxquels sont exposées les femmes

La violence domestique touche aussi bien les familles aisées que les familles pauvres. Le risque augmente lorsque des pressions supplémentaires s'exercent sur les familles, dans le cas d'une situation économique qui se détériore ou qui est incertaine pour certains ménages ou sur le plan sociétal. C'est ainsi que, en Roumanie, les changements sociaux rapides et les incertitudes politiques de la période de transition semblent s'accompagner d'une augmentation du taux de violence commise contre les femmes, y compris les violences domestiques.

Les divers problèmes auxquels sont confrontées les femmes victimes de violences domestiques se cumulent: les victimes souffrent de séquelles psychologiques autant que physiques qui entraînent une perte d'assurance et de confiance en soi. Les problèmes psychologiques limitent leur capacité à recourir à une aide, outre leur isolement social. Ces facteurs ont un effet négatif sur leur concentration et leur performance professionnelle qui peut amener les victimes à perdre ou à abandonner leur activité. De nombreuses femmes restent sur place sans espoir d'autres possibilités. Elles n'ont pas les moyens financiers de partir, la procédure de divorce est difficile ou onéreuse ou elles craignent que leur

agresseur ne les retrouve. D'autres obstacles institutionnels se présentent lorsque les mesures en place ne prévoient pas de moyens de soutien ou de départ en l'absence d'une reconnaissance officielle du problème dans la législation ou les procédures policières, et lorsque les dispositifs de soutien (conseils, refuge et relogement) sont absents ou inadéquats. Le viol conjugal, par exemple, n'est pas considéré comme un crime en Grèce. Les infrastructures d'aide aux victimes (lignes téléphoniques d'assistance, logement d'urgence, conseils, services juridiques) sont inadéquates en Grèce et à Malte et inexistantes en Roumanie.

Trafic d'êtres humains et prostitution féminine

Dans la société, le trafic humain et la prostitution sont alimentés par les problèmes socio-économiques. La pauvreté, liée à l'inadéquation des services juridiques, policiers et sociaux, crée les conditions qui permettent aux trafiquants de cibler les groupes défavorisés de jeunes femmes et d'enfants. Les personnes les plus vulnérables ont un faible niveau d'éducation et vivent dans des régions touchées par la pauvreté et le chômage massif, sont endettées ou toxicomanes ou ont subi des abus dans leur enfance ou un placement en institution.

Les disparités économiques entre pays sont responsables de flux migratoires de personnes prostituées qui incluent les victimes des trafiquants. La plupart de ces personnes viennent de pays en transition ou en développement et arrivent dans des pays riches. La chute du communisme a encouragé l'augmentation de la prostitution et du trafic humain en Europe du fait des bouleversements politico-économiques (allègement des contrôles frontaliers et des budgets alloués à la police, zones de conflit), ce qui s'est ajouté au trafic provenant d'autres régions du monde. Les flux de trafic ont augmenté vers l'UE et à l'intérieur de celle-ci. Certains pays représentent un lieu de départ et de destination. C'est ainsi que des femmes sont introduites en Pologne à partir de pays plus pauvres en dehors de l'UE, tandis que les Polonaises sont victimes de trafic ailleurs dans l'UE. Les pays les plus riches de l'UE sont surtout des pays de destination pour les femmes victimes du trafic d'êtres humains. Les chiffres relatifs à la Lituanie donnent une indication des profits réalisés: vers le milieu des années 90 des femmes étaient vendues à l'étranger pour le prix de 5 000 à 7 000 dollars américains, ce qui représente une somme importante par rapport aux revenus lituaniens.

Les femmes piégées par la prostitution et le trafic humain sont victimes des mêmes conditions que celles vécues par les victimes de violences domestiques (voir ci-dessus) et subissent des sévices additionnels: la séquestration, l'esclavage sexuel, les risques de maladies sexuellement transmissibles, la toxicomanie et les troubles psychologiques ainsi que la crainte d'être poursuivies en justice ou même déportées. Les modalités de piégeage, de coercition et d'abus des droits de l'homme appliquées par les trafiquants sont les mêmes, quel que soit le pays. De nombreuses femmes sont trompées par des offres d'emplois domestiques, de garde d'enfants ou dans l'hôtellerie. La plupart d'entre elles ne savent pas qu'elles vont devoir se prostituer. Une minorité de femmes sont vendues comme prostituées par leurs parents ou conjoint ou sont kidnappées par des gangs. Les trafiquants les piègent en leur retirant leur passeport et leurs pièces d'identité, en les emprisonnant et en utilisant la violence et la drogue. Elles n'ont pratiquement pas accès aux systèmes de protection sociale et leurs problèmes sont amplifiés par le fait qu'elles commettent un délit en se prostituant (les exceptions extraites de nos études de cas sont la Norvège et le Portugal).

9. Conclusions – Orientations des mesures d'intégration du genre et priorités pour les groupes défavorisés

La présente étude a montré qu'une analyse fondée sur le genre s'impose pour comprendre l'étendue et la forme de l'exclusion sociale qui frappe les groupes défavorisés et pour formuler et assurer le suivi des mesures appropriées.

Écarts fondés sur le sexe dans les risques de pauvreté liés à l'âge parmi les jeunes et les personnes plus âgées, taux de chômage et d'inactivité, pauvreté rurale, disparités hommes-femmes dans les modalités de l'exclusion sociale des invalides

Dans de nombreux pays les femmes sont plus exposées au risque de pauvreté quand elles sont jeunes, et dans tous les pays à l'exception des Pays-Bas lorsqu'elles sont âgées. L'ampleur des écarts fondés sur le sexe varie d'un groupe d'âge à l'autre, et entre pays; cela confirme l'importance des suivis sur le plan national. Par ailleurs, lorsque l'analyse porte sur les jeunes, on observe que, selon certains indicateurs, la situation des hommes est moins favorable (taux d'abandon scolaire dans la plupart des pays) tandis que selon d'autres les jeunes femmes sont les plus défavorisées (taux de «risque de pauvreté»).

La position défavorisée des femmes sur le marché de l'emploi fait qu'elles cumulent moins de droits individuels aux pensions et autres prestations sociales dans les régimes où les droits sont étroitement liés aux cotisations et aux salaires individuels. Les régimes qui prévoient des crédits de cotisation pour les périodes d'emploi à temps partiel ou pour les périodes d'inactivité liées aux responsabilités familiales permettent une indemnisation partielle. Cependant, cela ne compense pas entièrement l'impact négatif, sur les salaires et les pensions féminines, des inégalités hommes-femmes en matière de responsabilités de garde. Par conséquent, de nombreuses femmes dépendent des avantages obtenus en tant que conjointes ou de prestations sociales liées aux revenus. Ces deux dispositifs ne sont pas des formes adéquates de protection sociale comme en témoignent les taux de pauvreté élevés des femmes âgées. Tant que des inégalités de genre persisteront sur le marché du travail, les niveaux de revenu minimal assuré dans le cadre des régimes de couverture sociale constitueront un facteur clé pour mettre les femmes à l'abri de la pauvreté.

Une perspective sexuée est donc pertinente pour formuler et évaluer les ensembles de mesures relatives à l'éducation, la formation et l'éducation permanente; aux allocations de chômage et aux programmes du marché de l'emploi; aux mesures de conciliation travail-vie privée; au vieillissement actif, aux pensions et aux retraites; aux services de garde des personnes âgées. Cette perspective permet également de montrer la pertinence d'une analyse d'impact du genre pour toute une gamme de politiques, y compris la politique économique rurale.

Afin de mettre en place des mesures d'offre et de demande coordonnées qui visent l'inégalité hommes-femmes, il est nécessaire de prévoir une approche sexuée qui s'applique uniformément aux instruments politiques parallèles du Processus d'Inclusion Sociale et de la stratégie européenne pour l'emploi.

Les femmes représentent la majorité des parents isolés

Les taux de pauvreté sont élevés pour les familles monoparentales. Les désavantages peuvent être minimisés grâce aux systèmes d'emploi et de protection sociale des pays scandinaves qui offrent un «salaire social» élevé à tous les parents par le biais d'allocations liées à l'enfant et d'une infrastructure de garde étendue. Des mesures s'imposent dans plusieurs domaines afin d'augmenter les taux de participation des parents isolés dans les pays où ces taux restent faibles, d'augmenter les niveaux de rémunération auxquels ces personnes peuvent s'attendre lorsqu'elles occupent un emploi (par le biais de programmes de formation destinés aux parents isolés à faible niveau de qualification) et d'améliorer les dispositifs d'accueil des enfants et les allocations liées à l'enfant.

Les femmes roms

Les récentes directives européennes sur le racisme et la discrimination raciale ont élargi la protection juridique des Roms. Un nouveau Programme d'Action Communautaire et d'autres ensembles d'initiatives ont été lancés par les gouvernements des pays membres et les organisations internationales (par exemple la «Décennie de l'Inclusion des Roms 2005-2015»). Cependant, une évaluation récente réalisée pour la Commission européenne a conclu que seul un programme de mesures plus inclusif et coordonné ciblant les diverses sphères d'exclusion (santé, logement, éducation, emploi, services juridiques, racisme) pourrait traiter la situation défavorisée des Roms. Pour que ces mesures aboutissent, il est essentiel que les Roms soient consultés et impliqués dans la formulation et la mise en vigueur de ces programmes.

Un grand nombre de ces initiatives gardent le silence sur le problème des inégalités de genre. Pourtant, la combinaison du genre et de l'origine ethnique multiplie les handicaps subis par les femmes roms. Actuellement, les mesures qui visent les femmes se focalisent généralement sur leur rôle de mère afin d'améliorer la situation des enfants. Un élargissement sexué de ces programmes s'impose, qui incorpore des dispositions visant particulièrement les femmes roms.

Les efforts qui sont effectués pour élever les taux de qualification et de participation des femmes roms peuvent se trouver en conflit avec les valeurs traditionnelles de certaines communautés roms en ce qui concerne les rôles des hommes et des femmes. Il convient donc que la consultation et la participation soient conçues de sorte qu'elles touchent les divers groupes d'intérêts et qu'elles donnent la parole aux femmes comme aux hommes roms. Cela peut se révéler coûteux en termes de ressources, mais également productif («Les femmes roms peuvent le faire elles aussi» – E Romane Džuvlja Šaj).

Les indicateurs statistiques peuvent aider à mettre en évidence et à contrôler les inégalités hommes-femmes au sein des groupes ethniques, mais ils sont souvent absents ou restent limités dans de nombreux pays européens. L'élargissement du contrôle statistique aux Roms et à d'autres groupes ethniques est politiquement sensible dans de nombreux pays. Ce manque d'informations est à double tranchant: il peut offrir un certain degré de protection contre la surveillance et la persécution, mais il en résulte un manque de données pour évaluer les politiques ou pour lancer des campagnes d'information et de lutte contre le racisme et la discrimination. Il est essentiel qu'une ventilation sexuée soit intégrée dans tout élargissement du contrôle statistique.

Migrantes et immigrées

Les migrantes et les immigrées – particulièrement celles qui viennent de pays non occidentaux – sont mal intégrées dans le marché du travail. Elles connaissent généralement des taux d'emploi plus bas et de chômage plus élevés que les autres femmes du pays d'accueil. Leurs conditions d'emploi sont moins favorables étant donné qu'elles se concentrent dans des secteurs peu rémunérés et non régulés. Certains secteurs économiques dépendent de leur travail: la vente, la restauration, le nettoyage et d'autres emplois de service à bas salaires. Un nombre croissant de migrantes sont employées, souvent de manière informelle, chez des particuliers pour assurer la garde des enfants ou des personnes âgées et faire les travaux ménagers. Leur situation défavorisée sur le marché de l'emploi s'accompagne d'une protection sociale insuffisante, ce qui les expose encore davantage au risque de pauvreté. Certaines réformes publiques des systèmes d'aide sociale, au Danemark par exemple, ont réduit les droits accordés aux immigrés et augmenté leur risque d'exclusion du système.

Certains pays ont introduit des mesures qui visent à améliorer la situation des travailleurs migrants, mais si les disparités hommes-femmes quant aux compétences et aux besoins ne sont pas mises en évidence, ces mesures seront moins susceptibles de cibler les femmes. D'autres pays ont mis en place ou renforcé la législation antidiscriminatoire pour renforcer la protection accordée aux migrants. Mais lorsque les problèmes de discrimination de genre et de race sont traités séparément dans la législation et par les agences concernées, les problèmes spécifiques auxquels sont confrontées les migrantes, du fait de la discrimination sexuelle et raciale, risquent de ne pas être traités de manière adéquate à cause des cloisonnements institutionnels.

Afin d'aboutir à une compréhension plus fine des besoins et handicaps spécifiques des migrantes et des immigrées de provenances et destinations diverses, il est nécessaire d'effectuer plus de recherches pour intégrer le genre dans les politiques d'inclusion sociale.

Violence contre les femmes – L'exemple de la violence domestique, du trafic et de la prostitution

La violence et les abus sexuels que subissent les femmes sont loin d'être négligeables, mais l'ampleur de ce problème est souvent sous-estimée dans les politiques suivies et représente rarement un objectif prioritaire qu'accompagneraient un programme de mesures et un budget adéquat.

La dimension du genre est peu fréquemment invoquée de manière explicite ou traitée directement, le problème fondamental étant le fait que les violences et les abus sexuels sont en grande partie commis par des hommes contre des femmes et des enfants.

D'un pays à l'autre, les causes et effets de ces types de violence et d'abus sont les mêmes. Des disparités nationales sont observées au niveau des politiques suivies: solidité et étendue du cadre juridique, dispositifs de soutien et mesures de prévention. L'ampleur du phénomène peut aussi varier d'un pays à l'autre, selon qu'il s'agit d'un pays d'origine ou de destination pour le trafic. Des disparités nationales peuvent également concerner la prévalence des violences domestiques, mais l'absence de chiffres ne nous permet pas d'évaluer cet aspect.

La plupart des pays examinés dans ce chapitre ont introduit de nouvelles initiatives au cours des dernières années afin de lutter contre la violence domestique et le trafic humain: réformes législatives, sensibilisation de l'opinion publique et mise en œuvre de ressources pour combattre la violence domestique, élargissement et coordination de mesures nationales et transnationales pour répondre au trafic humain et aider les victimes. Il n'en demeure pas moins que certains problèmes persistent: dispositions juridiques insuffisantes, inadéquation considérable des ressources, manque de coordination entre les services policiers, judiciaires et sociaux, absence de collaboration transnationale par rapport au trafic humain, manque d'études, de services et de mesures d'inclusion sociale à long terme permettant de définir et de protéger les groupes les plus vulnérables.

Dans la majorité des pays, on note l'absence d'une approche systématique qui s'adresserait au comportement des hommes et réduirait le problème de la violence – par exemple des mesures ciblant les hommes afin de lutter contre les comportements violents et agressifs et pour réguler la demande à prédominance masculine de prostitution. L'accent est surtout mis sur des mesures juridiques permettant de poursuivre les hommes pris en délit de trafic, de gestion de la prostitution ou d'actes de violence domestique. La Norvège constitue un cas à part: les efforts entrepris ont visé à réduire la demande en interdisant aux fonctionnaires et aux forces armées d'acheter les services de personnes prostituées, mais ces mesures ont été critiquées comme étant trop restreintes en ne criminalisant pas l'achat de services sexuels. De manière plus générale, le rapport qui existe entre ces domaines particuliers et la réduction des inégalités hommes-femmes n'est pas toujours établi dans les déclarations officielles alors que le renforcement de l'indépendance économique des femmes et de leur statut social est une condition sine qua non pour les aider à éviter les situations abusives ou s'en échapper.

Trois considérations d'ordre général pour conclure

Premièrement, le Processus d'Inclusion Sociale doit mettre en œuvre un contrôle systématique des disparités hommes-femmes parmi des groupes défavorisés afin d'étayer l'analyse de l'impact du genre et l'intégration de la dimension sexuée au sein des Plans d'Action Nationaux. Le contrôle des écarts fondés sur le sexe moyens ne permet pas de dégager les causes principales ni de préciser où des progrès sont réalisés. Deuxièmement, l'intégration du genre souligne la pertinence de la perspective du parcours de vie pour les mesures d'intégration sociale. C'est ainsi que les mères isolées qui vivent dans le dénuement aujourd'hui risquent de devenir les femmes plus âgées de demain qui sont particulièrement exposées au risque de pauvreté. Troisièmement, certains problèmes auxquels les femmes sont confrontées ne peuvent être appréhendés et traités sans une approche transnationale; tel est le cas pour la force de travail migrante, le trafic d'êtres humains ou la taille de la population rom, lorsqu'une perspective européenne plutôt que nationale est adoptée.

Zusammenfassung

1. Einführung

Die durchgängige Berücksichtigung der Gleichstellung von Frauen und Männern (Gender-Mainstreaming) gilt als wesentliche Voraussetzung für den Prozess der sozialen Eingliederung. Dieser Ansatz für die Politikgestaltung und -überwachung steckt jedoch noch in den Kinderschuhen und kommt in den nationalen Aktionsplänen oft nicht zur Anwendung. Ziel dieses Berichts ist es, zu informieren und das Gender-Mainstreaming des Prozesses der sozialen Eingliederung durch die Auswertung der Ergebnisse der nationalen Berichte für 30 europäische Länder zu fördern. Er nimmt Unterschiede und Ungleichheiten zwischen den Geschlechtern bei den Risiken der Armut und sozialen Ausgrenzung unter die Lupe und schildert in den nachfolgenden Kapiteln die Situation benachteiligter Gruppen anhand von ausgewählten Beispielen, um die Bedeutung des Gender-Mainstreaming für die Politik der sozialen Eingliederung zu veranschaulichen.

2. Unterschiede und Ungleichheiten zwischen den Geschlechtern bei den Risiken der sozialen Ausgrenzung und Armut – ein kurzer Überblick

Unterschiede und Ungleichheiten zwischen Frauen und Männern sind ein grundlegendes Merkmal von sozialer Ausgrenzung und Armut. Für Frauen ist die Wahrscheinlichkeit, ein angemessenes persönliches Einkommen durch Beschäftigung zu erzielen, geringer. Dies zeigt sich durch die niedrigere Beschäftigungsquote von Frauen, ihre meistens geringere Bezahlung und am deutlichsten durch ihren niedrigeren Durchschnittsverdienst. Diese durchschnittlichen geschlechtsspezifischen Diskrepanzen bei der Beschäftigung sind für bestimmte Untergruppen ausgeprägter, so z. B. die Beschäftigungsquoten für ältere Beschäftigte. Frauen erwerben niedrigere Renten- und sonstige Ansprüche, wenn die Anspruchsgrundlage einkommensabhängig ist oder auf der individuellen Berufslaufbahn beruht. Die Gründe sind ihr niedrigerer Durchschnittsverdienst, die größere Wahrscheinlichkeit, dass sie ihre Beschäftigung unterbrechen oder weniger Stunden arbeiten, um Aufgaben in der Familie wahrzunehmen, und die höheren Arbeitslosenquoten, von denen Frauen in vielen Ländern betroffen sind. Die Sozialhilfesysteme in den meisten Ländern beruhen immer noch auf der implizierten und überholten Annahme, dass Frauen vom Einkommen eines männlichen Partners, des „Ernährers", oder abgeleiteten Leistungen als seine unterhaltsberechtigte Ehefrau versorgt werden oder versorgt werden sollten. Ungleichheiten zwischen Frauen und Männern bei der Beschäftigung in Verbindung mit unzulänglichen Konzepten in den Sozialhilfesystemen führen zu einer Situation, in der Frauen ungleich stärker von Armut betroffen sind, bzw. Armut zunehmend zu einem „weiblichen" Problem wird. Dennoch fehlt diese geschlechtsspezifische Perspektive oft bei politischen Debatten.

Die gemeinsamen statistischen Indikatoren, die für den Prozess der sozialen Eingliederung herangezogen werden, liefern einige Hinweise auf die Ungleichheiten zwischen Frauen und Männern bei Armut und sozialer Ausgrenzung. Das Armutsrisiko ist in 21 der 27 Länder für Frauen höher als für Männer, in sechs Ländern ist es für beide Geschlechter gleich und nur in Polen ist das durchschnittliche Armutsrisiko für Männer höher als für Frauen (es liegen keine Daten vor für IS, LI und NO). Mit diesem Indikator wird jedoch das Ausmaß des höheren Armutsrisikos von Frauen möglicherweise unterschätzt, da er davon ausgeht, dass die Haushaltsmittel in einen Topf geworfen und gleichmäßig aufgeteilt werden. Untersuchungen haben gezeigt, dass die Mittel zwischen den einzelnen Haushaltsmitgliedern ungleich verteilt sind. In Geringverdienerhaushalten ist es allgemein üblich, dass die Frauen das Haushaltsgeld verwalten und ihren eigenen Konsum (Lebensmittel, Kleidung, Heizung, wenn sie allein in der Wohnung sind, Freizeit usw.) zurückschrauben müssen, um den Lebensstandard ihres Partners und ihrer Kinder zu schützen.

Über einen längeren Zeitraum mit einem geringen Einkommen zu leben verursacht Stress, wirkt sich negativ auf die Wohnqualität und Gesundheit aus und führt zu sozialer Isolation. Frauen sind nicht nur stärker von Armut und niedrigem Einkommen betroffen, es gibt auch geschlechtsspezifische Unterschiede, wie Männer und Frauen den Stress und die soziale Isolation eines Lebens mit geringem Einkommen erleben, sowie geschlechtsspezifische Unterschiede bei der Gesundheit und Lebenserwartung und der Gefährdung, Opfer von Verbrechen oder obdachlos zu werden.

Klare geschlechtsspezifische Unterschiede zeigen sich auch bei vielen der anderen gemeinsamen Indikatoren von Armut und sozialer Ausgrenzung. Obwohl aus diesen Indikatoren oft deutlich wird, dass Frauen das größere Risiko tragen, sind bei einigen die Risiken für Männer größer. Des Weiteren hängt das Ausmaß der geschlechtsspezifischen Diskrepanz auch davon ab, welche Dimension der sozialen Ausgrenzung innerhalb eines Landes sowie länderübergreifend analysiert wird.

Eine geschlechtsbezogene Analyse ist für das Verständnis des Ausmaßes und der Form der sozialen Ausgrenzung benachteiligter Gruppen in der Bevölkerung aus drei verschiedenen Gründen entscheidend.

- Einige benachteiligte Gruppen werden zahlenmäßig von einem Geschlecht dominiert. Viele sind von Frauen dominiert, zum Beispiel Alleinerziehende, ältere Personen in Geringverdienerhaushalten und Opfer von häuslicher Gewalt und Frauenhandel. Andere sind männerdominiert, darunter ehemalige Häftlinge, bestimmte Wohnungslose und Obdachlose und Schulabbrecher oder Drogenabhängige in manchen Ländern.

- Eine geschlechtsspezifische Perspektive ist auch wichtig, wenn die Gruppenzugehörigkeit gleichmäßiger auf die Geschlechter verteilt ist, zum Beispiel bei den Roma, Migranten oder Behinderten. Dabei sind deutliche Unterschiede bei den Ursachen, beim Ausmaß und der Form der von Frauen und Männern erfahrenen sozialen Ausgrenzung festzustellen.

- Die Geschlechterverhältnisse – oder genauer gesagt das Verhalten der Männer – spielen eine zentrale Rolle bei zahlreichen sozialen Problemen: bei häuslicher Gewalt, Frauenhandel und Prostitution und den meisten anderen Verbrechensarten.

Der Begriff „Intersektionalität" ist vielschichtiger als der Begriff „doppelte Benachteiligung" und damit für das Verständnis geschlechtsbezogener Differenzen in Bezug auf verschiedene Arten der Diskriminierung und der sozialen Ausgrenzung besser geeignet. Zum Beispiel soll deutlich gemacht werden, wie Rassismus und Diskriminierung aufgrund des Geschlechts zusammenwirken und die Erfahrungen von Frauen aus ethnischen Minderheitengruppen bestimmen. Die Annahme der Intersektionalität ist, dass die Diskriminierung aufgrund des Geschlechts, der Rasse oder Klasse und andere Systeme der Diskriminierung

zusammenwirken und sich auf die relative Position von Frauen und Männern auswirken. Einige werden dabei an den äußersten Rand der Gesellschaft gedrängt, während andere besser integriert werden. Daher machen Frauen aus einer ethnischen Minderheitengruppe vollkommen andere Erfahrungen als Männer derselben Minderheitengruppe und Frauen aus der ethnischen Mehrheitsgruppe. Dieser Ansatz erkennt auch an, dass eine Person in der Gesellschaft sowohl Unterdrückung als auch Vorrechte erleben kann. So kann eine Frau zum Beispiel beruflich eine hohe Stellung haben und dennoch Rassismus oder häuslicher Gewalt ausgesetzt sein. Durch Anwendung des Konzepts der Intersektionalität ist es möglich, sowohl eine Gender-Mainstreaming-Perspektive bei der Politik der sozialen Eingliederung zu entwickeln als auch das Bewusstsein für Ungleichheiten unter Frauen bei Analysen, die sich mit der Darstellung der benachteiligten Position von Frauen gegenüber Männern in der Gesellschaft befassen, zu schärfen.

3. Die Intersektion von Geschlecht und Alter bei den Risiken der sozialen Ausgrenzung – junge und ältere Menschen

Die Intersektion von Geschlecht und Alter bei den Risiken der sozialen Ausgrenzung ist komplex und ändert sich laufend. So erreichen Frauen jetzt in den jüngeren Generationen Qualifikationsniveaus, die denen ihrer männlichen Altersgenossen entsprechen oder sie übertreffen. Dagegen bleiben andere geschlechtsspezifische Ungleichheiten, die junge Frauen benachteiligen, bestehen. Eine strenge Geschlechtertrennung nach Fachgebieten in Unterricht und Ausbildung bedeutet, dass junge Frauen oft in Bereichen überrepräsentiert sind, die in schlechter bezahlte Berufe münden. Und die stärkere Neigung von Frauen, ihre Berufstätigkeit aufzugeben, um Verantwortung in der Familie zu übernehmen, zeigt sich auch schon in den ersten Jahren ihrer Teilnahme am Arbeitsmarkt. Die Prozesse der Arbeitsmarktdiskriminierung bedeuten, dass Frauen immer noch geringere Erträge am Arbeitsmarkt erzielen (Einkommen, Karriereentwicklung) als Männer mit vergleichbaren Qualifikationen und Tätigkeitsmustern.

Das niedrigere Lebenseinkommen von Frauen wirkt sich auf ihre Renten aus, die einkommensabhängig sind und auf der individuellen Berufslaufbahn beruhen. Dadurch erhöht sich ihr Risiko, von Altersarmut betroffen zu werden. Dazu kommt, dass Frauen eine höhere Lebenserwartung als Männer haben, was dazu führt, dass sie unter den älteren Personen, die benachteiligter als die jüngeren Rentner sind (Sachgüter, Gesundheit, soziale Isolation), stärker vertreten sind. Daher gibt es unter den älteren Personengruppen nicht nur mehr Frauen als Männer; darüber hinaus gibt es auch geschlechtsbezogene Unterschiede bei dem Ausmaß und den Ursachen der sozialen Ausgrenzung bei älteren Personen.

Geschlechtsspezifische Diskrepanzen bei den Risiken der Altersarmut und der sozialen Ausgrenzung

Das Armutsrisiko ist in den meisten Ländern je nach Altersgruppe verschieden. In der Regel sind die jungen (16-24 Jahre) und die älteren (65+ Jahre) Altersgruppen die am häufigsten betroffenen. Frauen sind in beiden dieser Altersgruppen gefährdeter und die geschlechtsspezifische Diskrepanz ist bei älteren Menschen besonders ausgeprägt. Geschlechtsspezifische Ungleichheiten beim Armutsrisiko sind auch bei den dazwischen liegenden Altersgruppen festzustellen. Zusammenfassende Indikatoren gemeinsamer Tendenzen und Unterschiede in allen Ländern bei der Intersektion von alters- und geschlechtsspezifischen Diskrepanzen sind in Kasten 1 dargestellt.

Die nationalen Unterschiede beim Ausmaß oder der Richtung der geschlechtsspezifischen Diskrepanzen bei der Armut und der sozialen Ausgrenzung für verschiedene Altersgruppen resultieren aus den unterschiedlichen Arbeitsmarktbedingungen und Sozialhilfesystemen. So sind zum Beispiel in den sechs Ländern, in denen die jungen Männer das größere Armutsrisiko tragen, die Gründe mit hoher Wahrscheinlichkeit in den Schulabgangsmustern, der industriellen Umstrukturierung und in den nach Geschlechtern getrennten Beschäftigungsmöglichkeiten zu suchen (DE, CY, LU, PL, PT, SK). In ähnlicher Weise ist die Wahrscheinlichkeit für geschlechtsspezifische Diskrepanzen beim Armutsrisiko im Alter am geringsten, wenn das Rentensystem weitgehend auf der Staatsbürgerschaft anstatt auf der bisherigen Beschäftigung und dem bisherigen Einkommen beruht oder wenn Länder eine Gleichstellung der Geschlechter beim Lebenseinkommen und der Teilnahme am Arbeitsmarkt erreicht haben. Andere spezifische Beispiele für die geschlechtsspezifischen Auswirkungen verschiedener nationaler Maßnahmen für junge oder ältere Menschen werden ebenfalls erörtert. Dabei wird auf vier nationale Berichte Bezug genommen, die sich mit altersbezogenen Themen befassen (Island, Estland, Tschechische Republik, Spanien).

4. Geschlechtsspezifische Unterschiede bei langfristiger Arbeitslosigkeit und Nichterwerbstätigkeit, ländlicher Armut und der Ausgrenzung von Behinderten

Frauen haben in allen Mitgliedstaaten eine niedrigere Beschäftigungsquote als Männer, und die Diskrepanz ist in einigen Ländern besonders ausgeprägt. Dies ist ein Schlüsselfaktor, der dazu beiträgt, dass Frauen stärker dem Risiko der Armut und sozialen Ausgrenzung ausgesetzt sind. So sind sie von ihren individuellen Leistungsansprüchen, die sie ggf. haben, sowie Zuwendungen innerhalb des eigenen Haushalts (z. B. dem Einkommen eines Ehegatten oder Elternteils) abhängig. Sechs nationale Berichte untersuchten detailliert entweder die Langzeitarbeitslosen, die versteckten Arbeitslosen oder die nach einem Elternurlaub oder sonstiger Abwesenheit vom Arbeitsmarkt wieder ins Berufsleben zurückgekehrten Mütter (BG, CZ, HU, MT, PL, SK); drei Berichte deckten bestimmte Probleme von Nichterwerbstätigkeit und Unterbeschäftigung von Frauen in ländlichen Gebieten auf (IT, PL, SI) und zwei über geschlechtsspezifische Differenzen bei Menschen mit Behinderungen (IE, SI). Auf diese nationalen Beispiele wird in diesem Kapitel näher eingegangen.

Geschlechtsspezifische Diskrepanzen bei den Langzeitarbeitslosen- und Nichterwerbstätigenquoten und den damit verbundenen Armutsrisiken

Bei den Arbeitslosen-, Langzeitarbeitslosen- und Nichterwerbstätigenquoten gibt es große Unterschiede zwischen den einzelnen Ländern, aber in den meisten Fällen sind die Quoten für Frauen höher (Kasten 2). Muster und Ausmaß der geschlechtsspezifischen Diskrepanzen variieren zwischen den Ländern, wie es bei den altersbezogenen Vergleichen der Fall war. Dies zeigt erneut, wie wichtig eine Überwachung auf nationaler Ebene für die Politikgestaltung ist.

Geschlechtsspezifische Diskrepanzen können nicht angemessen beurteilt werden, ohne die Nichterwerbstätigenquoten zu berücksichtigen. So ist beispielsweise die Langzeitarbeitslosenquote für Frauen in Malta niedriger als die für Männer und ist auch im internationalen Vergleich relativ niedrig. Gleichzeitig ist jedoch in Malta die Quote der nichterwerbstätigen Frauen EU-weit die höchste. In ähnlicher Weise tritt das Ungleichgewicht zwischen den Geschlechtern in Bulgarien nur in Bezug

Kasten 1: Beispiele für statistische Indikatoren von geschlechtsspezifischen Diskrepanzen bei altersbezogenen Risiken der Armut und der sozialen Ausgrenzung und nationale Unterschiede bei der Intersektion von alters- und geschlechtsspezifischen Diskrepanzen

Junge Menschen

- Bei jungen Menschen ist das *Armutsrisiko* in 19 der 25 Mitgliedstaaten für Frauen höher (die Ausnahmen sind DE, CY, LU, PL, PT, SK).

- In den meisten Ländern ist die *Beschäftigungsquote* für junge Frauen deutlich niedriger als für junge Männer. Diese geschlechtsspezifische Diskrepanz liegt in Lettland, Spanien, Estland, Griechenland und Slowenien bei über 10%. Dagegen ist die geschlechtsspezifische Diskrepanz in den Niederlanden, in Dänemark und im Vereinigten Königreich gering bis nicht vorhanden, während die Beschäftigungsquote für junge Frauen in Schweden sogar diejenige junger Männer übersteigt.

- Bei *Schulabbrechern* ist das Risiko der Armut und der sozialen Ausgrenzung erhöht. Die Gesamtquoten sind in den einzelnen Ländern verschieden, aber in 25 der 29 untersuchten Länder (für Liechtenstein liegen keine Daten vor) ist der vorzeitige Abbruch der Schulausbildung unter jungen Männern viel verbreiteter. In weiteren drei Ländern ist die Quote für Jungen leicht erhöht (Deutschland, Vereinigtes Königreich und Island). Die Tschechische Republik bildet in dieser Hinsicht eine Ausnahme, da es dort mehr junge Frauen gibt, die die Schulausbildung vorzeitig abbrechen.

- Die durchschnittliche *Jugendarbeitslosenquote* in der EU ist für junge Männer etwas höher als für junge Frauen; es gibt jedoch bedeutende nationale Unterschiede beim Ausmaß und der Richtung der geschlechtsspezifischen Diskrepanz. Zum Beispiel sind die offiziellen Arbeitslosenquoten für junge Frauen in fünf Ländern (EL, ES, LU, PT, SI) höher als für junge Männer, während in sechs Ländern die Arbeitslosenquote für junge Männer mindestens zwei Prozentpunkte höher ist als für junge Frauen (CZ, DE, EE, LT, SK, UK).

- *Nichterwerbstätigkeit verbunden mit Mutterschaft* ist ebenfalls ein Faktor für einige junge Frauen, und hinter der Nichterwerbstätigkeit wegen der Übernahme familiärer Verantwortung kann sich auch eine versteckte Arbeitslosigkeit verbergen. Auf dieses Phänomen wird in Kapitel 4 ausführlicher eingegangen.

Ältere Menschen

- Das *Armutsrisiko* im Alter ist in allen Ländern außer den Niederlanden für Frauen viel größer.

- Die geschlechtsspezifische Diskrepanz bei der *Beschäftigungsquote* ist ausgeprägter als für die jungen Altersgruppen, und in der Altersgruppe der 55 bis 64-Jährigen ist die Quote in jedem Land für Frauen niedriger als für Männer. Die geschlechtsspezifische Diskrepanz ist in Finnland, Schweden, Frankreich und Estland am kleinsten und erreicht in Zypern und Malta 40%.

- Das *durchschnittliche Alter des Ausstiegs aus dem Berufsleben* ist für Frauen niedriger als für Männer (die Ausnahmen sind BE, HU, IE, IT, NO, RO).

auf die Nichterwerbstätigkeit, nicht jedoch in Bezug auf die Langzeitarbeitslosenquoten zutage. Gleichermaßen ist es wichtig, die geschlechtsspezifischen Risiken der Armut für bestimmte Kategorien der Beschäftigungslosen mit Bezug auf die geschlechtsspezifischen Ungleichheiten, die in anderen Dimensionen festgestellt wurden, zu analysieren, um die allgemeinen geschlechtsspezifischen Auswirkungen der Politik zu interpretieren. So ist beispielsweise in der Slowakei das Armutsrisiko unter den Arbeitslosen für Männer höher, obwohl im Verhältnis mehr Frauen langzeitarbeitslos oder nicht erwerbstätig sind und in einem Erwerbslosenhaushalt leben.

Das Ziel der Politik, die Beschäftigungsquoten von Frauen als eine Quelle des Schutzes gegen Armut zu erhöhen, deckt sich mit den Zielen der europäischen Beschäftigungsstrategie und erfordert die Gleichstellung von Mann und Frau bei den aktiven arbeitsmarktpolitischen Programmen und den Maßnahmen zur besseren Vereinbarkeit von Familie und Beruf (Kinderbetreuung, Arbeitszeitpolitik usw.). Außerdem bedeutet es eine große Herausforderung für die Politik der sozialen Eingliederung, da Frauen (und Männer), die ihre Beschäftigung reduzieren, um Aufgaben in der Familie wahrzunehmen, ihr persönliches

---

**Kasten 2: Geschlechtsspezifische Diskrepanzen bei den Arbeitslosen-, Langzeitarbeitslosen-
und Nichterwerbstätigenquoten sowie Beispiele für nationale Unterschiede beim Ausmaß
der geschlechtsspezifischen Diskrepanz**

- Die *Arbeitslosenquoten* sind in den meisten europäischen Ländern für Frauen höher als für Männer: 2003 galt das für 19 der 25 Mitgliedstaaten; die umgekehrte Situation wurde in sechs Ländern (DE, FI, HU, IE, SE, UK) festgestellt.

- Frauen haben außerdem in jedem Land höhere *Nichterwerbstätigenquoten* aufgrund häuslicher Verantwortungen. Das Ausmaß der geschlechtsspezifischen Diskrepanz variiert von Land zu Land und ist in den skandinavischen und baltischen Staaten am kleinsten.

- Die Quoten der *versteckten Arbeitslosigkeit* unter den Nichterwerbstätigen sind in 24 der 25 Mitgliedstaaten (Schweden ist die Ausnahme) für Frauen höher als für Männer.

- Die *Langzeitarbeitslosenquote* ist in 18 der 25 Mitgliedstaaten für Frauen höher als für Männer (die Ausnahmen sind EE, FI, HU, IE, MT, SE, UK), obwohl in vier der 18 Länder (DK, LV, NL, SI) die geschlechtsspezifische Diskrepanz gering ist.

- Das *Armutsrisiko* ist für die Nichterwerbstätigen und Arbeitslosen höher, und Ausmaß und Richtung der geschlechtsspezifischen Diskrepanz variieren zwischen den verschiedenen Gruppen und Ländern.

Armutsrisiko erhöhen. Dieses Problem wird in den Sozialschutzsystemen selten explizit bzw. angemessen berücksichtigt.

Zwei weitere Beispiele für Gender-Mainstreaming: ländliche Bevölkerungen und Menschen mit Behinderungen

Frauen in ländlichen Gebieten sind in einigen Mitgliedstaaten besonders häufig von sozialer Ausgrenzung, Isolation und Armut betroffen. Das Muster und die Ursachen für ländliche Armut variieren zwischen den einzelnen Ländern, was anhand der Beispiele Polen, Irland, Italien und Slowenien veranschaulicht wird. In der Regel haben Frauen in ländlichen Gebieten niedrigere Einkommen aus der Landwirtschaft und sind in Zusammenhang mit der Umstrukturierung der Landwirtschaft stärker von Arbeitslosigkeit und Unterbeschäftigung betroffen. Unter den Beschäftigten in der Landwirtschaft werden Frauen eher als „mithelfende Familienangehörige" anstatt als Selbstständige oder Arbeitnehmer bezeichnet, was bedeuten kann, dass sie nur über einen begrenzten Sozialversicherungsschutz verfügen. Wenn Frauen für einen landwirtschaftlichen Betrieb verantwortlich sind, ist es wahrscheinlicher, dass der Betrieb klein ist und geringe wirtschaftliche Erträge abwirft. Zu den ländlichen Gebieten können auch reiche sowie arme Haushalte gehören. In Slowenien sind zum Beispiel Frauen, die in einem landwirtschaftlichen Betrieb mitarbeiten, benachteiligter als nicht in der Landwirtschaft tätige Frauen vom Land. Andere Aspekte des Landlebens wirken sich ebenfalls auf die Lebensbedingungen der Frauen aus. Gesundheit, Ausbildung und öffentliche Verkehrsmittel sind oft begrenzter als in städtischen Gebieten, die Arbeit auf dem Land ist mit langen Arbeitszeiten und körperlich anstrengender Arbeit verbunden, und die ländliche Isolation kann zu sozialen Problemen beitragen.

Eine Gender-Mainstreaming-Perspektive ist auch wichtig, um Ungleichheiten und Differenzen bei den Erfahrungen von Menschen mit Behinderungen aufzudecken. In einigen Ländern, darunter Irland, gibt es mehr behinderte Frauen als Männer, und unter der behinderten Bevölkerung sind die Armutsquoten für Frauen höher. Behinderte Frauen im arbeitsfähigen Alter haben geringere Beschäftigungsquoten und niedrigere Einkommen als behinderte Männer. Nichterwerbstätige behinderte Frauen werden eher als „in häusliche Pflichten eingebunden" bezeichnet, während beschäftigungslose behinderte Männer eher als „arbeitslos" oder „Empfänger von Sozialleistungen für Behinderte" bezeichnet werden.

5. Alleinerziehende – eine frauendominierte Kategorie

Die Quote der Alleinerziehenden variiert zwischen den einzelnen europäischen Ländern und nimmt in den meisten Fällen zu. In allen Ländern handelt es sich mehrheitlich um Haushalte, die von weiblichen Personen geführt werden. Diese machen 80-95% aller Alleinerziehenden in den meisten Ländern aus. Die meisten werden zu Alleinerziehenden, weil ihre Beziehung zum Ehepartner oder Lebensgefährten zerbricht. Ledige Frauen, die Mütter werden, ohne zu heiraten oder mit einem Partner zusammenzuleben, sind weitaus seltener.

Frühere internationale Vergleichsstudien[1] haben gezeigt, dass Beschäftigung allein das wirtschaftliche Wohlergehen allein erziehender Mütter nicht sicherstellen kann. Sozialhilfesysteme, die einen hohen „sozialen Lohn" für Familien in Form von Leistungen speziell für Kinder und ihre Betreuer in Verbindung mit Kinderbetreuungsleistungen bereitstellen, senken die Risiken der Armut und Stigmatisierung für finanziell schlechter gestellte Eltern. Dies wird in diesem Kapitel genauer untersucht, indem auf die dreizehn nationalen Berichte Bezug genommen wird, die sich mit der Situation von Alleinerziehenden befassen (BG, EE, ES, FI, HU, IE, LI, LT, LU, MT, NO, SE, UK).

Die Risiken der sozialen Ausgrenzung und der Armut von Alleinerziehenden

Haushalte von Alleinerziehenden sind aus mehreren Gründen gefährdet, von Armut betroffen zu sein. Sie haben zusätzliche finanzielle Nachteile und größere Schwierigkeiten, Arbeit und Familie unter einen Hut zu bringen, wenn sie Kinder allein großziehen, im Vergleich zu den Ressourcen, die in Haushalten zur Verfügung stehen, in denen sich beide Elternteile die Verantwortung teilen. Der Druck, der einzige Ernährer zu sein, ist für Frauen deshalb noch schwerwiegender, weil die Löhne, die sie auf dem Arbeitsmarkt erzielen können, im Durchschnitt geringer sind als die von Männern. Allein erziehende Väter sind ebenfalls benachteiligt. Daten aus dem Vereinigten Königreich, Spanien und Irland zeigen, dass allein erziehende Väter höhere Beschäftigungsquoten haben als allein erziehende Mütter, jedoch niedrigere Beschäftigungsquoten als andere Männer. Die Minderheit von allein erziehenden Vätern ist möglicherweise in einigen Ländern auf bestimmte Weise benachteiligt. In Irland sind die Armutsquoten beispielsweise für allein erziehende Väter sogar höher.

Die gemeinsamen statistischen Indikatoren der EU zeigen, dass in jedem Mitgliedstaat das Armutsrisiko für Alleinerziehende viel höher ist als für andere Frauen und Männer. Die Diskrepanz ist in den skandinavischen Ländern der EU (DK, FI, SE, vergleichbare

Daten für Norwegen nicht verfügbar) am geringsten, was beweist, dass die sozialdemokratischen Sozialstaats- und Beschäftigungssysteme in diesen Ländern eine bessere soziale Integration für Alleinerziehende ermöglichen als dies unter den politischen Rahmenbedingungen anderer Länder der Fall ist. Allerdings sind Alleinerziehende in den skandinavischen Ländern verglichen mit der Situation von Haushalten, in denen beide Elternteile leben, immer noch wirtschaftlich benachteiligt.

Die Beschäftigung allein reicht nicht aus, um Alleinerziehende vor der Armut zu bewahren. In vielen Ländern gehen die hohen Armutsquoten allein erziehender Mütter einher mit einer Beschäftigungsquote, die derjenigen von Müttern in Paar-Haushalten entspricht oder sie sogar übertrifft, und dennoch tragen allein erziehende Mütter ein größeres Armutsrisiko. In einigen wenigen Ländern sind die Beschäftigungsquoten für allein erziehende Mütter niedriger als für Mütter, die in einer Partnerschaft leben. Dies ist eine aktuelle Entwicklung, die in Schweden und Finnland nach der wirtschaftlichen Rezession der 1990er Jahre begonnen hat und offenbar teilweise darauf zurückzuführen ist, dass viele der neuen Arbeitsplätze schlecht bezahlt sind oder flexible Arbeitszeiten erfordern. Daher ist es für Alleinerziehende schwieriger, ein ausreichendes Einkommen zu erzielen und Arbeit und Familie unter einen Hut zu bringen. Der Unterschied bei den Beschäftigungsquoten (und Armutsquoten) ist im Vereinigten Königreich besonders groß. Dort sind die Beschäftigungsquoten allein erziehender Mütter durch gezielte aktive arbeitsmarktpolitische Programme („New Deal for lone parents") gestiegen. Allerdings ist fast ein Drittel der Alleinerziehenden, denen durch das Programm eine Stelle vermittelt wurde, nach 12 Monaten nicht mehr beschäftigt, was auf Probleme mit der Qualität der Stelle oder der Kinderbetreuung, die ihnen zur Verfügung stand, schließen lässt.

In den vergangenen Jahren zielte die allgemeine Richtung der Alleinerziehendenpolitik in den europäischen Ländern darauf ab, ihre Beschäftigung zu fördern, d. h. das so genannte „adult-worker"-Integrationsmodell zu verfolgen. Dies beinhaltete eine Reform der Sozialleistungen, um den finanziellen Anreiz zu erhöhen, damit es sich wieder lohnt, zu arbeiten, in Verbindung mit aktiven arbeitsmarktpolitischen Pro-

---

(1)   Lewis, J. und Hobson, B. (1997) „Introduction" in Lewis, J. (ed.) Lone Mothers in European Welfare Regimes: Shifting Policy Logics, London: Jessica Kingsley.

grammen und Unterstützung bei der Kinderbetreuung. Die Ausgestaltung und Auswirkungen dieser Reformen sind von Land zu Land unterschiedlich. Obwohl dieser Politikansatz helfen kann, allein erziehende Mütter wieder in die Beschäftigung zu bringen, kann die Beschäftigung an sich ihre Armut nicht lindern, wenn die verfügbaren Stellen gering bezahlt oder unsicher sind oder wenn sie keinen Zugang zu einer guten Kinderbetreuung haben und es keine flexiblen Arbeitszeitregelungen gibt. Daher müssen die Auswirkungen des „adult-worker"-Modells unter bestimmten nationalen Rahmenbedingungen überwacht werden. Trotz der Barcelona-Ziele wird es sicherlich in vielen Ländern weiterhin Probleme mit der Verfügbarkeit und den Kosten der Kinderbetreuung geben.

In einigen Ländern gab es kürzlich Reformen, deren Ziel es war, den finanziellen Beitrag der abwesenden Väter zu erhöhen. Diese Initiativen waren jedoch nicht immer erfolgreich, wie die Beispiele aus Litauen, Bulgarien und dem Vereinigten Königreich zeigten.

6. Die Intersektion von Geschlecht und ethnischer Zugehörigkeit bei der sozialen Ausgrenzung – die Roma

Es gibt möglicherweise über zehn Millionen Roma in ganz Europa, und ca. 1,5 Millionen Roma kamen durch den Beitritt der zehn neuen Mitgliedstaaten im Mai 2004 in die EU. Die Bevölkerung der Roma ist größer als die Bevölkerung einiger Mitgliedstaaten und stellt die größte ethnische Minderheitengruppe innerhalb der EU dar.

Systematische statistische Daten fehlen in den meisten Ländern, aber die verschiedenen verfügbaren Studien zeigen, dass die Gemeinschaft der Roma von einigen der extremsten Formen der sozialen Ausgrenzung und Armut in Bezug auf alle Lebensbereiche betroffen sind. Dazu gehören politische Beteiligung und Bürgerrechte, Gesundheit, Wohnsituation, Ausbildung, Benachteiligungen am Arbeitsmarkt, Einkommen und soziales Wohlergehen. Diskriminierungen, Rassismus und ausgrenzende Behandlung durch die Mehrheit der Bevölkerung sind weit verbreitet und schränken ihren Zugang zu öffentlichen Dienstleistungen ein. In einigen Ländern gibt es zusätzliche Probleme wie Sprachbarrieren, fehlende Dokumente einschließlich Staatenlosigkeit oder hohe Raten erzwungener Betreuung von Roma-Kindern durch staatliche Einrichtungen. Das vorherrschende Muster

wirtschaftlichen Überlebens ist eine Existenz am Rande der Gesellschaft mit informeller Arbeit zur Bestreitung des Lebensunterhalts kombiniert mit der Abhängigkeit von Sozialhilfe, oft in abgetrennten Gemeinschaften in entlegenen oder wirtschaftlich benachteiligten Gebieten.

Die stark benachteiligte Situation der Roma hat ihre Wurzeln in einer Geschichte aus Verfolgung, Rassismus und aufgezwungenen Assimilationsprogrammen. Die Bedingungen haben sich während des wirtschaftlichen und politischen Umbruchs des Übergangszeitraums in vielen der ehemals kommunistischen Länder noch verschlechtert. Hinzu kamen erneute Probleme mit Verfolgung und Staatenlosigkeit in der gesamten EU und in Nicht-EU-Mitgliedstaaten.

Über Ungleichheiten zwischen Frauen und Männern innerhalb der Roma liegen noch weniger Informationen vor. Die verfügbaren Informationen lassen darauf schließen, dass Roma-Frauen mit zusätzlichen Nachteilen kämpfen müssen. Wir stützen uns dabei auf die Angaben aus acht nationalen Berichten (BG, CY, CZ, EL, HU, RO, SI, SK).

Die besonderen Probleme von Roma-Frauen

Geschlechtsbezogene Unterschiede bei der Stellung innerhalb der Familie und im Wirtschaftsleben bedeuten, dass Roma-Frauen und -Männer unter verschiedenen Formen und Ausmaßen von Armut und Ausgrenzung zu leiden haben. Die besonderen Probleme, von denen Frauen betroffen sind, sind folgende:

● *Die traditionelle Roma-Kultur schreibt für Frauen eine Rolle innerhalb der Familie vor, die ihre Teilnahme am öffentlichen und politischen Leben einschränkt*

Die Hauptaufgabe der Frauen ist die Arbeit in der Familie, und eine Teilnahme am Arbeitsleben, am bürgerlichen oder politischen Leben ist unerwünscht. Die Frauen sind sehr jung, wenn sie heiraten und zum ersten Mal schwanger werden (14-16 Jahre ist nicht ungewöhnlich für Mädchen), und sie haben viele Kinder. Diese traditionellen Familienrollen bedeuten, dass Roma-Frauen sogar stärker vom politischen und bürgerlichen Leben der Hauptgesellschaft ausgeschlossen sind. Eine Folge davon ist, dass sie einen beschränkteren Zugang zu Rechtsberatung und -vertretung und anderen politischen Maßnahmen haben, deren Ziel die Gleichstellung von Männern und Frauen ist, als Nicht-Roma-Frauen.

● *Roma-Frauen haben zusätzliche Gesundheitsrisiken in Zusammenhang mit frühen und häufigen Schwangerschaften*

Die Gesundheitsrisiken werden durch ihre Armut und ihren schlechten Zugang zu Gesundheits- und Familienplanungsleistungen noch verstärkt.

● *Die Auswirkungen der Programme zur erzwungenen Sterilisation, die unlängst in einigen Ländern angewandt wurden*

Es gab bis jetzt noch keine Entschädigung oder öffentliche Entschuldigung für die Frauen, die gemäß den Regierungsprogrammen zur Sterilisation gezwungen wurden. Diese Programme wurden in einigen Ländern (z. B. in der Tschechischen Republik und der Slowakei) bis in die frühen 1990er Jahre angewandt.

● *Schlechte Wohnbedingungen, hohe häusliche Arbeitsbelastung und Ausschluss von lokalen Dienstleistungen*

Die Rolle und das Arbeitspensum im Haushalt sind bei Roma-Frauen anstrengender als bei vielen Nicht-Roma-Frauen: Sie müssen sich um mehr Kinder kümmern, sie müssen mit schlechten Wohnbedingungen und Behausungen, in denen die Grundausstattung (laufendes Wasser, Heizung) fehlt, zurechtkommen und haben schlechten Zugang zu lokalen Dienstleistungen (Gesundheit, Ausbildung usw.), was es für sie schwierig macht, sich um ihre eigenen Bedürfnisse und die ihrer Familien zu kümmern.

● *Der Bildungsnachteil der Roma – ein hoher Anteil an Analphabeten und niedrige Qualifikationsniveaus – ist für Roma-Frauen sogar noch ausgeprägter*

● *Hohe Arbeitslosenquoten und Nachteile am Arbeitsmarkt*

Roma-Frauen sind sogar noch mehr als Roma-Männer beschränkt auf eine begrenzte Auswahl an niedrig bezahlten und unsicheren Arbeiten, oft in der Schattenwirtschaft (Straßenverkäufer, Hausarbeiten, Arbeiten in der Landwirtschaft). Das liegt zum einen daran, dass Frauen nach der traditionellen Kultur der Roma ihren Platz in erster Linie in der Familie haben, und zum anderen an ihren schlechteren Bildungsmöglichkeiten. Bei diesen Arbeiten gibt es keinen Sozialversicherungsschutz. Dadurch kommen die Frauen in Situationen, in denen sie häufig geringe Bezahlung und Ausbeutung in Kauf nehmen müssen.

● *Abhängigkeit von Sozialhilfe*

Viele Roma sind von der Sozialhilfe abhängig, erleben jedoch oft Diskriminierungen oder negative Behandlungen durch Beamte. Zusätzliche Schwierigkeiten haben die Nomaden. Frauen sehen sich oft noch größeren Hürden gegenüber, weil bei ihnen die Wahrscheinlichkeit, dass sie einen individuellen Anspruch auf Versicherungsleistungen durch die Teilnahme am Arbeitsmarkt erworben haben, noch geringer ist. Hinzu kommt, dass traditionelle Roma-Eheschließungen im offiziellen Recht selten anerkannt werden. Dies kann erhebliche Nachteile in Bezug auf die ehegattenbasierte Anspruchsberechtigung für bestimmte Leistungen, Besuchsrechte für Ehegatten in Gefängnissen und Krankenhäusern usw. haben.

● *Prostitution und Frauenhandel*

In einigen Ländern sind Roma-Frauen eine der Gruppen, die aufgrund der extremen und sich verschlechternden wirtschaftlichen Bedingungen besonders häufig bei Prostitution und Frauenhandel erwischt werden. Dies ist jedoch kein allgemeines Phänomen in ganz Europa, da die traditionelle Roma-Kultur die Prostitution verbietet.

● *Häusliche Gewalt*

Bei den Roma-Gemeinschaften treffen oft mehrere Aspekte ihrer Lebensumstände zusammen und erhöhen so das Risiko häuslicher Gewalt. Dazu gehören die materiellen und psychischen Schwierigkeiten, unter Bedingungen der Armut und der sozialen Ausgrenzung zu leben, der zusätzliche Druck wirtschaftlicher Probleme und Schwierigkeiten, die Belastung durch Eheschließung und Elternschaft im Teenager-Alter und ein Familiensystem, das traditionell den Männern Macht und einen höheren sozialen Status verleiht. Für Frauen ist es allgemein schwierig, aus Situationen häuslicher Gewalt auszubrechen, aber Roma-Frauen sehen sich zusätzlichen Hürden gegenüber, wenn sich die einzig verfügbaren Unterstützungsleistungen außerhalb der Roma-Gemeinschaft befinden.

7.　Immigranten und Migranten

In diesem Kapitel betrachten wir die Risiken der sozialen Ausgrenzung von Immigranten und vor kurzem zugewanderten Migranten aus einer Gender-Mainstreaming-Perspektive und stützen uns auf die Informationen der nationalen Experten für zwölf Länder (AT, BE, CY, DE, DK, FR, IS, IT, LV, NL, NO, PT). Immigrantinnen/Migrantinnen machen in den meisten der zwölf Länder, in denen entsprechende Fallstudien durchgeführt wurden, 5-9% der weiblichen Bevölkerung aus, in den Niederlanden sogar 19%. In den meisten dieser Länder nimmt die Anzahl der Migranten unter der Bevölkerung zu. Zu dieser Entwicklung tragen auch die grenzüberschreitenden Ungleichheiten bei den wirtschaftlichen und politischen Bedingungen bei. In einigen Ländern gibt es neue politische Initiativen, deren Ziel es ist, die besondere Situation der weiblichen Immigranten und Wanderarbeitnehmer zu verbessern, z. B. in Portugal, Frankreich und den Niederlanden. In einigen anderen Ländern wie z. B. in Österreich oder Lettland hat Gender-Mainstreaming in der Politik nur einen geringen oder gar keinen Stellenwert

Nicht alle Migranten sind benachteiligt. Diejenigen, die aus Ländern mit einem ähnlichen oder höheren Lebensstandard im Vergleich zum Bestimmungsland stammen, haben kaum Nachteile (insbesondere wenn sie dieselbe Hautfarbe und denselben kulturellen Hintergrund haben). In der EU sind daher in der Regel Migranten aus Afrika, Asien und Lateinamerika, der Türkei und in letzter Zeit aus den mitteleuropäischen Ländern (Nicht-EU-Mitglieder sowie EU-Mitglieder) am meisten benachteiligt. Angezogen durch die Aussicht auf einen höheren Lebensstandard und gezwungen durch politische und wirtschaftliche Probleme in ihrem Heimatland wandern sie in reichere Länder aus. Oft haben sie bei ihrer Ankunft nur geringe Chancen auf dem Arbeitsmarkt. Meistens werden sie eingestellt, um freie Stellen für schlecht bezahlte und unqualifizierte Arbeiten zu besetzen, einige davon in der Schattenwirtschaft. Sie werden durch eine Kombination aus wirtschaftlichen und soziokulturellen Faktoren benachteiligt: Sprachbarrieren, schlechte Ausbildung oder Qualifikationen, die nicht anerkannt sind, Rassendiskriminierung und Ausländerfeindlichkeit sowie beschränkte gesetzliche oder wirtschaftliche Rechte. Die nicht angemeldeten Arbeiter, die illegale Migranten sind, sind in einer noch heikleren Lage. Das Ausmaß und die Form der Ausgrenzung hängt von den nationalen politischen Rahmenbedingungen in ihrem Gastland ab (Antidiskriminierungsgesetze, Schulungssysteme, Anspruch auf Sozialhilfe usw.).

Die besonderen Probleme von Immigrantinnen/ Migrantinnen

Weibliche Migranten können zusätzliche Nachteile haben. Einige kommen als wirtschaftlich abhängige Ehefrauen in das Gastland, wodurch ihre Rechte, selbstständig eine Beschäftigung aufzunehmen oder ihre Ansprüche auf eigene Sozialhilfeleistungen möglicherweise eingeschränkt werden. Sie kommen häufig aus einem kulturellen Hintergrund, bei dem Frauen begrenzte Bildungsmöglichkeiten haben und wo es im Vergleich zu den Werten und Praktiken der Bevölkerung des Gastlandes weniger akzeptiert ist, dass Frauen arbeiten gehen. Sie sind Diskriminierungen aufgrund des Geschlechts sowie anderen diskriminierenden Behandlungen und Rassismus ausgesetzt.

Anmeldung und Status

Durch verschiedene nationale politische Rahmenbedingungen kann es für Wanderarbeitnehmerinnen schwieriger sein, die größere gesetzliche Sicherheit eines „angemeldeten" anstelle eines „nicht angemeldeten" Arbeitnehmers zu erlangen. So deckt zum Beispiel die Arbeitserlaubnis für Arbeitnehmer im öffentlichen Sektor in Österreich Hausarbeiten nicht ab, sodass viele dieser Arbeiten inoffiziell und nicht reguliert ausgeführt werden.

Der verheirateten Frauen, die einwandern, um ihrem Ehegatten nach den Einwanderungsbestimmungen zur Familienzusammenführung nachzukommen, zugewiesene Status kann so sein, dass die Frauen als wirtschaftlich Abhängige ohne das Recht, eine Arbeit zu suchen, eingestuft werden. Dadurch wird ihre wirtschaftliche Abhängigkeit von ihrem Ehegatten noch verstärkt.

Beschäftigungs- und Arbeitslosenquoten

Männliche Migranten haben in der Regel höhere Erwerbsquoten als männliche Nicht-Migranten, einschließlich höherer Arbeitslosenquoten. Migrantinnen haben oft niedrigere Erwerbsquoten als Nicht-Migrantinnen, aber nicht immer. Für Frauen spielt die Dynamik des Herkunftslandes eine entscheidende Rolle – sowohl kulturelle Faktoren, z. B. betreffend die traditionelle wirtschaftliche Rolle der Frau, als auch ihre Qualifikationsniveaus und die Frage, ob die Frauen als abhängige Familienmitglieder (Ehefrauen, Töchter) oder als unabhängige (allein stehende) Wirtschaftsmigrantinnen einreisen, sowie der wirtschaftliche Zeitraum, in dem die Migrantinnen in das Land kommen. All diese Faktoren haben Einfluss auf die Integration der Migrantinnen in den Arbeitsmarkt und prägen auch die Erfahrungen, die die zweite und die nachfolgenden Generationen von Frauen machen werden. Ein Beispiel dafür sind die Arbeitsmarktmuster von Frauen nach ihrer ethnischen Herkunft im Vereinigten Königreich.

Arbeitsplatzqualität und Arbeitsbedingungen von Migranten

Die Arbeitsmärkte sind stark nach Rassen und dem Status Migrant/Nicht-Migrant sowie nach Geschlechtern getrennt. Migranten, die einer Beschäftigung nachgehen, sind überproportional in gefährlichen und gering bezahlten Stellen sowie in der Schattenwirtschaft vertreten. Einige arbeiten zusammen mit Arbeitern ohne Migrantenhintergrund in besser bezahlten Wirtschaftsbereichen. Dort haben sie jedoch Nachteile in Form von schlechteren Arbeitsbedingungen und einem größeren Risiko, bei einer Konjunkturschwäche ihre Stelle zu verlieren.

Immigrantinnen/Migrantinnen werden noch stärker in ein enges Segment schlecht bezahlter und weitgehend frauendominierter Jobs gedrängt als Nicht-Migrantinnen. Sie sind vor allem bei persönlichen Dienstleistungen und Verkaufstätigkeiten und insbesondere bei Reinigungsarbeiten und Arbeiten in privaten Haushalten vertreten. Ein Grund dafür ist, dass viele Migrantinnen niedrigere Bildungsniveaus haben. Andere sind hoch qualifiziert, aber ihre Fähigkeiten kommen zu wenig zum Einsatz und nehmen im Laufe der Zeit aufgrund von Diskriminierung, Marginalisierung und Ausgrenzung ab.

Eine wachsende Zahl von Migrantinnen ist in privaten Haushalten beschäftigt (Betreuungsleistungen für Kinder und ältere Menschen, Hausarbeit). Viele sind inoffiziell beschäftigt, und ihr sozialer Schutz oder ihre Arbeitnehmerrechte sind beschränkt. Diese Form der Beschäftigung hat besonders in Italien stark zugenommen, wo eine große Schattenwirtschaft ein allgemeines Strukturmerkmal der Wirtschaft ist und wo eingeschränkte staatliche Sozialleistungen bei den Familien eine Nachfrage nach Haushaltshilfen geschaffen haben, die bei der Betreuung älterer Verwandter behilflich sind.

Die Arbeitsbedingungen von Migrantinnen mögen im Vergleich zu den dürftigen Alternativen, die es in ihrem Herkunftsland gibt, günstig erscheinen. Dies rechtfertigt jedoch nicht die schlechten Arbeitsbedingungen, unter denen sie in wohlhabenderen Ländern arbeiten. Außerdem nimmt die Wahrscheinlichkeit, dass sie unter schlechten Arbeitsbedingungen arbeiten müssen zu, da die Marginalisierung am Arbeitsmarkt ihre Fähigkeiten untergräbt und schlechte Bezahlung und lange Arbeitszeiten es unmöglich machen, vollständig am gesellschaftlichen Leben teilzunehmen und es schwer machen, eine eigene Familie zu gründen oder für sie zu sorgen.

- ● **Ausbildung und Schulung (einschließlich Sprachkenntnissen) und aktive arbeitsmarktpolitische Programme**

Schlechte Qualifikationsniveaus sind bei vielen Migrantinnen die Regel, und einige haben das zusätzliche Hindernis der Sprachbarrieren. Manche Gruppen sind dagegen sehr gebildet und arbeiten unter ihrem Qualifikationsniveau, zum Beispiel viele Haushaltshilfen, die aus Mittelosteuropa eingewandert sind.

- ● **Wohlfahrts- und Sozialschutzsysteme**

Die schlechtere Stellung auf dem Arbeitsmarkt für Frauen aus Migranten-/Immigrantengruppen bedeutet, dass sie noch weniger Möglichkeiten haben, vollständige Ansprüche nach dem Sozialschutzsystem zu erwerben, insbesondere wenn sie größtenteils im informellen Sektor tätig sind. Die Rentenansprüche sind oft minimal, auch für diejenigen, die einen großen Teil ihres Arbeitslebens im Gastland verbracht haben. Die Probleme sind in einigen Ländern, zum Beispiel Österreich, besonders gravierend. Auch bei Wohlfahrtssystemen, die größere Teile der Bevölkerung abdecken, wie z. B. das niederländische System, kann es aufgrund der Struktur der Anspruchsberechtigung Probleme für Migrantinnen geben, insbesondere für Frauen, die nur eine Berufstätigkeit von wenigen Jahren nachweisen können oder die als abhängige Partner durch die Familienzusammenführung in das Gastland kommen.

Staatliche Reformen, deren Ziel es ist, Arbeit finanziell wieder attraktiver zu machen, können die Leistungsempfänger unter den Migranten möglicherweise härter treffen als die Anspruchsberechtigten unter den Nicht-Migranten, wenn sie schlechtere Perspektiven auf dem Arbeitsmarkt haben, wie z. B. die jüngsten Reformen in Dänemark.

Der Zugang zu Kinderbetreuung ist ebenfalls ein wichtiger Aspekt der Arbeitsmarktintegration für Migrantinnen, die Mütter sind. Dies kann auch in Ländern mit einer relativ guten Gesamtversorgung wie beispielsweise Norwegen für Migrantinnen ein Problem sein.

Die französische Politik bemüht sich intensiv um die Förderung der sozialen Eingliederung von Immigranten und ethnischen Minderheitengruppen, während dieses Thema in vielen nationalen Aktionsplänen in anderen Ländern nur einen geringen Stellenwert hat. Zahlreiche Reformen sind positiv, doch, obwohl frühere nationale Aktionspläne das Problem der „doppelten Diskriminierung" von Migrantinnen und Frauen aus ethnischen Minderheitengruppen erkannt haben, besteht bei der Gender-Mainstreaming-Analyse der Intersektion von Geschlecht und Herkunft in der Politik der sozialen Eingliederung noch Entwicklungsbedarf.

8. Gewalt und sexueller Missbrauch gegen Frauen – häusliche Gewalt, Menschenhandel und Prostitution

Thema dieses Kapitels ist Gewalt und sexueller Missbrauch gegen Frauen in zwei Bereichen – häusliche Gewalt und Menschenhandel und Prostitution. Informationsgrundlage sind hauptsächlich die nationalen Berichte für acht Länder (BG, CY, EL, LT, MT, NO, PL, RO).

Die Mehrheit der Angreifer und Kunden sind Männer, und die Mehrheit der Opfer sind Frauen, obwohl auch einige Jungen und erwachsene Männer Opfer häuslicher Gewalt werden. Benachteiligte junge Männer sind außerdem gefährdet, durch Obdachlosigkeit oder Drogenabhängigkeit in die Prostitution (vor allem gleichgeschlechtlich) hineingezogen zu werden.

Das Ausmaß von häuslicher Gewalt, Menschenhandel und Prostitution wird oft unterschätzt, insbesondere wenn die Schätzungen auf Statistiken von gemeldeten Verbrechen beruhen. Aber auch wenn man nur von den erfassten Fällen ausgeht, ist das Problem weit verbreitet. Die britische Regierung schätzt zum Beispiel, dass es in den Jahren 2000 und 2001 15,4 Millionen Fälle häuslicher Gewalt gab, wovon sich 84% gegen Frauen waren, und dass jede Woche zwei Frauen infolge häuslicher Gewalt sterben. Etwa eine Viertel- bis eine halbe Million Frauen und Kinder werden gemäß einer Studie jedes Jahr in Europa Opfer von Menschenhandel, und das Problem breitet sich in der ganzen Welt mit hoher Geschwindigkeit aus. Mittelosteuropa, Afrika und Lateinamerika sind dabei die Hauptherkunftsländer für den Menschenhandel.

Gefährdung von Frauen durch häusliche Gewalt

Häusliche Gewalt kommt in reichen und armen Familien vor. Frauen können noch mehr gefährdet sein, wenn Beziehungen unter zusätzlichem Belastungsdruck stehen, z. B. durch die Verschlechterung oder Ungewissheit der wirtschaftlichen Bedingungen für bestimmte Haushalte oder die Gesellschaft allgemein. In Rumänien scheint es beispielsweise im Zuge der schnellen sozialen Veränderungen und der politischen Unsicherheiten der Übergangsperiode einen Anstieg der Gewalt gegen Frauen, einschließlich der häuslichen Gewalt, gegeben zu haben.

Die Probleme, mit denen Frauen konfrontiert sind, die Opfer häuslicher Gewalt sind, sind vielfältig und kumulativ: Die Opfer erleiden sowohl psychische als auch körperliche Schäden, die zu einem Einbruch des Selbstbewusstseins und Selbstvertrauens führen. Dieser psychische Schaden begrenzt ihre Fähigkeit, Hilfe zu suchen, was oft noch durch ihre soziale Isolation verstärkt wird. Er wirkt sich auch negativ auf die Konzentration und Leistung am Arbeitsplatz aus, was zum Verlust oder zur Aufgabe des Arbeitsplatzes führen kann. Viele bleiben, weil sie keine Alternative sehen – ihnen fehlen die wirtschaftlichen Mittel zur Flucht, eine Scheidung ist schwer zu erreichen oder teuer, oder sie haben Angst, dass ihr Angreifer sie verfolgen und finden wird. Zusätzliche institutionelle Hindernisse stellen sich in den Weg, wenn die Politik keine Mittel zur Unterstützung und zum Entkommen anbietet, weil das Problem in der Gesetzgebung oder den polizeilichen Verfahren nicht anerkannt ist und wenn Unterstützungsleistungen (z. B. Beratungsdienste, Zufluchtsorte und Hilfe für den Wohnungswechsel) fehlen oder unzureichend sind. In Griechenland ist zum Beispiel die Vergewaltigung in der Ehe kein Verbrechen, und die Infrastruktur zur Unterstützung der Opfer (telefonische Hilfsdienste, Notunterkünfte, Beratungsdienste, Rechtsberatung) sind in Griechenland und Malta unzureichend und fehlen in Rumänien ganz.

Menschenhandel und Prostitution von Frauen

Menschenhandel und Prostitution werden durch schlechte soziale und wirtschaftliche Bedingungen in der Gesellschaft noch verstärkt. Armut in Kombination mit unzureichenden Rechtsberatungs-, Polizei- und sozialen Diensten schafft Bedingungen, unter denen Menschenhändler effektiv benachteiligte junge Frauen und Kinder ködern können. Die am meisten Gefährdeten sind Frauen mit schlechter Bildung, die in Gebieten mit hoher Arbeitslosigkeit und Armut leben, insbesondere diejenigen mit Problemen mit Schulden oder Drogenabhängigkeit oder diejenigen, die als Kind missbraucht wurden oder in einem Heim aufgewachsen sind.

Wirtschaftliche Ungleichheiten zwischen den Ländern führen zu grenzüberschreitenden Prostituiertenströmen, einschließlich der Frauen, die in andere Länder geschleust werden. Die meisten stammen aus armen Ländern in der Übergangsphase oder Entwicklungsländern und werden in reichere Länder verschleppt. Der Zusammenbruch des Kommunismus führte wegen der wirtschaftlichen und politischen Umbrüche (weniger Grenzkontrollen und Mittel für politische Maßnahmen, Konfliktgebiete) zu einer Zunahme der

Prostitution und des Menschenhandels in ganz Europa zusätzlich zu dem von vielen anderen Teilen der Welt aus stattfindenden Menschenhandel. Die Menschenhandelsströme haben sowohl in die EU als auch innerhalb der EU zugenommen. Einige Länder sind sowohl Ursprungs- als auch Zielländer. Frauen werden zum Beispiel aus ärmeren Nicht-EU-Ländern nach Polen geschleust, während polnische Frauen in andere EU-Länder geschleust werden. Die reichsten EU-Mitgliedstaaten sind die Hauptzielländer für verschleppte Frauen. Anhand der Daten für Litauen bekommt man eine ungefähre Vorstellung von dem Gewinn, der mit Menschenhandel erzielt wird. Mitte der 90er-Jahre wurden Frauen für einen Durchschnittspreis von 5 000-7 000 USD ins Ausland verkauft, was verglichen mit den Einkommensniveaus in Litauen ein sehr lukratives Geschäft ist.

Frauen, die Opfer von Prostitution und Menschenhandel werden, geraten durch ähnliche Faktoren wie die Opfer von häuslicher Gewalt (siehe oben) sowie durch zusätzliche Faktoren in die Falle: die Tatsache, dass sie gewaltsam gegen ihren Willen festgehalten werden, Sexsklaverei, sexuell übertragbare Krankheiten, weit verbreitete Drogenabhängigkeit und psychische Probleme sowie Angst vor Verfolgung und Abschiebung. Das Muster der Fallen, der Kontrolle und der Verletzung der Menschenrechte von Menschenhändlern ist ähnlich, unabhängig von dem Land, in dem es geschieht. Viele Frauen werden mit falschen Versprechungen wie Arbeitsangeboten als Haushaltshilfen, Kindermädchen oder Hotelangestellte geködert. Die meisten wissen nicht, dass sie als Prostituierte arbeiten werden. Eine Minderheit von ihnen wird von ihren Eltern oder Ehemännern in die Prostitution verkauft oder von Menschenhändlerringen entführt. Die Menschenhändler kontrollieren sie, indem sie ihnen den Ausweis und die Identitätspapiere wegnehmen, indem sie sie einsperren, ihnen Gewalt antun und Drogen geben. Sie haben natürlich kaum Zugang zum Sozialschutzsystem, und ihre Probleme werden in vielen Ländern missverstanden, weil sie durch ihre Arbeit als Prostituierte ein Verbrechen begehen (Ausnahmen in unseren Fallstudien sind Portugal und Norwegen).

9. Schlussfolgerungen – Richtlinien und Prioritäten für eine Gender-Mainstreaming-Politik für benachteiligte Gruppen

Dieser Bericht hat gezeigt, dass eine geschlechtsbezogene Analyse für das Verständnis des Ausmaßes und der Form der sozialen Ausgrenzung benachteiligter Gruppen entscheidend ist, um ein politisches Regelwerk auszuarbeiten und zu überwachen.

Geschlechtsspezifische Diskrepanzen bei den altersbezogenen Armutsrisiken unter jüngeren und älteren Menschen, bei den Arbeitslosen- und Nichterwerbstätigenquoten, bei ländlicher Armut, geschlechtsspezifische Ungleichheiten bei Mustern für die soziale Ausgrenzung von Behinderten

Frauen tragen in vielen Ländern ein höheres Armutsrisiko, wenn sie jung sind, und in allen Ländern, wenn sie alt sind, wobei die Niederlande eine Ausnahme darstellen. Das Ausmaß der geschlechtsspezifischen Ungleichheiten variiert zwischen den Altersgruppen und den einzelnen Ländern. Dadurch wird deutlich, wie wichtig es ist, Entwicklungen auf nationaler Ebene zu beobachten. Des Weiteren zeigt die Analyse für junge Leute, dass bei einigen Indikatoren die Lage für Männer schlechter ist (Quote der Schulabbrecher in den meisten Ländern), während bei anderen die jungen Frauen in der schlechtesten Lage sind (Armutsquoten).

Die benachteiligte Situation von Frauen auf dem Arbeitsmarkt bedeutet, dass sie weniger individuelle Rentenansprüche und sonstige Sozialversicherungsansprüche in Systemen erwerben, bei denen die Anspruchsberechtigung stark von den bisher einbezahlten Beiträgen oder den erzielten Einnahmen abhängt. Systeme, in denen Beiträge in Zeiten einer Teilzeitbeschäftigung oder einer Nichterwerbstätigkeit wegen einer Familienauszeit gutgeschrieben werden, bieten eine teilweise Entschädigung. Dies ist jedoch kein vollständiger Ausgleich für die negativen Auswirkungen von geschlechtsspezifischen Ungleichheiten bei der Wahrnehmung familiärer Aufgaben auf die persönlichen Einkommen und Renten von Frauen. Infolgedessen sind viele Frauen von abgeleiteten Leistungen als Ehefrauen oder von Sozialhilfe gegen Bedürftigkeitsnachweis abhängig; derzeit sind jedoch beide ungeeignet, um einen guten sozialen Schutz zu bieten, wie das Beispiel der hohen Armutsraten im Alter bei Frauen beweist. Solange es geschlechtsspezifische Ungleichheiten am Arbeitsmarkt gibt, wird die Höhe des nach den Sozialhilfesystemen garantierten Mindesteinkommens daher ein Schlüsselfaktor für die Verbesserung des sozialen Schutzes von Frauen vor Armut bleiben.

Daher ist eine geschlechtsspezifische Perspektive maßgeblich für die Ausarbeitung und Bewertung einer Reihe von politischen Maßnahmen. Dazu gehören Ausbildung, Schulung und lebenslanges Lernen, Arbeitslosenunterstützung und Arbeitsmarktprogramme, Maßnahmen zur besseren Vereinbarkeit von Arbeit und Familie, Förderung der Aktivität im Alter, Renten und Ruhestand, Betreuungsdienstleistungen für ältere Menschen. Es macht auch deutlich, wie wichtig eine Analyse der geschlechtsspezifischen Auswirkungen anderer Politiken wie der Landwirtschafts- oder Wirtschaftspolitik ist.

Um eine Politik zu erreichen, die Angebot und Nachfrage angemessen berücksichtigt und geschlechtsspezifische Ungleichheiten in den Griff bekommt, ist daher ein Gender-Mainstreaming-Ansatz erforderlich, der konsequent bei allen parallel eingesetzten politischen Instrumenten des Prozesses der sozialen Eingliederung und der europäischen Beschäftigungsstrategie angewandt wird.

Alleinerziehende sind meistens Frauen

Die Armutsquoten sind für Alleinerziehende höher. Ihr Nachteil wird in den Sozialstaats- und Beschäftigungssystemen der skandinavischen Länder, die einen hohen „sozialen Lohn" für alle Eltern durch kinderbezogene Leistungen und umfassende Kinderbetreuungsleistungen bieten, minimiert. Politische Maßnahmen sind in einer Reihe von Bereichen erforderlich – um die Beschäftigungsquoten von Alleinerziehenden in Ländern, in denen diese niedrig sind, zu erhöhen, um das Lohnniveau, das sie bei einer Arbeitsstelle erzielen können, zu erhöhen (z. B. Schulungsprogramme für gering qualifizierte Alleinerziehende) und für bessere Kinderbetreuungsleistungen und kinderbezogene Leistungen.

Roma-Frauen

Die jüngsten Richtlinien zum Schutz gegen Rassismus und Rassendiskriminierung haben den Rechtsschutz der Roma ausgeweitet. Es gibt auch ein neues Aktionsprogramm der Gemeinschaft und verschiedene andere politische Initiativen von nationalen Regierungen und internationalen Behörden (z. B. „Dekade zur Eingliederung der Roma 2005-2015"). Eine kürzlich abgeschlossene Bewertung für die Europäische Kommission kam jedoch zu dem Schluss, dass die Benachteiligung der Roma-Bevölkerung nur mit einem koordinierteren, umfassenden Politikprogramm bekämpft werden kann, das die verschiedenen Ausgrenzungsbereiche zusammen berücksichtigt (Gesundheit, Wohnsituation, Ausbildung, Beschäftigung, Rechtsberatung, Rassismus). Darüber hinaus sei eine umfassende Befragung und Einbeziehung der Roma in die Ausgestaltung und Umsetzung der Politik ein entscheidender Faktor für den Erfolg von Programmen.

Viele dieser politischen Initiativen schweigen zum Problem der Ungleichheit zwischen Frauen und Männern, obwohl die Intersektion von ethnischer Zugehörigkeit und Geschlecht die Benachteiligungen von Roma-Frauen verschärft. Wenn heutzutage Maßnahmen speziell für Frauen entworfen werden, konzentrieren sie sich in der Regel auf ihre Rolle als Mutter, um letztendlich die Situation ihrer Kinder zu verbessern. Es ist eine weiter gefasste Herangehensweise an alle Programme unter Berücksichtigung des Gleichstellungsaspekts erforderlich, die gezielte Bestimmungen für Roma-Frauen umfasst.

Bemühungen, die Ausbildung und Beschäftigung von Roma-Frauen zu verbessern, können mit traditionellen Werten in Bezug auf die angemessenen Rollen der Geschlechter in einigen Teilen der Roma-Gemeinschaften in Konflikt kommen. Daher müssen die Befragung und Einbeziehung der Roma bei der Politikgestaltung so organisiert werden, dass die verschiedenen Interessengruppen und die Stimmen der Roma-Frauen sowie die der Roma-Männer erreicht werden. Dies kann ressourcenintensiv, aber produktiv sein, wie ein Beispiel eines in Slowenien eingeführten Programms zeigt („Roma women can do it" – E Romane Romane Džuvlja Šaj).

Statistische Indikatoren sind wichtig, um Ungleichheiten zwischen Frauen und Männern innerhalb ethnischer Gruppen zu erkennen und zu überwachen. Derzeit fehlen diese in vielen europäischen Ländern oder sind zumindest eingeschränkt. Die Erweiterung der statistischen Überwachung der Roma und einiger anderer ethnischer Gruppen ist in vielen Ländern ein politisch heikles Thema. Dieser Informationsmangel ist jedoch ein zweischneidiges Schwert. Er kann einen gewissen Schutz vor Überwachung und Verfolgung bieten, bedeutet jedoch auch, dass Belege für eine Politikbewertung oder für Informationskampagnen gegen Rassismus und Diskriminierung fehlen. Der Kernpunkt ist hier, dass eine geschlechtsbezogene Aufschlüsselung in eine Erweiterung der statistischen Überwachung einbezogen werden muss.

Migrantinnen und Immigrantinnen

Migrantinnen und Immigrantinnen – insbesondere diejenigen aus nicht-westlichen Ländern – sind schlecht in den Arbeitsmarkt integriert. Normalerweise haben sie

niedrigere Beschäftigungsquoten und höhere Arbeitslosenquoten als Nicht-Migrantinnen im Gastland und
schlechtere Arbeitsbedingungen, weil sie gehäuft in
besonders niedrig bezahlten und nicht regulierten Teilen der Wirtschaft arbeiten. Einige Wirtschaftssektoren
sind auf ihre Arbeitskraft mehr oder weniger angewie-
sen, so z. B. der Verkauf, die Gastronomie, der Reini-
gungssektor und andere gering bezahlte Dienstleis-
tungsjobs. Immer mehr Migrantinnen sind oft inoffiziell
in privaten Haushalten beschäftigt, um Kinder oder
ältere Verwandte zu betreuen und im Haushalt zu
arbeiten. Zu der Benachteiligung auf dem Arbeitsmarkt kommt noch der schlechte soziale Schutz hinzu,
wodurch die Frauen einem höheren Armutsrisiko ausgesetzt sind. Einige Regierungsreformen der Sozialhilfesysteme, zum Beispiel in Dänemark, haben die Rechte von Immigranten eingeschränkt und ihr Risiko der
Verarmung erhöht.

Einige Länder haben politische Maßnahmen eingeführt, deren Ziel es ist, die Situation von Wanderarbei-
tern zu verbessern, aber wenn geschlechtsspezifische
Unterschiede bei den Bedürfnissen und Fähigkeiten
nicht berücksichtigt werden, dann könnten die Programme möglicherweise nicht den gewünschten
Erfolg erzielen, wenn es darum geht, Frauen zu erreichen. Einige Länder haben neue oder strengere Antidiskriminierungsgesetze eingeführt, die den Schutz,
den Migranten erwerben können, erhöhen. Wenn
jedoch die Themen Rassendiskriminierung und Diskriminierung aufgrund des Geschlechts in verschiedenen
Gesetzen behandelt werden und dafür verschiedene
Behörden zuständig sind, besteht die Gefahr, dass die
spezifischen Probleme, die Migrantinnen aufgrund der
Kombination von Rassendiskriminierung und Diskriminierung aufgrund des Geschlechts haben, nicht angemessen berücksichtigt werden, weil die Verantwortung an verschiedene Einrichtungen aufgeteilt ist.

Um ein besseres Verständnis der spezifischen Bedürfnisse und Benachteiligungen von Migrantinnen/Immi-
grantinnen aus verschiedenen Herkunftsländern und
in verschiedenen Zielländern zu erzielen, ist als
Grundlage für eine Politik der sozialen Eingliederung
auf der Basis von Gender-Mainstreaming mehr For-
schungsarbeit erforderlich.

Gewalt gegen Frauen – die Beispiele häusliche Gewalt sowie Frauenhandel und Prostitution

Gewalt und sexueller Missbrauch von Frauen sind
weit verbreitet. Dennoch wird das Ausmaß des Problems in der Politik oft unterschätzt und ist selten ein

vorrangiges Ziel, für das ein umfassendes Aktionsprogramm entwickelt und ein angemessenes Budget
bereitgestellt wird.

Die geschlechtsspezifische Dimension wird selten aus-
drücklich anerkannt und unmittelbar berücksichtigt –
das grundlegende Problem ist, dass ein großer Teil
der Gewalt und des sexuellen Missbrauchs in der
Gesellschaft von Männern gegen Frauen und Kinder
begangen wird.

In den einzelnen Ländern sind die Ursachen und Auswirkungen dieser Arten von Gewalt und Missbrauch
ähnlich. Die nationalen Unterschiede sind politischer
Art: die Stärke und die Reichweite des gesetzlichen
Rahmens, der Unterstützungsleistungen und Vorbeu-
gungsmaßnahmen. Ein weiterer Unterschied zwischen
den Ländern ist das Ausmaß des Problems, insbesondere wenn es ein Herkunfts- oder Zielland für Menschenhandel ist. Es kann außerdem nationale Unterschiede bei der Verbreitung von häuslicher Gewalt
geben, aber es liegen keine Informationen vor, um
dies zu beurteilen.

In den meisten der in diesem Kapitel genannten Länder gab es in den letzten Jahren neue politische Initiativen, um die Probleme häusliche Gewalt und
Menschenhandel anzugehen. Dazu gehörten eine
Rechtsreform, Sensibilisierungskampagnen und
neue Ressourcen für Dienste zur Bekämpfung von
häuslicher Gewalt, erweiterte und koordinierte
nationale und grenzüberschreitende Programme zur
Bekämpfung des Menschenhandels und zur Unterstützung von Frauen, die in die Hände von Menschenhändlern gelangt sind. Zu den noch ungelös-
ten Problemen gehören unzureichende gesetzliche
Regelungen, vollkommen unzureichende Ressourcen, eine schlechte Koordinierung zwischen den verschiedenen Polizei-, Gerichts- und Sozialbehörden,
fehlende länderübergreifende Zusammenarbeit bei
dem Problem des Menschenhandels, unzureichende
Forschungsarbeiten, Dienstleistungen und politische
Maßnahmen zur langfristigen sozialen Eingliederung, um stark gefährdete Risikogruppen zu erkennen und zu schützen.

Was in den meisten Ländern fehlt, ist ein systematischer
politischer Ansatz, um das Verhalten der Männer zu
ändern und um das Ausmaß des Problems zu reduzieren – auf Männer ausgerichtete Initiativen, um gewalttä-
tige und aggressive Verhaltensweisen zu unterbinden
und um die männerdominierte Kundennachfrage in der
Sexindustrie zu regulieren und zu reduzieren. Der

Schwerpunkt liegt weitgehend auf rechtlichen Maßnahmen, um Männer, die beim Menschenhandel, bei der Zuhälterei oder bei häuslicher Gewalt erwischt wurden, strafrechtlich zu verfolgen. Norwegen hat sich etwas Besonderes einfallen lassen. Dort gab es Bemühungen, die Nachfrage nach Prostitution zu reduzieren, indem den Staatsbediensteten und den Streitkräften verboten wurde, Sex käuflich zu erwerben. Diese Maßnahme wurde jedoch kritisiert, weil sie nicht weit genug ging und z. B. den käuflichen Erwerb von Sex nicht kriminalisierte. Allgemeiner ausgedrückt wird die Verbindung zwischen diesen spezifischen Politikbereichen und der Reduzierung von geschlechtsspezifischen Ungleichheiten in offiziellen politischen Erklärungen nicht immer hergestellt. Dies ist jedoch erforderlich, da die Verbesserung der eigenen wirtschaftlichen Mittel und des sozialen Status von Frauen eine Voraussetzung ist, um den Frauen zu helfen, Missbrauchssituationen zu vermeiden oder ihnen zu entkommen.

Abschließend drei allgemeine Punkte...

Erstens muss für den Prozess der sozialen Eingliederung eine systematische Überwachung der Unterschiede zwischen Frauen und Männern innerhalb der benachteiligten Gruppen entwickelt werden, um die Analyse der geschlechtsspezifischen Auswirkungen und das Gender-Mainstreaming bei den nationalen Aktionsplänen zu unterstützen. Die Überwachung der durchschnittlichen geschlechtsspezifischen Unterschiede ist für das Aufzeigen der genauen Ursachen und das Feststellen, wo es Fortschritte bei der Behebung der geschlechtsspezifischen Diskrepanzen gibt und wo nicht, unwirksam. Zweitens hebt Gender-Mainstreaming die Bedeutung einer Lebensbahnperspektive für die Politik der sozialen Eingliederung hervor. Zum Beispiel könnten die Alleinerziehenden, die heute in Armut leben, später die älteren Frauen sein, die ein besonders hohes Armutsrisiko im Alter haben. Drittens können einige Probleme, von denen Frauen betroffen sind, ohne eine grenzüberschreitende Herangehensweise nicht vollständig erfasst und angegangen werden. Dazu gehören Wanderarbeiter, Menschenhandel oder die Größe der Roma-Bevölkerung bei einer Betrachtung aus einem europäischen anstatt einem nationalen Blickwinkel.

1. Introduction

Gender mainstreaming has been emphasised as a key requirement in the Social Inclusion Process since the process began in 2000. This was re-emphasised and accorded an even higher profile in the 2002 common objectives which state 'the importance of taking the role of gender fully into account in the development, implementation and monitoring of National Action Plans (NAPs) (Council of the European Union, 2002).

However, assessments to date conclude that the extent of gender mainstreaming achieved so far in the NAPs for social inclusion is at best patchy and in many cases absent from the national reports (European Commission, 2005; Fagan and Hebson, 2006; Fagan et al., 2005; Rubery et al. 2003, 2004). Similar problems with the uneven development and implementation of gender mainstreaming are also present in the NAPs for employment (Rubery et al., 2003, 2004). The aim of this report is to help inform and develop the gender mainstreaming of the Social Inclusion Process by focusing upon the gender dimension to the different dimensions of poverty and social inclusion. It is based on national reports for 30 European countries, which review gender differences and inequalities in the risks of poverty and social exclusion and include a focus on selected examples of disadvantaged groups to illustrate the relevance of gender mainstreaming for effective social inclusion policy.

The national reports were prepared by the 30 national experts in the EGGSIE network, using a common work programme devised by the coordinating team in discussion with the European Commission. The national experts for the 15 pre-2004 Member States were asked to make a smaller contribution to this piece of work because they had the additional task of preparing an evaluation of the gender mainstreaming of the National Action Plans on social inclusion submitted by their governments in 2005 (see Fagan et al., 2005). Hence the 15 pre-2004 Member States were asked to prepare either one or two case studies of 'disadvantaged groups' while the other 15 national experts prepared three or four case studies. The details of the work programme are presented in Appendix 1, along with a table listing the disadvantaged groups which were selected for the focus in each national report (Appendix Table A1).

The following chapter identifies the gender dimension in risks of poverty and social exclusion. Chapters 3 to 8 focus on discussing the situation of selected disadvantaged groups which have been chosen for analysis to highlight key issues for developing gender mainstreaming for social inclusion policy. Conclusions are drawn in Chapter 9.

2. Gender differences and inequalities in the risks of social exclusion and poverty – a brief review

Gender differences and inequalities are a fundamental feature of social exclusion and poverty which are exposed by a range of statistical indicators. Employment is identified in European policy debates as a key mechanism for offering protection against social exclusion and poverty; yet in this arena there are marked gender inequalities (for evidence from the 2004 round of NAP/employment reports see Rubery et al., 2004; also Rubery et al., 2003). The employment rate for women is still lower than that for men in most countries, despite some narrowing of the gender gap in most countries over the past two decades or so. The gender gaps in employment rates are more pronounced for particular groups within the populations, such as among older workers. Women are still more likely than men to interrupt their employment or to work part-time/reduced hours to attend to family care responsibilities. On average, employed women are less likely to secure a decent income than employed men, as indicated by their greater exposure to low pay and more broadly by the persistent gender pay gap, and in turn more likely to have inferior pensions and other social protection entitlements. In every country there is a sizeable gender pay gap for hourly earnings. National data show that the pay gap is smaller among the low paid, but a higher proportion of women are paid at or close to the minimum

wage and hence their individual risk of in-work poverty is very dependent on the levels at which minimum wages are set (see Appendix Table A2 for more details on national gender pay gaps and trends in minimum wages). Gender-segregated working conditions also give rise to marked differences between women and men in their exposure to health and safety risks (Fagan and Burchell, 2002), which in turn contribute to gender differences in overall health and the incidence of a range of health problems (e.g. musculo-skeletal, cancers, heart disease).

Turning to the situation of the non-employed as well as the employed, a body of research has brought a gender lens to the study of poverty and revealed that it is disproportionately experienced by women, or is 'feminised'. The earliest systematic studies which demonstrated this were conducted nearly 20 years ago (e.g. Glendinning and Millar, 1987; updated in 1992), yet such a gender perspective is often absent from policy debates.

Some hints of the gender inequalities in poverty and social exclusion can be gathered from the common indicators of poverty and social exclusion published in the joint reports on social inclusion (European Commission, 2002, 2004a, 2005a), which show that in

---

Box 2.1: The at-risk-of-poverty common indicator

The at-risk-of-poverty rate is the proportion of persons with an equivalised disposable household income below 60% of the national equivalised median income. The household's total disposable income is taken to be the total net monetary income by the household and its members. This includes all income from work, private income from investment and property, plus all social cash transfers received including old-age pensions, net of any taxes and social contributions paid. The ECHP income data does not include some resources which are major determinants of living standards for some groups (receipts in kind, transfers paid to other households, imputed rent or interest payments). The income figures are scaled according to household composition (1 for the first adult, 0.5 for any other household member aged 14 and over and 0.3 for each child aged under 14). The resulting figure is attributed to each household member, whether adult or child.

Source: Eurostat.

most countries the at-risk-of-poverty rate is higher for women. However, it is important to note that the common indicators may underestimate the magnitude of women's greater risk of poverty. This is because the indicator is calculated on the assumption that household resources are pooled and shared equally (see Box 2.1-p.51 for the exact methodology), yet household-based calculations may underestimate differential individual exposure to poverty within the household. For example, gender differences in exposure to poverty and social exclusion in the United Kingdom have been identified in recent reports by the UK Equal Opportunities Commission and the government's Women's Equality Unit, and these features are summarised in Box 2.2. They show that women are more at risk of poverty and that the full extent of the gender gap may be underestimated. This is because resources are not always shared equally within households and women are more likely to 'go without' when money is tight.

Living on low income for a sustained period causes stress and has negative impacts on housing quality, health and social isolation. In addition to women's greater exposure to poverty and low-income, there are gender differences in how men and women experience life on a low income, as well as gender differences in health and life expectancy, the experience of crime, and homelessness (see Box 2.2 and Table 2.1-p.53).

Box 2.2: Gender, poverty and social exclusion in the United Kingdom

Poverty and low income

- Women are more likely than men to be living in poverty. After housing costs, 25% of women and 22% of men live in low-income households (equivalent incomes below 60% of the median). This means that women are 14% more likely than men to live in households with incomes below this level.

- The extent of women's greater risk of poverty may be underestimated because income and other resources are not always shared equally within households. In particular, when resources are tight, women are more likely than men to go without. In households where money is in short supply women also tend to have the stressful burden of budgeting and managing debt.

- A broken employment history because of child rearing, high rates of part-time employment, concentration in low-paid, low status work, and the gender pay gap all contribute to women's exposure to poverty and low income. Women with lower educational qualifications are particularly vulnerable and have the lowest earnings potential.

- The gender gap in income opens up over the lifecourse. While on average women's annual income is 69% of men's, the gender difference is smallest for those aged under 25 years (90%), widens to around 60% for those currently in their mid-30s to late 50s, followed by narrowing of the gap for those aged 65 years and older (70%).

- There is often an implicit policy assumption that women have, or should have, access to a male partner and his income, and that women's main role is as a carer.

- Given men's higher average lifetime income, many women in households without a male income suffer from poverty. Two groups at particular risk are lone mothers and retired women who live alone. It is estimated that only 49% of women pensioners received their full basic state pension, compared with 92% of men.

- Living for a long time on low income restricts social activity, causes stress in relationships and becomes a dominant feature of everyday life. There is evidence that women and men may experience poverty in different ways.

Other dimensions of inequality and social exclusion

- Lack of money impacts negatively on housing quality, health and social isolation.

- A higher proportion of women than men worry day-to-day about how to afford the things their household needs, and they are more likely to feel isolated and depressed because of a lack of money.

- Social isolation impacts differently by gender among those living on low income. Young men tend to have wider social networks, participate more in sport and make more use of subsidised leisure facilities than young

Box 2.2: Gender, poverty and social exclusion in the United Kingdom (continued)

women; in later life women tend to have better social relationships and to be less isolated, due largely to the networks they build around their caring responsibilities.

- Women feel more restricted in their movements outside of their house because they feel unsafe.

- Men are more likely to be victims of violent crime and attacks by strangers.

- Women are more likely to be victims of domestic violence, and 70% of violence against women is either domestic or committed by an acquaintance.

- Men commit more crime, and the crimes they commit are more likely to involve violence or a drug offence. The highest rates of criminal offence are for young men aged 15 to 20 years.

- Men have a lower life expectancy and are more likely to die from most of the principle causes of death (heart disease, lung cancer, suicide).

- Women are more likely to have symptoms of mental ill-health or distress.

- Men account for the majority of 'rough sleepers' among the homeless, women's lack of housing is more associated with temporary provision which is overcrowded or poor quality. More than half of the women and young girls who become homeless do so due to domestic violence or sexual abuse, and they are more likely to secure temporary accommodation with family or friends or to be accepted for emergency re-housing by local government under the statutory provisions.

Sources: Equal Opportunities Commission (2003), Bradshaw et al. (2003); Women and Equality Unit (2004, 2005a, Table 6.13; 2005b); Crisis (1999).

Table 2.1: Gender differences in different dimensions of social exclusion in the United Kingdom

	Women	Men
Restricted movement outside the home because they feel unsafe	42.1	16.5
Social activity excluded	22.9	17.4
Labour market excluded	21.3	12.9
Disengaged from all activities	11.1	12.5
No daily contact with friends or family	9.6	15.0
Service excluded	5.6	2.6

Source: Poverty and social exclusion survey, Gorden et al (2000), cited by the Equal Opportunities Commission, (2003).

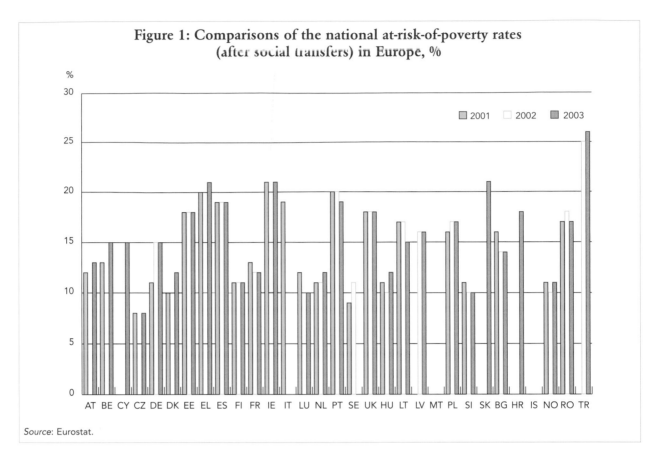

Figure 1: Comparisons of the national at-risk-of-poverty rates (after social transfers) in Europe, %

Source: Eurostat.

Figure 1 presents the overall national at-risk-of-poverty rates across Europe, while Table 2.2 (p.55) provides a gender breakdown. The rate in each country is expressed relative to the national median income; it does not compare actual living conditions across countries.[2] Despite the limitations which we have just discussed concerning measuring individual poverty derived from household income, Table 2.2 does provide some indication of the greater risk of poverty faced by women. In 21 of the 27 countries shown, the at-risk-of-poverty rate is higher for women (no data are available for IS, LI, NO). This indicator records a gender equal risk of poverty in six Member States (FI, LV, MT, PT, RO, SK) and it is only in Poland that the average at-risk rate is higher for men than women. In those countries where women are more at risk of living in a household at risk of poverty, the magnitude ranges from women being 5.3% more likely in Italy to over 15% more likely in nine others (AT, BU, CY, CZ, DE, EE, LU, SE, SI). Inspection of the table shows that the countries with the largest gender gap include both those with relatively low proportions of the population living on less than 60% of the national median income (e.g. CZ, LU) and those with higher proportions of the population with this living standard (e.g. DE, EE).

Clear gender differences are apparent in many of the other EU common indicators on poverty and social exclusion, such as exposure to persistent poverty, long-term unemployment, residency in a jobless household and early school leaving. While these indicators often show that women face the greater risk, this is not always the case. For some dimensions of social exclusion, men are more at risk. Furthermore, the magnitude of the gender gap varies according to which dimension of social exclusion is being analysed within a country, as well as across countries, as the example in Table 2.2 shows.

A gender-based analysis is essential for understanding the extent and form of social exclusion among disadvantaged groups within the population, for several distinct reasons. Firstly, certain vulnerable or disadvantaged groups are numerically dominated by one sex. Many are female-dominated, for example lone parents or older persons in low-income households, and women and girls constitute the majority of those who are the victims of domestic violence and sex trafficking. Other situations are male-dominated, including ex-prisoners, some types of homelessness (sleeping rough),

(2)   Hence for example, the at-risk rate is similar for Hungary and for Luxembourg but the material living standards are not the same for those in poverty in both counties. Similarly, the at-risk rate is higher in the United Kingdom than in Bulgaria, but the material living conditions of the poor in the former more affluent country may be higher than those for the poor in Bulgaria.

Table 2.2: At-risk-of-poverty rates (relative poverty) in 27 European countries, 2003 (%)

	All	Men	Women	Percentage point gap (women:men)	Percentage rate gap
AT	13	12	14	+ 2	16.7
BE	16	15	17	+ 2	13.3
CZ	8	7	9	+ 2	28.5
CY	15	14	17	+ 3	21.4
DE	15	13	17	+ 4	30.7
DK	12	11	12	+ 1	9.1
EE	18	17	20	+ 3	17.6
EL	21	20	22	+ 2	10.0
ES	19	18	20	+ 2	11.1
FI	11	11	12	+ 1	9.1
FR[a]	12	12	13	+ 1	8.3
HU[a]	10	9	10	+ 1	11.1
IE	21	20	22	+ 2	10.0
IT[b]	19	19	20	+ 1	5.3
LT[a]	17	16	17	+ 1	6.3
LU	10	9	11	+ 2	22.2
LV[a]	16	16	16	–	0
MT[c]	15	15	15	–	0
NL[a]	12	11	12	+ 1	9.1
PL[a]	17	17	16	– 1	– 5.8
PT[b]	20	20	20	–	0
SE[a]	11	10	12	+ 2	20.0
SI[a]	10	9	11	+ 2	22.2
SK	21	21	21	–	0
UK	18	17	19	+ 2	11.8
BG[a]	13	12	15	+ 3	25.0
RO[a]	18	18	18	–	0

Notes: Data is for 2003, except (a) = 2002, (b) = 2001, (c) = 2000. This series does not include data for the other three countries covered in this report (IS, LI, NO). The at-risk-of-poverty rate is the proportion of persons with an equivalised disposable household income below 60% of the national equivalised median income. The percentage rate gap = the percentage point gap/the poverty rate for men, e.g. for BE = 2/15 = 13%.

Source: Eurostat database (http://epp.eurostat.cec.eu.int).

and patterns of early school leaving or drug abuse in some countries; and men have a lower average life expectancy. Secondly, a gender perspective is still relevant for analysing vulnerable groups where the membership is more evenly split by sex in order to identify salient differences in the causes, extent and form of social exclusion experienced by women and men, for example among the Roma, migrants or the disabled. Thirdly, because gender relations, or more precisely men's behaviour, is centrally implicated in a number of social problems: most domestic violence is carried out by men on women, trafficking and prostitution is largely organised and used by men and, overall, most crime is committed by men (with violent crime and major acts of corporate fraud being particularly male-dominated).

Gender-based differences in exposure to different dimensions of social exclusion, for example the particular experiences of women and men from ethnic minority groups, is sometimes referred to as a 'double disadvantage' for women who face the additional burden of racism as well as gender discrimination. An alternative, and more nuanced analytical tool is the concept of 'intersectionality', which starts from the premise that people live in multiple, layered identities and are members of more than one 'identity community' at the same time (AWID 2004, George 2001). Hence, gender discrimination, racism, class inequalities and other systems of discrimination structure the relative position of women and men and combine to push some to the extreme margins of society, while others are more included and still others occupy privileged positions. The result is that women from an ethnic minority group have a substantively distinct experience to that of both men from the same minority group, and from women of the ethnic majority group. This conceptual approach also acknowledges that an individual can experience both oppression and privilege in society; for example a woman may occupy a high status professional position yet still be exposed to racism or domestic violence. In sum:

'Intersectionality is an analytical tool for studying, understanding and responding to the ways in which gender intersects with other identities and how these intersections contribute to unique experiences of oppression and privilege'

(Association for Women's Rights in Development, 2004)

Thus, through applying the concept of intersectionality, it is possible to both develop a gender mainstreaming perspective on social inclusion policy and inject a greater awareness of inequalities among women into an analysis which focuses on exposing the disadvantaged position of women vis-à-vis men in society.

The focus of this report is on advancing our understanding of how gender mainstreaming – supported by gender impact analysis – is a necessary tool for analysing the causes and dimensions of social exclusion and poverty, for identifying policy priorities, and for policy design, monitoring and evaluation. Table 2.3 (p.57) shows the disadvantaged groups that were selected by the national experts (and Appendix Table A1 provides the information organised by country) for a focused discussion in this report.

The experts based their selection on a number of considerations. The basic condition was that the group was disadvantaged in terms of above-average risks or particular dimensions of poverty and social exclusion. A second practical consideration was that at least some secondary information sources existed as a basis for the case-study discussion. The third counterbalancing consideration was that experts should also endeavour to focus attention on certain disadvantaged groups which are marginalised in policy debates about social inclusion, in part because there is a lack of statistical evidence or detailed research studies to inform the debate. The other selection criterion to consider was if the socioeconomic situation of the groups was deteriorating and/or membership was growing. Finally, the study was designed to focus on the disadvantaged position of women, but national experts could also focus on a case study where men were the more disadvantaged if they so chose.

Some experts (e.g. CY, EL) emphasised that they had selected disadvantaged groups which were the most invisible in public debate, such as women who had experienced domestic violence, or the socioeconomic situation of Roma women. Some (e.g. SI) emphasised that the disadvantaged groups they had selected were not the most disadvantaged in their country according to the gravity of their situation, but were particularly important in order to develop the gender mainstreaming perspective in social exclusion debates. Others focused on female-dominated disadvantaged groups which were growing quite rapidly (e.g. lone parents in many countries) or were already sizeable and women predominated (e.g. inactivity, among the unemployed in some countries, disadvantaged older persons) but where the gender mainstreaming of policy was under-developed. Some case-study groups were chosen because they have a more numerically even gender profile but men and women have different experiences or degrees of exclusion (e.g. migrants in some countries, rural populations, the Roma, young people).

Hence the selection covers a wide range of disadvantaged situations, but it was not designed to be a comprehensive review. Rather the case-study focuses have been chosen to expose the main issues to consider as a basis for bringing gender mainstreaming into social inclusion policy design and monitoring. Hence separate chapters discuss younger and older people (Chapter 3), long-term unemployment and inactivity (Chapter 4), lone parents (Chapter 5), the Roma (Chapter 6), immigrants and migrants (Chapter 7), and trafficking, prostitution and domestic violence (Chapter 8).

Table 2.3: Summary of the disadvantaged groups which were selected as a focus for analysis in the national reports

Disadvantaged group	National reports
Lone parents	BG, EE, ES, FI, HU, IE, LI, LT, LU, MT, NO, SE, UK
The long-term unemployed and/or inactive women	BG, CZ, HU, LV, MT, PL, SK
Roma women	BG, CY, CZ, EL, HU, SI, SK, RO
Immigrant/migrant women	AT, BE, CY, DE, DK, FR, IS, IT, LV, NL, NO, PT
Trafficking and prostitution of women	BG, CY, LT, MT, NO, PL, RO
Domestic violence	EL, MT, RO
Older women	CZ, ES, IS
Young women (16 to 24 years)	IS, LV
Early school leavers	EE
Rural women	SI, PL
Women with disabilities	IE, LV, SI
'Erased men'/'unattached men'	EE, SI
Homeless	LT

3. The intersection of gender and age in risks of social exclusion – young and older people

At every stage of the lifecourse, women are more at risk of experiencing poverty. This emerges from a variety of sources; the main ones being inequalities and discrimination in education and labour market opportunities and the impact on both of these of family care responsibilities which women take on at different stages.

Poor access to education is a major source of poverty and social exclusion. Among older generations it was the case that women had fewer educational opportunities and lower qualification levels. However, this is not the situation for younger generations, for the gender gap has been transformed over the past 25 to 35 years. Today, in most countries, the qualification level reached by younger generations of women matches or exceeds that for their male peers. This may mean that young women are less exposed than young men to the risks of early school leaving or youth unemployment. Yet other gender inequalities remain which disadvantage young women: marked gender segregation by subject area persists, and women are often over-represented in areas which feed into low-paid occupations. Furthermore, the labour market returns for a given qualification are on average lower for women than men in terms of earnings and career advancement. Hence the intersection of gender and youth is complex and changing, and this signals that a gender perspective is relevant for social inclusion policy design and monitoring.

There is a vast body of evidence which records gender inequalities in the labour market, and this is detailed, for example, in gender mainstreaming evaluations of the National Action Plans on employment (e.g. Rubery et al., 2004). The main message is that in many countries employment rates for women still fall markedly below those for men and in all countries women's hourly and lifetime earnings are lower than those for men, as indicated by the higher proportion of women working at minimum wage levels and the persistent gender pay gap. Econometric modelling shows that this earnings penalty for women persists even when efforts are made to check for any gender-related differences in 'earning power' – including education and women's greater propensity to reduce their labour market involvement in connection with family responsibilities (maternity/parental leave, periods working part-time, economic inactivity associated with family responsibilities). Furthermore, there is a cumulative effect over the lifetime, for example in the United Kingdom a period of part-time employment has a negative 'scar' effect on the earnings of women for many years afterwards, even if they resume full-time employment (Francesconi and Gosling, 2005).

It is the lower lifetime earnings of women, and the associated impact on their pensions, which is a major cause of women's greater risk of poverty in old age. In addition, while women benefit from a greater life expectancy compared with men, this also means that they predominate among the elderly who are more disadvantaged than the younger retired. The elderly have higher risks of poverty than the recently retired due to the consumption of their assets and perhaps the erosion of the real value of the pension they retired on, higher risks of ill-health and incapacity due to physical ageing, and higher risks of social isolation through bereavement of spouses and friends. Hence, not only do women predominate among the older age groups, but there are also gender-related differences in the extent and causes of social exclusion for older persons.

In this section we provide an overview of age-related differences in risks of poverty and social exclusion. We also draw on national reports which provided a case-study focus on young or older people: the national reports for the Czech Republic and Iceland examined the situation of older women; the Spanish report provided information on older women in the context of a wider trend towards the individualisation of society; and the national reports for Iceland and Estonia provided some information about the disadvantages facing young people and early school leavers respectively.

3.1. A profile of the age-related poverty and social exclusion risks

We have already seen that in the majority of countries women face a higher average risk of poverty (see Section 1). Table 3.1 explores the gender differences according to age group. It shows that only five countries have a poverty profile with limited age-related variation, including no marked increase in rates for the oldest age group (CZ, EE, HU, LT, LV). In six countries, young people have much higher poverty risks than any other age group (DE, IT, LU, NL, PL, SK). Of the other 14 countries shown in the table, seven countries display risk rates that are similar across age groups until the oldest one (65+ years) where the rate increases markedly (AT, BE, CY, EL, IE, MT, SI), and seven have higher poverty risks for both the youngest and oldest age groups (DK, ES, FI, FR, PT, SE, UK). Against these different national profiles of poverty across age groups, we also see some differences in the relative exposure of women and men to poverty. The poverty risk is higher for women for those aged 16 to 24 years in all but six of the 25 countries shown (CY, DE, LU, PL, PT, SK) and in all but four of the countries for the 25 to 49 years age group (FI, LT, SE, SI). In the six countries where it is young men who face the greater risk of poverty, the reasons are likely to lie in patterns of early school leaving and gender segregated employment opportunities. For example, in Germany industrial restructuring over the 1990s led to large job losses from the male-dominated manufacturing sectors, and the limited service sector job growth which has occurred has provided more openings for young women than young men (Fagan et al., 2005).

The picture for the 50 to 64 year age group is more variable – here men are more at risk of poverty in six countries (CZ, DE, EE, IE, PL, SK). However, among the oldest age group in all countries except the Netherlands, women are more at risk of poverty, with a particularly marked gap of at least nine percentage points found in Austria, Estonia, Finland, Ireland, Lithuania, Slovenia, Sweden and the United Kingdom. Women are exposed to greater risks of poverty in old age in pension systems which are closely based on an employment record of contributions, particularly when women's employment profiles are punctuated by periods of absence or part-time employment. That women are not at greater risk of poverty in old-age in the Netherlands is largely attributable to the fact that the pension system is largely citizenship-based rather than dependent on an employment history of contributions (Ginn and Arber, 1998). In most countries the employment profiles of women are becoming more continuous over the lifecourse, and hence the pension situation of younger generations is improving in contribution-based pension systems. However, the persistent pattern of gender earning gaps among the employed means that the average value of women's pensions will remain lower than those of men in systems where there is a large earnings-related element.

3.2. Gender and employment entry for young people

Across Europe, those at the beginning and the end of their working life have lower employment rates than those in the core period of their working life (25 to 54 years). The lower employment rates for young people aged 18 to 24 years stem mainly from inactivity due to education and training, plus youth unemployment. Economic inactivity connected with motherhood is also a factor for some young women, and inactivity due to family responsibilities can also mask some hidden unemployment; this is discussed separately in Chapter 4.

Educational attainment offers some protection from risks of social exclusion, in particular by increasing the opportunities to secure well-paid employment; conversely early school leaving increases the risks of poverty and social exclusion. Across Europe, young women now achieve a higher educational attainment than young men, which reverses the pattern for older generations (Rubery et al., 2004). Table 3.2 (p.63) shows that rates of early school leaving are much higher in some countries than in others, but in most countries young men are more likely to leave school with a low level of qualification. In 25 of the 29 countries shown (no data for LI), early school leaving is more prevalent for young men. Of the other four countries shown, the rate is slightly higher for boys in Germany, Iceland and the United Kingdom, while the Czech Republic is somewhat exceptional, with young women being more exposed to early school leaving.

Hence, in most countries, young men are more at risk of early school leaving and the risks of social exclusion and poverty which this entails. The higher average educational attainment of young women in most countries affords them some resources to secure employment; however, two points should be noted here for developing gender impact analysis. Firstly, students can also be at risk of poverty, for they are reliant on income from their families, any educational grants provided by the state and also part-time or casual employment. Secondly, even though education is usually a springboard into better-paid employment compared with the options facing early school leavers, there are still gender-differentiated outcomes. Gender-segregated educational specialisms and labour market discrimination means that even among the most educated graduate pool women tend to enter lower-paid professions. Furthermore, in some countries the earnings secured by women with intermediate level qualifications may only match those obtained by men with lower qualifications (see Box 3.1-p.64).

Regarding unemployment rates, while overall female unemployment rates still tend to exceed those for men in the EU (see Chapter 4), among young people the gender gap tends to be reversed. The youth unemployment rate in the EU is one percentage point higher for young men (Table 3.3-p.65). However, there is considerable variation between the countries: recorded unemployment rates are higher for young women in five countries (EL, ES, LU, PT, SI), while they are at least two percentage points higher for young men in six countries (CZ, DE, EE, LT, SK, UK). Hence, across the EU there are important national differences in gender inequalities in exposure to unemployment among young people.

Table 3.1: At-risk-of-poverty rates in EU countries by age group and gender, 2001 and 2002 (%)

	At-risk-of-poverty by age group				Gender gaps (women:men)			
	16 to 24	25 to 49	50 to 64	65+	16 to 24	25 to 49	50 to 64	65+
AT	11	8	9	24	+ 7	+ 2	+ 3	+ 16
BE	12	10	12	26	+ 1	+ 3	+ 3	+ 2
CY	9	9	15	58	− 1	+ 3	+ 10	+ 4
CZ	9	8	5	4	+ 2	+ 2	− 1	+ 5
DE	16	9	10	12	− 2	+ 4	− 1	+ 5
DK	21	7	5	24	+ 6	−	−	+ 2
EE	21	17	19	16	+ 2	+ 1	− 2	+ 14
EL	19	14	21	33	+ 3	+ 1	+ 3	+ 5
ES	20	15	17	22	+ 2	+ 2	+ 3	+ 4
FI	23	7	9	23	+ 9	− 1	+ 3	+ 19
FR	21	12	13	19	−	+ 2	+ 1	+ 4
HU	11	9	8	8	+ 2	−	+ 1	+ 5
IE	12	17	16	44	+ 5	+ 1	− 4	+ 16
IT	25	18	16	17	−	+ 2	+ 1	+ 3
LT	19	17	15	12	+ 1	− 1	−	+ 9
LU	20	11	9	7	− 5	+ 1	+ 1	+ 1
LV	18	16	17	10	−	−	+ 1	+ 7
MT	10	14	12	20	−	+ 1	+ 4	+ 2
NL	22	10	7	4	− 3	−	+ 1	− 2
PL	21	17	11	7	− 1	−	− 3	+ 4
PT	18	15	16	30	− 6	−	+ 1	+ 3
SE	18	7	5	16	+ 4	− 1	−	+ 10
SI	10	7	10	19	−	− 1	−	+ 13
SK	23	21	14	13	− 1	+ 1	− 2	+ 1
UK	20	12	11	24	+ 3	+ 4	+ 2	+ 9
EU	**19**	**12**	**12**	**17**	**+ 1**	**+ 2**	**−**	**+ 5**

Sources: For new Member States and EU average: 2002 data except CY (1997), MT (2002) and EU (various years) from European Commission (2005a), Table 8a, p. 190. For the EU-15: 2001 data from European Commission (2004a), Table 2, p. 230.

Table 3.4 (p.66) shows that the total employment rate for young people ranges from 20.3% (Lithuania) to 65.9% (the Netherlands). These country differences arise from differences in national education systems and school leaving ages and from rates of unemployment (see Rubery et al., 2004, for more detail). Our focus here is on gender gaps in employment rates for the youngest age group. In most countries the employment rate for young women is notably lower than that for young men. The widest gender gap is in Latvia, closely followed by Spain, Estonia, Greece and Slovenia. All of these Member States have a gap greater than 10 percentage points. In contrast, in Sweden a higher proportion of young women are in employment than men, and in Finland there is no gender gap at all. The Netherlands, Denmark and the United Kingdom all have a small gender gap in favour of men in this age group.

The Icelandic and Estonian national reports included a focus on young people. In both countries, young people experience higher rates of unemployment than other age groups. The main theme in the Estonian report is that there is a link between educational attainment and the labour market status of young people, with a particular concern being the growing number of people who drop out from school with only a basic or unfinished basic education (see Box 3.2-p.64).

In Iceland too, inadequate education is seen to contribute to youth unemployment, but the expert's emphasis here is on the misalignment of training/education provision and labour market requirements (see Box 3.1-p.64). The other problems identified in the national report for Iceland are the lack of adequate state support for young people, both in terms of inadequate benefits and inadequate help to enter employment. Benefits for the young unemployed do not cover the minimum cost of living in most cases, which puts those without parental support at risk of poverty. For those living with parents, the high marginal tax rate on moving from benefit into work (38.58%) acts as a disincentive to take a low-paid job. Young people are also less likely to participate and more likely to drop out of active labour market programme (ALMP) schemes. A particular problem that the expert identifies is that those who are claiming unemployment benefit cannot undertake education and training until they have been out of work for six months.

The indicators on early school leaving, unemployment and employment for young people illustrate how the intersection of youth and gender varies in outcome across the different countries. In many, but not all, young men are more at risk of leaving school early and with low qualification levels. Risks of unemployment are higher for young men in some countries but for young women in others, while the gender gap is slight in others still. In most countries, the youth employment rate is much higher for men, with the magnitude of the gap particularly pronounced in some. The other side of the coin is that women's greater propensity to be economically inactive, associated with domestic responsibilities (see Chapter 4), starts to open the gap in this age group. Furthermore, even when women secure higher qualification levels, this does not automatically translate into higher earning rates than for men with lower qualifications; an example of this is Iceland (see also Rubery et al., 2004, for a broader discussion of gender inequalities in the labour market). Thus young men and women face different forms of risk and disadvantage in relation to securing qualifications and a decent foothold in the labour market.

3.3. Gender, employment and retirement for older people

Gender gaps in employment rates are greater for the population aged 25 years and over, and are particularly pronounced for the older age group. In most countries, the employment rate is lower for those in the 55+ age group, and the average employment rate for this group across the EU is 41% , compared with 76.8% for those aged 25 to 54 years. There are also marked national variations in the employment rate of older people, ranging from 26.2% in Poland to 69.1% in Sweden. Among those aged 55 to 64 years the employment rate for women is lower than that for men in every country (Table 3.5-p.67). The gender gap is smallest in Finland, Sweden, France and Estonia and reaches 40 percentage points in Cyprus and Malta. Hence the particular issue of the low employment rates for older women is central to the policy objective of securing a higher employment rate for older people in the European Employment Strategy.

Employment rates for older persons are lower for a combination of 'push' and 'pull' reasons: discrimination stemming from ageism, early retirement policies designed to alleviate unemployment, age-related increases in ill health (particularly for those in physically demanding jobs) and other factors such as income adequacy and desire to devote time to other activities (grandchildren, travel, etc.). In addition

Table 3.2: Early school leavers: percentage of the population aged 18 to 24 with at most lower secondary education and not in further education or training, 2004

	All young people	Young women	Young men	Gender gaps (women:men)
AT	8.7	7.9	9.5	– 1.6
BE	11.9	8.3	15.6	– 7.3
CY	18.4	14.3	23.3	– 9.0
CZ	6.1	6.5	5.8	0.7
DE	12.1	11.9	12.2	– 0.3
DK	8.1	5.8	10.4	– 4.6
EE[a]	12.6	9.6	15.6	– 6.0
EL	14.9	11.6	18.3	– 6.7
ES	31.1	24.1	37.8	– 13.7
FI	8.7	6.9	10.6	– 3.7
FR	14.2	12.3	16.1	– 3.8
HU	12.6	11.4	13.7	– 2.3
IE	12.9	9.7	16.1	– 6.4
IT	22.3	18.7	26.2	– 7.8
LT	9.5	7.4	11.6	– 4.2
LU[b]	17.0	19.6	14.4	5.2
LV	15.6	10.7	20.5	– 9.8
MT	45.0	43.1	46.6	– 3.5
NL	14.5	12.6	16.4	– 3.8
PL	5.7	3.7	7.7	– 4.0
PT	39.4	30.6	47.9	– 17.3
SE	8.6	7.9	9.3	– 1.4
SI	4.2	2.6	5.8	– 3.2
SK	7.1	6.4	7.8	– 1.4
UK	16.8	16.5	17.1	– 0.6
EU	15.7	13.3	18.1	– 4.8
BG	21.4	20.7	22.1	– 1.4
IS	26.3	26.1	26.4	– 0.3
NO	4.5	3.7	5.2	– 1.5
RO	23.6	22.4	24.9	– 2.5

Notes: (a) = 2002 data, (b) = 2003 data. No data are available for Liechtenstein.
Source: Eurostat (2005).

some labour market policies which are designed to provide more security for older workers may have the opposite, unintended effect by deterring employers from hiring older workers. One such example is the greater job security afforded older workers in Iceland (see Box 3.3-p.68).

The markedly lower employment rate for older women in some countries is in part due to lower labour market participation earlier in their working lives. To some extent this is a 'generational effect' which is being eroded as younger generations of women pursue a higher and more continuous profile of labour market

Box 3.1: Education/training and youth unemployment in Iceland

The recent growth in youth unemployment in Iceland is explained by the expert as resulting from a mismatch in skills and labour market demands – as the educational system favours general education, and the influx of immigrant workers from eastern Europe with vocational skills. Young men are more likely to be unemployed, an important explanatory factor being that young women are more likely to enter education after becoming unemployed whilst young men continue to search for a job. A greater 'incentive' for young women to complete secondary education is that it is only with such a level of qualification that they can gain wages comparable to those of men with only primary education.

Source: national report.

Box 3.2 Provisions for early school leavers in Estonia

For early school leavers, it is possible to complete basic education at an adult secondary school or to undertake 'preparatory vocational training' at a vocational school. Vocational schools have no right to give basic education so they have to find schools to supplement their curricula. The problems with the current system include insufficient places, the inflexibility of the rules covering vocational training, and economic problems for adults wanting to return to education. Recommendations to the Parliament made by the State Audit Office include allowing vocational schools to provide basic education to those aged over 17, and supporting adults who wish to return to education.

Source: national report.

participation. However, while the gender gap may be reduced among future generations it is unlikely to disappear in the foreseeable future.

In most countries the state retirement age for women is now the same as for men and set somewhere between 60 and 67 years, although for some, including the United Kingdom, this is a recent introduction and transitional mechanisms are in place for older generations. Of the European OECD countries, only Austria, the Czech Republic and Poland do not have an equal retirement age for men and women in place (Table 3.6-p.69).

The average exit age of both sexes is almost universally lower than the official retirement age (the only exception is for women in Hungary), but women typically retire earlier than men in all the countries shown except six (BE, HU, IE, IT, NO, RO). The largest gender gap is in Slovakia (4.1 years).

In the Czech Republic, legislation has been passed to increase the retirement age. At the same time, the expert reports that people who are approaching the retirement age are facing increasing pressures to exit the labour market. Their point has resonance across European countries. An increase in the state retirement age will reduce the number of people eligible for a pension, but unless older people have opportunities to be employed until a higher age, this will make them more reliant upon other forms of benefit and at greater risk of poverty if the benefits they are eligible for are less than pension rates. Some state policies provide additional support for unemployed older workers in acknowledgement of the greater difficulties which they face in securing employment. However, where these provisions rest upon previous social security contributions, it may be more difficult for women to secure eligibility, since women typically have more interrupted employment records. This negative gender impact exists in the provisions for older workers in Spain, for example (see Box 3.4-p.68).

Some people work beyond state pension age. Financial reasons play a major part, but for some it is also because they gain enjoyment and other non-financial rewards from their employment. Again in the Czech Republic, in 2001, 19% of all senior citizens continued to work in some form after the state retirement age. This work was generally ad hoc and occasional, with retired persons willing to work for lower wages than other age groups. The expert concludes that proposals to allow older workers to take a 'flexible retirement' are welcome and should be extended, for one advantage would mean that this would enable older persons to continue in their pre-retirement occupation instead of being obliged to switch to low-paid, irregular employment to supplement their pension at the end of their working life. Iceland is one country with provisions for flexible retirement, and the government has recently proposed an extension of the arrangements (see Box 3.5-p.70).

Pension entitlements are typically based upon a time dimension – the number of contributory years, sometimes defined narrowly in terms of years in paid

Table 3.3: Unemployment rates for young people (15 to 24 years) by gender, 2004

	Total	Women	Men	Gender gaps (women:men)
AT	5.6	5.4	5.7	– 0.3
BE	7.5	7.3	7.6	– 0.3
CY	4.5	4.7	4.2	0.5
CZ	7.4	6.1	8.6	– 2.5
DE	6.0	4.9	7.2	– 2.3
DK	5.6	4.9	6.2	– 1.3
EE	7.5	6.2	8.8	– 2.6
EL	9.9	12.1	7.6	4.5
ES	9.9	10.5	9.4	1.1
FI	10.3	9.5	11.1	– 1.6
FR	8.1	7.7	8.5	– 0.8
HU (a)	4.3	3.5	5.1	– 1.6
IE	4.7	4.2	5.2	– 1.0
IT	8.5	8.6	8.4	0.2
LT	5.9	4.9	7.0	– 2.1
LU	4.8	6.0	3.7	2.3
LV	6.8	6.6	6.9	– 0.3
MT	9.2	8.7	9.5	– 0.8
NL	5.7	5.7	5.7	–
PL	14.2	13.4	15.0	– 1.6
PT	6.7	6.9	6.5	0.4
SE	8.0	7.6	8.4	– 0.8
SI	6.5	6.8	6.2	0.6
SK	13.0	11.1	14.9	– 3.8
UK	7.6	6.4	8.7	– 2.3
EU	8.3	7.8	8.8	– 1.0

Note: (a) The national expert regards the EU statistics as an underestimate of unemployment in Hungary. National statistics show unemployment rates in the second quarter of 2005 to be 20.2% for men and 18.1% for women.
Source: European Commission: Employment, Social Affairs and Equal Opportunities DG (2005b), *Indicators for monitoring the 2004 employment guidelines: 2005 compendium*, updated 14.10.2005, p. 74.

employment, and an earnings dimension – the amount earned through wages over a working life (or a shorter qualifying period, or final earnings). Women are disadvantaged across both of these dimensions in that they accrue lower individual pension entitlements, due to less continuous employment profiles and the gender wage gap. This is behind the much greater risks of poverty in old age faced by women, as shown in Table 3.1 (p.61). Hence while the moves across Europe to promote flexible and later retirement as a means to facilitate 'active ageing' will provide women with opportunities to increase their pensions. The impact of such policies is likely to be highly gender differentiated in terms of both employment patterns among older workers and the financial returns from prolonged employment.

Table 3.4: Employment rates for young people (15 to 24 years) by gender, 2004

	Total	Women	Men	Gender gaps (women:men)
AT	51.9	47.9	56.0	– 8.1
BE	27.8	25.4	30.1	– 4.7
CY	37.3	33.6	41.5	– 7.9
CZ	27.8	25.4	30.1	– 4.7
DE	41.9	40.2	43.6	– 3.4
DK	62.3	61.1	63.4	– 2.3
EE	27.2	21.6	32.8	– 11.2
EL	26.8	21.3	32.3	– 11.0
ES	35.2	29.3	40.8	– 11.5
FI	39.4	39.4	39.4	–
FR	30.4	26.7	34.0	– 7.3
IE	47.7	44.7	50.7	– 6.0
HU	23.6	20.8	26.3	– 5.5
IT	27.6	23.1	32.1	– 9.0
LT	20.3	16.5	24.0	– 7.5
LU	21.4	19.5	23.3	– 3.8
LV	30.5	24.4	36.4	– 12.0
MT	47.7	43.2	52.0	– 8.8
NL	65.9	65.4	66.3	– 0.9
PL	21.7	18.6	24.8	– 6.2
PT	37.1	32.5	41.5	– 9.0
SE	39.2	39.7	38.6	1.1
SI	33.8	28.6	38.8	– 10.2
SK	26.3	24.6	28.0	– 3.4
UK	55.4	54.1	56.6	– 2.5
EU	**36.8**	**33.8**	**39.8**	**– 6.0**

Source: European Commission: Employment, Social Affairs and Equal Opportunities DG (2005b), *Indicators for monitoring the 2004 employment guidelines: 2005 compendium*, updated 14.10.2005, p. 65.

The poorer individual pension entitlements accumulated by women over the lifecourse means that among the retired population women are more dependent than men on other forms of welfare. For example, the national reports for Spain, Slovakia and the Czech Republic report that women receive a significant portion of their pension income from widow's pensions. The experts for Spain and Slovakia present contrasting evidence of the adequacy of women's pension entitlements based on their late husband's contributions: in Spain 60% of older women receive a means-tested widow's pension but it is insufficient to lift them out of poverty (Box 3.6-p.70), while in Slovakia the widow's pension serves to raise the income of older women and partly compensates for their lack of an individual pension (Box 3.7-p.71).

A final consideration in relation to older people is care services for the elderly, including both services to assist independent living in their own homes and residential services. The care of the elderly is a gendered issue as the responsibility for caring for an elderly relative (other than spouses) most often falls

Table 3.5: Employment rates for the 55 to 64 year age group by gender, 2004

	Total	Women	Men	Gender gaps (women:men)
AT	28.8	19.3	38.9	-19.6
BE	30.0	21.1	39.1	-18.0
CY	50.1	30.4	70.9	-40.5
CZ	42.7	29.4	57.2	-27.8
DK	60.3	53.3	67.3	-14.0
DE	41.8	33.0	50.7	-17.7
EE	52.4	49.4	56.4	-7.0
EL	39.4	24.0	56.4	-32.4
ES	41.3	24.6	58.9	-34.3
FI	50.9	50.4	51.4	-1.0
FR	37.3	33.8	41.0	-7.2
HU	31.1	25.0	38.4	-13.4
IE	49.5	33.7	65.0	-31.3
IT	30.5	19.6	42.2	-22.6
LT	47.1	39.3	57.6	-18.3
LU	30.8	22.9	38.5	-15.6
LV	47.9	41.9	55.8	-13.9
MT	30.9	11.4	52.2	-40.8
NL	45.2	33.4	56.9	-23.5
PL	26.2	19.4	34.1	-14.7
PT	50.3	42.5	59.1	-16.6
SI	29.0	17.8	40.9	-23.1
SK	26.8	12.6	43.8	-31.2
SE	69.1	67.0	71.2	-4.2
UK	56.2	47.0	65.7	-18.7
EU	**41.0**	**31.7**	**50.7**	**-19.0**

Source: European Commission, Employment, Social Affairs and Equal Opportunities DG (2005b), *Indicators for monitoring the 2004 employment guidelines: 2005 compendium*, updated 14.10.2005, p. 11.

on women. The number of frail elderly in need of assistance in their daily lives is increasing in parallel with growing strains on family-based forms of support: women are more likely to be employed during the latter part of their working life, which is the period in which care responsibilities for older parents typically increase. In addition the type of support families can provide in some societies may be changing due to geographical mobility and distance, and the impact of divorce on inter-generational relationships in some families. The expansion of elderly care services presents a number of difficulties in many countries, in part because of expenditure constraints but also because of recruitment and retention problems in areas such as 'home help', which have traditionally been female-dominated jobs (Anxo and Fagan, 2005). In some countries, carer's benefits exist to support family-based forms of care but, if these benefits are means tested or only available to carers who give up employment, this can create disincentives for employment among older workers and may even mean that there is more demand on the more costly state care services as a result (see Box 3.8-p.71).

> ### Box 3.3: Explanations of employer reluctance to employ older people in Iceland
>
> Since the early 1990s, an agreement has been in force in the private sector (which employs around 90% of all employees) granting workers aged 55 and over a longer period of notice, so it takes longer for employers to dismiss older workers. The length of the term of notice is four months for those aged 63 and over. For workers below the age of 54 the period is three months. This policy contributes to the smaller flow of older workers from employment to unemployment, compared with younger staff (a positive development for older workers) but also a smaller flow of older workers from unemployment to employment (a negative development). Employer reluctance to recruit older people, due partly to this policy, has led to older people being the most likely group in Iceland to become long-term unemployed – with older women who lose their job the worst affected. Early retirement schemes are not available in Iceland, and people can remain on unemployment benefit until the age of 70. The other major factor contributing to employer reluctance to recruit older people is that they are deemed to have inadequate skills. In particular, older people are less likely to be recruited to work in the ICT sector, and older workers are least likely to participate in job-related education and training.
>
> *Source:* national report.

> ### Box 3.4: Spanish benefits for pre-retirement workers
>
> The difficulties for older workers to find or stay in employment are such that the Spanish social security system allows people over the age of 52 to remain on unemployment assistance until the retirement age. However eligibility is conditional on previous social contributions and many older women do not qualify because their work history contains more interruptions than those of men. A gender impact analysis of eligibility would provide the basis for reforming the eligibility conditions so that more women qualified for this form of social protection.
>
> *Source:* national report.

3.4. Concluding assessment: gender mainstreaming the policy direction and priorities for disadvantaged groups of younger and older people

Gender intersects with age-based risks of exposure to poverty and social exclusion. The gender pattern is least clear-cut for young people; for young men and women face different forms of risk and disadvantage in relation to securing qualifications and a decent foothold in the labour market. But overall, the poverty risks are higher for young women than young men in the majority of countries. Women also have higher risks of poverty than men among those aged 25 years or older in most age bands and in the majority of countries, with the disadvantage which women face being particularly visible among the older, retired age groups. Hence a gender perspective is relevant in the design and evaluation of a range of policies directed at redressing disadvantage among young and older people: education and training, unemployment benefits and labour market programmes, pensions and retirement, and elderly care services.

The four national case studies which focused on young and older people (CZ, EE, ES, IS) reached similar policy recommendations. For both young and older people the experts point to the inadequacy of benefit levels for the unemployed and retired. In relation to active labour market programmes for the unemployed and the promotion of 'active ageing' through flexible retirement policies the Icelandic expert's comments are pertinent: that young people and those close to the retirement age should be encouraged to participate in the labour market through means other than the threat of poverty.

In pension systems built upon employment contributions and lifetime earnings, women are more at risk than men of failing to accumulate a decent pension, due to the persistent gender wage gap and because women have more interruptions to employment or periods of part-time employment for family care responsibilities. For similar reasons, women are also less likely to meet the contributory requirements for unemployment insurance benefits. Care-related credits for periods of part-time employment or non-employment can provide some partial financial redress but are inadequate or absent in some state pension systems. For example, if

Table 3.6: State retirement ages and average exit age from the labour force, 2003

	State retirement age		Average exit age from the labour force		
	Females	Males	All	Females	Males
AT	60	65	58.8	58.2	59.4
BE	65	65	58.7	58.7	58.6
CY			62.7	(:)	(:)
CZ[a]	59–63	63	60.0	59.0	61.2
DE	65	65	61.6	61.4	61.9
DK	65	65	62.1	62.0	62.3
EE			60.8	(:)	(:)
EL	65	65	63.2	62.5	63.9
ES	65	65	61.4	61.3	61.6
FI	65	65	60.3	60.0	60.7
FR	60	60	59.6	59.6	59.7
IE[b]	66	66	64.4	62.8	62.0
HU[c]	62	62	61.6	62.1	60.9
IT	65	65	61.0	61.0	60.9
LT[d]	62.5	58.5	63.3	(:)	(:)
LU	65	65	(:)	(:)	(:)
LV			60.3	(:)	(:)
MT			58.8	(:)	(:)
NL	65	65	60.4	59.9	61.0
PL	60	65	58.0	56.4	59.8
PT	65	65	62.1	60.6	63.7
SE	65	65	63.1	62.8	63.5
SI			56.2	(:)	(:)
SK[e]	62	62	57.8	55.9	60.0
UK	65	65	63.0	61.9	64.2
EU	n/a	n/a	61.0	60.5	61.5
BG			58.7	57.5	60.1
NO	67	67	62.8	62.8	62.8
RO			62.8	62.9	62.6

Notes: The state retirement ages shown include all legislated changes up to 2002, even when these take effect in the future. The average exit age data is weighted by the probability of withdrawal from the labour market. Some figures are provisional values.
(a)   The Czech female retirement age depends on the number of children.
(b)   Irish data on male and female average exit age from the labour force are for 2002.
(c)   The national expert reports that the female retirement age will reach 62 years in 2009 (it is currently 60 years). It is surprising that the female average exit age is both higher than the state retirement age and the male average exit age, so the expert doubts the validity of these data.
(d)   State retirement age data for 2003 were provided by the national expert. Since 1995, there has been an annual increase in the state retirement ages, by 4 months for females and two months for men.
(e)   The national expert reports that the retirement age of 62 will be achieved for all men in 2007 and for all women in 2014.
(:)   Not available.

Sources: OECD (2005), Table 2.1, pp. 29–30; Eurostat Average exit age from the labour market, by gender, supplemented by information provided by the national experts.

such credits were introduced into the Czech pension scheme this would help to improve the financial position of women, particularly since the statutory parental leave system permits mothers (and more recently fathers) to be on leave until the child is four years old. Similarly, credits and other financial support for care responsibilities for older parents and other adults would redress gender gaps in income in old age, given that

women constitute the majority of this group of carers too (as well as many of the elderly relatives being cared for, given women's greater life expectancy). The Spanish national expert advocates another solution to the gender inequalities in old age incurred through contribution-based systems: a guaranteed minimum income above the poverty line for the retired.

Box 3.5: Flexible retirement provisions in Iceland

The official retirement age in Iceland is 67. Public-sector employees can postpone retirement until 70, allowing them to build up a higher pension entitlement. These workers are able to take partial retirement between the ages of 60 and 70, and support themselves through a combination of a part-time wage and a pension during this period. While public-sector workers are prohibited from working beyond 70, there is no such restriction in the private sector. Many occupational pension schemes allow members to receive a pension from 65, but no pension schemes in Iceland allow private-sector workers a flexible retirement before the age of 65, forcing some older workers to leave their job and claim unemployment benefits in their early 60s. The inflexibility of retirement rules has been criticised by a committee appointed by the prime minister in 2001, which has recommended giving workers the options of working until the age of 72, and taking partial retirement before or after the official retirement age of 67. These recommendations have not yet been implemented, but would have a positive impact on the employment integration of older men and women.

Source: national report.

Box 3.6: Inadequacy of single women's pension entitlements in Spain

Among the over-65s who live alone, only 31% of women receive a retirement pension compared with 88% of men. In contrast, 60% of women receive a widow's pension, compared with only 3% of men. The widow's pension is partly means-tested, and in 2003 the average level was EUR 403 per month. The 31% who receive an individual pension includes both those who receive a non-means-tested, contributions-based pension (the most well-off group, receiving an average EUR 442 per month in 2003) and those who did not have a husband with a contributions-based pension and are therefore reliant on only means-tested benefits (the poorest group, receiving EUR 269 per month in 2003). All three income sources for single older women are insufficient alone to raise incomes above the poverty threshold (EUR 491 per month in 2003), so the poverty rate of older single women can be expected to be in excess of the 50.3% estimate for all single older people. The widow's pension is criticised by the expert as a 'residual of the past' that is received by many widows and widowers who do not need it and is at an insufficient level for those who are reliant upon it. An increase in the level of the non-contributory pension to put those excluded from the contributory scheme above the poverty line would have a positive impact on the pension situation of women.

Source: national report.

Box 3.7: Importance of widow's pensions in Slovakia

Despite Slovakian women having lower average *individual* pension entitlement than men, their *total* pension income seems to be typically higher where they receive a widow's pension. In contrast, Slovakian men have only been granted entitlement to a widower's pension since 2004.

Source: national report.

Box 3.8: The need for more state support for carers in the Czech Republic

In Czech society, it is generally taken as given that adult children and their families will support and help elderly parents. In the main, this responsibility falls on women, 80% of whom combine caring with paid employment. Where the older person is infirm, a benefit is available to a family member to care for them full-time. This is set at a low level (1.6 times the living minimum), and taking this benefit can lead to a large reduction in total household income. Alternatively, an infirm person can be placed in a state-run care institution. The cost to the state of this second option is significantly higher than the benefit available, and the expert suggests that a higher carer's benefit should be paid to relatives to reduce this gap. Such a change could actually reduce total state expenditure.

Source: national report.

4. Gender differences in rates of long-term unemployment and inactivity, rural poverty and the exclusion of disabled people

One of the priorities of the European Employment Strategy is to secure a higher employment rate for women; for their employment rate is lower than that of men in all Member States, and in many countries the gender gap is pronounced. This lower employment rate for women is a key factor contributing to women's greater exposure to poverty and social exclusion, making them reliant on whatever individual benefit entitlements they have plus intra-household transfers (e.g. the earnings of a spouse or parent).

In most European countries, unemployment rates are higher for women than for men; in 2003 this applied to 19 of the 25 Member States, with the reverse situation found in six countries (DE, FI, HU, IE, SE, UK). Inactivity rates are also higher for women. The economically inactive are a heterogeneous group: students in full-time education, older persons who have retired early, and those who are not seeking employment due to care responsibilities (mainly mothers)[3] or disability/chronic sickness. Inactivity can also hide 'latent unemployment' for those who want employment but are not recorded as unemployed. In the Czech Republic, for example, the national expert argues that the numbers of those in full-time education or taking early retirement reflects a response to poor labour market conditions and 'latent unemployment'. When the definition of this group of 'job seekers' is set to include those who do not want a job immediately but do within a specified period of a year or so, this constitutes a sizeable group within the European working-age population, and particularly for economically inactive women (e.g. Fagan, 2001).

The main reason why economic inactivity rates are higher for women than for men is that a much higher proportion of women report that they are inactive due to care responsibilities; more precisely, it is mainly that mothers are constrained in their labour market options because the primary responsibility for putting time into child-raising still falls to women. While in some countries there are some care-related payments which are received directly by women in their roles as mothers or carers for older or incapacitated relatives, the level of support provided is usually relatively low.

Six national experts in the EGGSIE network produced reports considering long-term unemployed women and/or women who are not active in the labour market: Bulgaria, the Czech Republic, Hungary, Malta, Poland and Slovakia. The main focus of the national expert reports is on three disadvantaged groups of unemployment and inactivity:

- the long-term unemployed[4], who remain formally classified as economically active and may receive some or all of their income through unemployment insurance benefits;

- those who are economically inactive, but who would ideally prefer to be in employment; women in this group may be supported by state benefits whether means-tested or circumstances-based (e.g. having pre-school children) and/or by the wage of their partner;

---

(3)   In some countries, periods of parental leave are treated as economic inactivity; in others, those on parental leave are defined as employed (albeit absent from work).
(4)   Unemployment is deemed to be 'long-term' when it has lasted for over 12 months.

a subgroup of those registered as inactive that receive particular attention from the experts is women who have recently had children and are potential 'returning mothers' to the labour market; these women may have extra state benefits available to them through maternity/parental leave schemes whilst they remain formally economically inactive.

In addition, some national experts provided a case-study focus on the particular issues of inactivity and under-employment of women in rural areas (IT, PL, SI) and gender differences among people with disabilities in labour market integration (IE, SI). These case studies are also discussed in this chapter.

4.1. A profile of gender gaps in long-term unemployment and inactivity rates

Based on the most recent data available (Eurostat, 2005), across the EU, 46% of those who are unemployed are classified as long-term unemployed. The national report for Poland records that long-term unemployment constituted 45.8% of all unemployment in 2002, while in the Czech Republic the expert reports that since 2000 more people have been in long-term unemployment than in unemployment for a period of less than 12 months. The most recent data shows a range in this proportion from 68% of the unemployed in Slovakia to 19% of the unemployed in Sweden.

The proportion of the economically active population who are identified as 'long-term unemployed' varies significantly across the EU (Table 4.1). In all but seven of the countries shown (EE, IE, FI, HU, MT, SE, UK) the long-term unemployment rate is higher for women than for men; although in four of the 18 countries (DK, LV, NL, SI) where the rate is higher for women the gender discrepancy is slight.

Gender differences in long-term unemployment rates should not be assessed in isolation from data on inactivity rates. This can be illustrated by the example of Malta, where the long-term unemployment rate for women is lower than that for men and is also two percentage points below the EU average long-term unemployment rate for women. Table 4.2 (p.77) shows that Malta has the highest inactivity rate in the EU for women aged 15 to 64 years and also for the overall population as a result. It is the only Member State where the female inactivity rate exceeds 50%. Part of the explanation for this very high level lies in the relatively low retirement age in

Malta (61 years for men, 60 years for women) and that more women attend university (57.1% of university graduates in Malta are women); but by far the most important reason is the division of household labour. According to national statistics, 62.9% of inactive women do not work because of personal or family commitments, compared with only 3.1% of inactive men. This indicates that the low level of female long-term unemployment in Malta is partly a consequence of low female participation in the labour market. For Malta, the combination of low female long-term unemployment rates and very high female inactivity rates can both be seen to stem from social norms and practices that sustain a pronounced gender division of labour and place the onus to perform household responsibilities on women.

The gender division of household responsibilities and its manifestation in gender gaps in inactivity rates is most extreme in the case of Malta, but exists in every Member State. The smallest gender gaps are found in the Nordic states (Sweden 3.9, Finland 4.4, and Denmark 7.8) and the Baltic States (Lithuania 7.2, Estonia 8.4 and Latvia 9.0). Furthermore, in 24 of the 25 Member States, a higher proportion of inactive women than inactive men are 'hidden unemployed' who want employment; producing an overall EU-25 rate of 5.8% of inactive women and 3.5% of inactive men. The exception is Sweden where there is no gender gap (Rubery et al. 2004, based on the employment context indicator No 18 for the European Employment Strategy).

National data for the Czech Republic and Poland illustrate the greater exposure of women to both inactivity and long-term unemployment rates, while in Bulgaria the gender imbalance emerges in relation to inactivity but not long-term unemployment rates (see Box 4.1-p.78). Among the different categories of inactivity it is particularly inactivity due to family/household responsibilities where women are over-represented, as was already observed in the earlier cross-country discussion. Both the Czech and Polish national experts highlight that this over-representation of women in this category of economic inactivity is connected to the way policies shape the labour market options available to and selected by women with care responsibilities. Hence the inadequacy of work–family reconciliation measures, and employer-based discrimination steer women into economic inactivity when they become mothers or take on elderly care responsibilities. (For a more detailed discussion of parental leave and other reconciliation policies across Europe see also Fagan and Hebson, 2006, and Plantenga and Remery, 2005.)

Table 4.1: Total long-term unemployed population (12 months or more) as a proportion of the total active population (by gender) 2004

	Total	Men	Women
AT	1.2	1.1	1.3
BE	3.8	3.4	4.3
CY	1.1	0.8	1.5
CZ	4.2	3.4	5.3
DE	5.4	4.8	6.1
DK	1.2	1.1	1.2
EE	4.8	5.6	4.1
EL	5.6	3.0	9.4
ES	3.5	2.3	5.3
FI	2.1	2.3	2.0
FR	3.9	3.5	4.4
HU	2.6	2.6	2.5
IE	1.6	2.0	0.9
IT	4.0	2.9	5.5
LT	5.5	5.2	5.9
LU	1.0	0.8	1.1
LV	4.3	4.2	4.4
MT	3.4	3.8	2.7
NL	1.6	1.5	1.6
PL	10.2	9.5	10.9
PT	3.0	2.6	3.4
SE	1.2	1.4	1.0
SI	3.1	3.0	3.2
SK	11.7	11.0	12.5
UK	1.0	1.2	0.6
EU-25	4.1	3.6	4.7

Note: Data for Cyprus is for 2003.
Source: European Commission (2005b), Key indicator 6, p. 15.

In Hungary, unemployment rocketed in the early 1990s from previously very low levels in the 'socialist' period. Unemployment then fell in the period 1994–2003, which in the mid-1990s was partly due to people moving from unemployment to inactivity rather than from unemployment to employment. The mid-1990s saw a growth in the number of people attending Hungary's universities, and the encouragement of people to remain economically inactive through early retirement schemes and extended parental leave. Recent data suggests that there is little hidden unemployment among those who are inactive, as of 2.6 million inactive people, only 14%

would like a job. However the majority of these hidden unemployed are women (60%).

4.2. The poverty and social exclusion risks experienced by the long-term unemployed and economically inactive

The common indicators for monitoring social inclusion in the EU Member States show that the economically inactive and unemployed have high risks of poverty, and there are gender differences in the risks (European Commission, 2005a, Table 8a). Long-term unemployment also increases exposure to poverty due to an exhaustion of insurance-based welfare benefits and resources such as savings. The six national case studies (BG, CZ, HU, MT, PL, SL) provide additional discussion of the risks of poverty associated with long-term unemployment and inactivity.

In Bulgaria, the poverty risk increases with unemployment and rises again with long-term unemployment. All unemployed people have an at-risk-of-poverty rate of 41.1% compared with 23.1% for the economically inactive and 12.1% for the employed. The poverty rate for the long-term unemployed is nearly twice as high as that for those who have been unemployed for less than three months. Among the economically inactive there are also some hidden or 'latent' unemployed with neither earned income nor eligibility for social benefits. Women are over-represented among this group and their experience of poverty is likely to be underestimated using aggregate household calculations of living standards (see Chapter 1).

Polish data on the experience of the long-term unemployed shows them to be the group most likely to report that they have insufficient resources to meet basic needs such as food, rent and medical care. Women in this situation are likely to face a constant lack of time as they cannot afford more expensive ready-made products and services. Long-term unemployment also has a negative psychological dimension, but findings from a Polish study suggest that it impacts most on men's subjective well-being (Klonowicz, 2002, cited by Plomien, 2005).

In Slovakia, data shows a high at-risk-of-poverty rate for all unemployed people at 47% , with the risk being higher for unemployed men than unemployed women. However, in the context of high and persistent unemployment, proportionately more women are long-term unemployed or inactive (see Tables 4.1-p.75 and 4.2-p.77) and they are more likely to live in a jobless household. The proportions of workless households and 'unemployable' young people is growing in Slovakia: data for 2004 show that 10% of men, 11.6% of women and 12.8% of children live in jobless households, with potentially negative effects on motivation and long-term social cohesion. Young people aged 20 to 24 years old constitute 20% of total long-term unemployment and are a group that the expert identifies as one that should be targeted by active labour market programmes.

In Malta, it is inactivity rates rather than long-term unemployment that are the central concern of the expert. The very high level of female inactivity contributes to women forming the majority of those who are at risk of poverty (51.5%).

A point raised by both the Bulgarian and Czech experts is that prolonged periods out of work, whether in long-term unemployment or 'latent' unemployment among the inactive, can lead to women subsequently filling low quality jobs on their return to employment. These may be part-time, temporary or low-paid jobs. One indication that women have lower average expectations from their job than men is found in the Bulgarian report, where 2003 data shows only 3.9% of women who left a job did so due to dissatisfaction with labour conditions, compared with 5.3% of men, even though women's jobs are inferior on dimensions such as wage levels and job security. A Czech study involving interviews with potential 'returning mothers' also found that such women have very low employment expectations.

Rates of unemployment, particularly long-term unemployment, and inactivity are highest for those with low education levels. This well-known feature of labour markets is reinforced by the six national case studies. National data shows that over half of the inactive people in Poland have a low level of education, over half of unemployed women in Hungary have only primary education, and three-quarters of unemployed women in the Czech Republic have only primary or lower secondary education. Those with a university degree have less risk of being unemployed (for example, in Hungary) but in Bulgaria the expert points out that a degree is no guarantee against long-term unemployment in a context of low labour demand, as 2003 data show that graduates constituted 11% of the long-term unemployed women. In Slovakia, there has been an increase in the proportion of long-term unemployed people who have secondary and professional education. Thus, even the highly educated are not immune to unemployment when it is widespread; however, they are still likely to be better placed to compete for a position towards the front of the 'job queue'.

4.3. Limitations in current policy provision for the long-term unemployed and economically inactive from a gender mainstreaming perspective

Gender differences in employment patterns and earnings in the period prior to unemployment can place women at a disadvantage when claiming benefits in

Table 4.2: Inactivity rate – share of population of working age (15 to 64) that are neither employed nor unemployed, 2004

	Total	Men	Women
AT	28.7	21.5	35.8
BE	34.1	26.6	41.8
CY	27.4	17.0	37.1
CZ	30.0	22.1	37.8
DE	27.4	20.8	34.2
DK	19.9	16.0	23.8
EE	30.0	25.6	34.0
EL	33.5	21.0	45.9
ES	31.3	19.6	43.2
FI	25.8	23.6	28.0
FR	30.5	24.8	36.1
HU	39.5	32.8	46.0
IE	30.5	20.1	41.0
IT	37.3	25.1	49.4
LT	30.9	27.2	34.4
LU	35.3	25.2	45.7
LV	30.3	25.7	34.7
MT	41.7	19.6	64.0
NL	23.4	16.1	30.8
PL	36.0	29.9	42.1
PT	27.0	20.9	33.0
SE	22.8	20.9	24.8
SI	30.2	25.5	35.0
SK	30.3	23.5	37.0
UK	24.8	18.0	31.4
EU	30.3	22.5	38.0

Source: Authors' calculations based on European Commission (2005b), Key indicator 24, p. 46.

unemployment insurance systems. The Polish case is one such example. In Poland, there has been a systematic decline in the proportion of unemployed people with the right to contributions-based unemployment benefit since 2000 (see Box 4.2-p.80 for details of entitlement). By the end of 2000 the rate was low for both sexes but particularly for women (25.7% of unemployed men and 15.9% of unemployed women), and by 2004 the rate had fallen to only 17% of unemployed men and 11.6% of unemployed women. This has additional repercussions for pension income because credits are only made into the pension fund for periods of unemployment when contributory unemployment ben-

efit is received and no credits are made for periods during which social assistance is claimed. Furthermore, social assistance is paid at a lower level than unemployment benefit, so those receiving social assistance face 'most severe financial hardships' (Plomien, 2005, p. 15). A higher proportion of women than men are reliant on 'non-employment related' sources of benefit (i.e. sources other than unemployment benefit) in both rural (50.6% compared with 20.7%) and urban (46% compared with 24%) areas.

Another issue concerning benefits is raised by the Czech and Hungarian experts in relation to rights to parental leave. These countries have long parental leave entitlements, up to four years in the Czech Republic, and as many as 10 or more years for some parents in Hungary (see Box 4.3-p.81). These entitlements are seen by the experts as partly reflecting a government attempt to reduce the number of people registered as unemployed through defining many women with children as economically inactive. The Czech expert regards many women on parental leave as experiencing 'latent' unemployment and the Hungarian expert views the entitlement (particularly the GYET – see Box 4.3-p.81) as contributing 'to the conservation of the traditional division of labour both at the workplace and in the household' (Nagy, 2005). Following a period of extended parental leave, there are problems for women in returning to the labour market, as their skills may have been eroded. Furthermore, employers' knowledge of the parental leave entitlement makes them reluctant to employ young women, a problem which is also noted for Bulgaria and Slovakia. Similar problems of the reintegration of women following extended periods of parental leave are identified in a number of other European countries (see Fagan and Hebson 2006). In situations where the legal framework of equal treatment is insufficient to ensure employer compliance, or where there is insufficient opportunity for inactive women to undergo training to renew their skills, or where childcare shortages oblige women to take longer periods of parental leave, the benefits of parental leave entitlements can be turned to the disadvantage of women.

Thus, the experts prioritise various policy reforms to enhance the reconciliation options open to women with childcare responsibilities. The Czech expert identifies a lack of provision by the state employment bureau for reintegrating mothers in the labour market. She suggests that the situation would be improved if more provision was made for mothers to use state-provided childcare facilities during parental leave beyond the current right to a maximum of five days a month. The national experts for Malta and Hungary also emphasise that more extensive childcare provision for 0 to 3 years is needed. The Maltese, Czech and Slovakian experts also identified the need for a wider range of working options to be developed in the economy to facilitate work–family reconciliation, such as job sharing, part-time hours and teleworking. It is also necessary to evaluate the operation of the social security system in relation to periods of reduced or flexible working hours. For example, the Maltese social security system penalises those who take a break in employment, as an interrupted working history leads to benefit entitlements ultimately being inadequate. It also acts as a disincentive to part-time employment, which might be a preferred option for returning mothers, because the

---

Box 4.1: National examples of the over-representation of women among the long-term unemployed and inactive

In **Poland**, women constitute the majority of long-term unemployed people (57.6 %), but this proportion has fallen significantly since 1998 (73.3 %) as male unemployment has increased. Of the 14 million inactive persons in Poland in 2004, the majority were retired (35.1 %), engaged in education or training (25.6 %), or unable to work due to disability or illness (21.1%). Women are over-represented in each of these groups, but particularly among those who are inactive due to family/household responsibilities (9.1% of all inactive people). Within this group, there were 1.15 million women and only 16 000 men in 2004, pointing to the inadequacy of family and work reconciliation policies in Poland. Women were also over-represented in other smaller groups of inactive people: those who were not willing to work (300 000 women compared with 145 000 men) and those who wanted to work but were discouraged by not being able to find employment (230 000 women compared with 174 000 men).

In the **Czech Republic**, unemployment benefit is paid for only six months, which leads to many people subsequently being classified as inactive, disguising the true level of long-term unemployment. Women are over-represented among both the long-term unemployed and the economically inactive. The expert regards both of these observations as being due to interruptions in labour market participation and the long duration of parental leave. It is more difficult for young women to find work due to employer concerns about imminent interruption in their participation and the extended period of parental leave which keeps women out of the labour market following child birth.

National data for **Bulgaria** show that during the period 1998–2003 there were consistently around 150 000 long-term unemployed women. Women constituted 45.1% of long-term unemployed people in 2003. The female inactivity rate is four times that for men.

Source: national reports.

social security contributions required of part-time employees are disproportionately high. Disincentives and penalities such as these have to be tackled so that social protection systems are in tune with the demands of work–family reconciliation.

Access to active labour market policies for women who are inactive as well as unemployed is important. Gender mainstreaming is more advanced in this part of employment policy, although gender inequalities in access still remain (see for example, Rubery et al. 2004). Active labour market programmes and training initiatives targeted at women exist in a number of countries (see Rubery et al., 2004 for additional information), including Poland and Hungary, while Bulgaria is an example of where the efforts for women focus on reconciliation measures (see Box 4.4-p.82). However, the scale of active labour market programmes is insufficient for the size of the unemployment problem in some countries. For example, the Polish expert identifies not only a reduction in the coverage of unemployment insurance benefits (discussed above), but also a low level of expenditure on active labour market programmes (ALMPs). In 1997, 0.3% of GDP was spent on ALMPs, constituting 15% of total labour market programme spending, compared with EU averages of 1.1% and 36% respectively. The expert also notes that the number of participants in such programmes fell between 2003 and 2004. The coverage of active labour market programmes is also limited in Hungary, and their function is not well understood by many in the population. In Slovakia, only 1.5% of unemployed men and 2.3% of unemployed women aged over 25 were participants in training activities in 2003. These figures are low for the EU despite the high incidence of unemployment in Slovakia, although it is of note that participation rates in the programme are slightly higher for unemployed women than unemployed men.

4.4. Gender mainstreaming and other disadvantaged groups with high rates of inactivity or under-employment: the examples of rural women and women with disabilities

In some Member States, women in rural areas are particularly vulnerable to social exclusion. This is in part a consequence of the high proportion of rural women who are unemployed, for example in Poland and Italy, where the problem is particularly pronounced for young rural women (Box 4.5-p.82). It can also be because of the larger size of rural families in some countries (e.g. Poland) or where the rural population is ageing (e.g. Slovenia) due to processes of agricultural decline and migration of young people to urban areas.

Poland and Slovenia have large but declining agricultural sectors. In Poland, the agricultural sector suffers from low productivity and low income per capita, and moves toward the development of non-agricultural rural workplaces has been slow and confined to coastal areas where agro-tourism is more viable. Among the rural population, women have higher education levels than men, but qualification levels are lower for both sexes in rural areas compared with urban ones. Similar proportions of women and men are employees (48.2%) but men are more likely to be self-employed (31.9%) than helping family members ('family workers', 9.5%), while the reverse applies for women (20.7% are self-employed and 21.9% are family workers). Rural women are therefore less likely than men to be managing a farm and, where they do, they are usually smaller farms of less than five hectares, using less capital-intensive methods, and more likely to be engaged in subsistence farming. Those who help out in a family farm may not be included in the social protection system.

In Slovenia, women make up nearly half of the agricultural workforce (48%), which is higher than the EU average (37%). It is 'farm women' rather than 'rural women' in Slovenia who are defined as a disadvantaged group by the Office for Equal Opportunities. One indicator of this is education levels, with 'rural women' having education levels which are higher than the national average, and 'farm women' having the lowest. For example, the proportion of women aged 25 to 44 years who have primary level education or lower is 8.7% for rural women, 19.6% for all women and 21% for farm women (the proportions with graduate level qualifications are 26%, 21.6% and 18.6% respectively).

The lower educational attainment of farmers and related agricultural workers makes them vulnerable to displacement and poverty as the sector declines and few alternative sources of employment are created in rural areas. In these circumstances women can be particularly vulnerable to unemployment and under-employment, even when they have higher qualification levels than rural men, as in the example of Poland. The national experts for Slovenia and Poland conclude that the main problems facing rural women is their reliance on a declining agricultural sector and their location in social

Box 4.2: Rules concerning entitlement to unemployment benefit in Poland

A person registered as unemployed, between the ages of 18 and 59 (women) or 64 (men), able and ready to take on employment, not owning an agricultural holding with arable land exceeding 2 hectares, not receiving a monthly income exceeding half of the minimum pay, and who was employed during the preceding 18 months for at least 365 days has the right to unemployment benefits for six months in general, for 12 months in areas affected by particularly high unemployment, and for a maximum 18 months if the regional unemployment rate is more than double the national average and the unemployed has been employed for at least 20 years (Kowalski and Bialas, 2004, cited by Plomien, 2005).

Source: national report.

settings where 'traditional' gender roles are more pronounced than in urban areas. In addition, there are sources of social exclusion which are distinctive to rural areas. These include spatial isolation and lack of access to health and other services; the long hours and lack of free time for farmworkers. One indicator of the lack of education/access to information in rural areas provided by the Polish expert is the much lower levels of computer ownership (24.8% in rural households compared with 51.6% in urban households) and Internet access (6.4% and 27.9% respectively). Some social problems can also be more pronounced in rural areas, for example in Slovenia the incidence of alcoholism is much higher in rural areas, and mainly affects men.

From this brief discussion of the situation of women in rural areas it is evident that gender mainstreaming is relevant for exposing how the problems of agricultural decline hit men and women differently, and that this is pertinent for the design of social inclusion policies for rural areas.

The problems of social exclusion and poor labour market integration experienced by people with disabilities is another important example of how a gender mainstreaming perspective is necessary for exposing inequalities and differences in men's and women's experiences.

Ireland is one of several Member States in which there are more women than men defined as being disabled[5]. This group has a very high risk of poverty in Ireland, and the risk is highest for disabled women (Box 4.6-p.83). This is partly because half of all disabled women in Ireland are aged over 65 years, and older women as a whole face a high risk of poverty (see Chapter 3). Disabled men and women have lower educational participation rates and lower labour market participation rates than their non-disabled counterparts, and those who are employed have lower earnings.

However, the way that the 'disability gap' operates has a particular gender dimension in Ireland. Young disabled women are more likely to be in education than young disabled men, reflecting the broader national pattern of gender differences, but the gap in rates between the disabled and non-disabled is higher for women than men. The labour market participation rate of disabled women is very low and, if employed, their earnings levels are lower than those of non-disabled women, thus making them even more vulnerable to being low paid. The national expert argues that more effective legislation is needed to prevent discrimination against the disabled population, in conjunction with better education and training opportunities, more accessible transport, and welfare reform to remove 'benefit traps' and to improve the labour market integration of disabled women and men.

A particular problem faces disabled women with a long-term condition in Ireland. If they are not employed they are less likely to receive welfare payments than disabled men; and, connected with this, they are more likely to define themselves as 'engaged in home duties' than disabled men, who are more likely to define themselves as unemployed.

Gender disparities among the disabled in their risks of social exclusion and poverty are also identified in the case-study example of Slovenia. There is no gender disaggregated data on disability for Slovenia, or indeed for some other Member States (including the Czech Republic), but approximately 8.5% of the population are classified as disabled in Slovenia (roughly 170 000 people), of which approximately 28 000 are employed and 9 000 are registered as unemployed. Survey data reveals that both men and women with

(5)   According to data in the expert reports, other countries in which this is the case are France, Greece, Hungary, Lithuania, Poland and Spain. Fewer women than men are categorised as disabled in Belgium, Estonia, Luxembourg and the Netherlands. Disability is a social as well as a physical category, as the classification of people as disabled in some official sources is linked to criteria for national benefit and employment systems.

Box 4.3: Parental leave benefit provision in Hungary

	Basis of entitlement	Age of child	Amount paid per month
GYED	Insurance-based: recipient must have been employed for 180 days in year before childbirth	0 to 2	70% of previous income up to a maximum of HUF 83 000 per month
GYES	Universal	0 to 3	The amount of the minimum state pension (HUF 23 200 per month in 2004 and HUF 24 700 per month in 2005)
GYET	For those with three or more children where one parent stays at home	0 to 8	The amount of the minimum state pension (HUF 23 200 per month in 2004 and HUF 24 700 per month in 2005)

If a parent is eligible to receive GYED for the first two years of a child's life, he/she is subsequently eligible to GYES for one additional year. Professional/managerial women with GYED entitlement are less likely than lower income women to take the full three years.

The GYET was introduced in the early 1990s (a time of rising unemployment and conservative government) to enable/encourage women with three or more children to remain economically inactive. Those with three or more children who utilise the full parental leave entitlements will be economically inactive for a minimum of 10 years (until the youngest child reaches eight years of age). As the length of time out of employment increases the potential difficulties of re-entry, the expert sees GYET recipients as potentially the most disadvantaged in this way.

Source: national report.

disabilities have lower levels of educational attainment than the national average, but a key gender disparity is living standards. Disabled women have inferior material living conditions to their male counterparts, owning fewer consumer goods and being more constrained in their expenditure on holidays and entertainment. Disabled people with mobility constraints have different sources of support according to their gender. For women, relatives are most important, especially children, whereas men rely more on their partners as well as typically wider networks of friends, co-workers and neighbours.

4.5. Concluding assessment: gender mainstreaming the policy direction and priorities for the long-term unemployed and economically inactive

Women aged 15 to 64 years have higher economic inactivity rates, higher rates of hidden unemployment among the inactive, and in most countries a higher proportion are long-term unemployed as a proportion of the population in this age group. More broadly, in many countries the overall unemployment rate is higher for women than for men.

Hence a gender perspective on unemployment and economic inactivity is necessary in order to identify and monitor gender inequalities in the risks and as a means for designing appropriate policy measures. Three main areas for policy reform are identified by the authors of the national case studies as priorities to improve the situation of women who are currently inactive or in long-term unemployment. Two of these relate directly to enabling women to access employment.

Firstly, four of the experts identify a need for more flexible, family-oriented patterns of employment to be encouraged so that particularly returning mothers, but also early retirees, are better able to participate in the labour market (BG, HU, MT, PL). On the particular issue of part-time work this may need to be accompanied by social security reform so that this form of employment is not penalised. For example, social security reform is needed in Malta so that part-time work is not penalised through high social contributions by employees and low entitlements to future benefits. More extensive and affordable childcare provision is also needed; which was emphasised by the experts from Hungary, Malta and Poland.

A second area for improvement is in education and lifelong learning, highlighted by experts from Hungary,

Box 4.4: Active labour market programmes and training initiatives aimed at women in Bulgaria, Hungary and Poland

Bulgaria

Efforts to enhance women's employment integration according to the national employment action plan 2005 include policies aimed at supporting the combination of work, family and child-raising responsibilities, stimulating self-employment among women, and developing childcare services.

Hungary

The PHARE programme: a programme to assist women to take jobs, become self-employed or start their own business.

Human resource development operative programme: A programme with the aim of promoting labour market participation for 3 200 women.

Family-Friendly Workplace Award: Established in 2001, this programme concerns the reintegration of young parents returning from parental leave. The main forms of integration are training opportunities, job-specific information, keeping contact, introduction of part-time jobs, teleworking, etc. However, the award itself is not able to urge companies to set up reconciliation projects.

Poland

Training programme for all women: One of the strategic goals of the second phase of the National Action Plan for women for 2003–05 is to increase employment opportunities for women. This is to be achieved by professional training and retraining for all women, and particularly for the long-term unemployed, lone mothers, disabled women, or women from rural areas.

Re-employment programme: The Polish Agency for the Development of Entrepreneurship implements a programme called 'Professional integration and reintegration of women', which aims at increasing re-employment chances of long-term unemployed, lone mothers, or mothers returning to the labour market after child-caring duties. This programme covers 1 800 women in two regions, and involves counselling and training.

Source: national reports.

Box 4.5: High unemployment among rural young women in Poland and Italy

In Poland, rural women have similar employment rates to urban women; however, they experience particular problems of unemployment and labour market exclusion. Among the rural population, unemployment rates are higher for women (21.2%) than for men (18.6%), and rates are especially high among young women. Data for 2002 show the unemployment rate for young women (15 to 24 years) in rural areas was 32.7% more than twice the national average (the national rate was 13.4% for young women in 2004) and was also higher for rural than urban women in the 25- to 34-year-old age group. This is one of the factors why young women are the keenest part of the rural population to move to urban areas.

Data for Italy from 2003 show an overall female at-risk-of-poverty rate of 10.8%. However, within this figure there is considerable regional difference, with the figure being lower in northern and central Italy (5.6% and 5.2% respectively) and much higher in the (more rural) south (24.2%). The female employment rate is considerably lower in the south (Mezzogiorno): in 2005 it was 30.1% compared with the national average of 45.1%. The lack of labour market integration of young women (aged 15 to 24 years) is particularly acute, with an unemployment rate of 47.2% in the south, compared with the national average of 28.1%. Some young women who are looking for formal employment enter the underground economy in low-paid, casual jobs. The proportion of them becoming discouraged by their poor prospects of finding formal employment is increasing and leads them to exit the labour market on getting married or having a first child.

Source: national reports.

Box 4.6: Disability and gender disparities in Ireland

Current data indicates that 10.6% of females in Ireland have a disability, more than twice the proportion among males (4.2%). Disabled women also have a higher risk of poverty (58%) than disabled men (52%), but both figures are very high. Half of all disabled women are over 65, and this group has a particularly high risk of poverty. Legislation was introduced in the late 1990s and early 2000s to protect disabled people from discrimination in the labour market, but a range of exemption clauses and the incorporation of the concept of 'undue cost' on employers restrict the effects of such initiatives.

There is a 'disability gap' in education participation rates among 15- to 19-year-olds. Young disabled women are more likely to be in education than young disabled men (66.9% compared with 62%), reflecting the pattern of higher education participation rates for women among the non-disabled population (82.2% for women and 72.9% for men). However, the 'disability gap' is more pronounced for women than for men. Among working-age disabled women the labour market participation rate is very low at 12.5% , compared with 25.5% among disabled men, and rates are lower for older working-age people with disability. Women without a disability have an employment rate four times higher (42.2%) than that of disabled women (10.1%), demonstrating the greatly disadvantageous labour market position that women with a disability face.

For those disabled women in work, the gender pay gap is exacerbated by a further 'disability gap' in pay. This is partly due to their tendency to work fewer hours. More highly educated disabled people fare better in terms of pay, indicating the need for improved access to training and education for disabled women in order to improve their labour market integration.

The Irish benefit system does not provide disabled women with individualised, non-means-tested sources of income. Disabled women with a long-term condition who are not in employment are less likely to receive welfare payments than disabled men, and are more likely to categorise themselves as 'engaged in home duties' than as unemployed. Of the disabled men and women who receive benefits a higher proportion of women receive short-term allowances. Women with disabilities who have a partner lack the status of an individual direct claimant. Consequently single disabled women in receipt of the means-tested allowance are likely to lose their entitlement if they marry/cohabit with a partner in employment or in receipt of non-means-tested benefits; and women who are living with a partner and working in the home at the time when they become disabled are effectively excluded from direct income maintenance support and certain employment and training programmes.

Source: national report.

Poland, Slovakia and Bulgaria. The latter two experts emphasise the need for training to match patterns of labour market demand, whilst the Hungarian expert sees the priority as being to provide more training for potential returning mothers.

The third suggestion that is found in several reports, and is perhaps the most difficult to achieve, is that responsibility for household labour should be more evenly distributed between women and men. The Czech and Hungarian experts argue for incentives and support measures to encourage men to take parental leave and to be more involved in childcare. Similarly, the Maltese expert, in urging for a broader change in culture, argues that initiatives are needed to encourage and 'empower' men to contribute more to domestic work. It may be that an important part of an effective policy package to encourage more women to participate in the labour market is

to help men to be able to reduce the proportion of time they spend at work (see the previous reports by Fagan and Hebson, 2006, and Plantenga and Remery, 2005, for further discussion of this topic).

The above three recommendations emphasise labour supply considerations – gender mainstreaming the design of education and training and other aspects of active labour market programmes, flexible working options and care services for those with family responsibilities, and measures to promote a more gender-equal division of household labour. Demand-side policies are also important causes of women's greater risks of unemployment, family-connected inactivity and poverty. The examples of women in the rural economy in Italy, Poland and Slovenia expose the gender-differentiated impact of agricultural restructuring whereby women in rural areas are more vulnerable than rural men to unemployment and poverty and also show a marked difference in the social exclusion risks faced by rural and urban women. Similarly the Irish and Slovenian case studies of disability expose pronounced gender disparities in the extent and form of disadvantage experienced by women and men with disabilities. In this respect, the Irish expert emphasises the importance of establishing effective anti-discrimination legislation as well as better access to education and training, accessible transport and welfare reform to remove benefit traps and introduce individualised non-means-tested benefits, so that disabled women have access to an independent income. To achieve coordinated supply and demand-side policies which tackle gender inequalities thus requires a gender mainstreaming approach which is applied consistently across the parallel policy tools of the Social Inclusion Process and the European Employment Strategy.

5. Lone parents – a female-dominated category

A lone parent can be defined as someone living without a partner, who has the daily care responsibility for a dependent child (Kjeldstad and Skevik, 2004, cited in Ellingsæter, 2005). Within this definition, however, there are a number of ambiguities that make cross national comparison difficult. Firstly there is the question of the age at which a child ceases to be dependent. The most common threshold used across the countries is 18 years (used in data in national case studies for Estonia, Hungary and Lithuania) but other national data draw the line at 20 (Ireland) and 15 (Norway – in some national statistics, although children are legally dependent in Norway until the age of 18). Other national data does not specify an age, so it is difficult to make precise comparisons of the scale of lone parenthood across Europe. There are further ambiguities in the definition and situation of a lone-parent household (LPH), according to whether or not a non-resident parent is involved in supporting or looking after the child(ren), at what point a new partnership constitutes a transition from lone parenting to a couple, and the distinction between lone parents who live in separate households and those who live with their own parents in an extended family unit.

Despite these definitional and conceptual issues, previous international studies that focused on lone parents (Lewis, 1997, 2001; Millar and Rowlingson, 2001) have identified a link between high rates of lone parenthood and features of a country. Rich, predominantly Protestant and northern European countries (DK, NO, SE) have been observed to have much higher rates of lone parenthood than poor, predominantly Catholic southern European countries (ES, IT, PT) in terms of lone-parent households as a percentage of all families with children (Rowlingson, 2001, pp. 171–3).

As we document below, the majority of lone parents are mothers. With regard to international comparison of the situation of lone parents, Lewis and Hobson (1997, p. 13) argue that lone mothers' well-being is greatest

'... where there is income from employment and from transfers; where benefits are universal for mothers and for children rather than categorical for either lone mothers or their children; and where the 'social wage' is high, especially in respect of childcare provision'.

It is in the Scandinavian countries that most of these criteria are met. Lewis and Hobson go on (op. cit., pp. 15–18) to set out two ideal types of care regime, both of which involve low rates of solo mother poverty and stigmatisation. The 'caregiver social wage model' supports mothers through social transfers, whilst the 'parent–worker model' involves high rates of labour market participation and a high 'social wage' – as employment alone cannot ensure lone-mother well-being. Sweden exemplifies the latter. The Netherlands was more akin to the former model at the end of the 1990s, but recent reforms to Dutch lone-parent policy have started to shift the policy emphasis towards the 'parent–worker model' as well.

Thirteen national experts in the EGGSIE network produced reports on lone parents for the following countries: Bulgaria, Estonia, Finland, Hungary, Ireland, Liechtenstein, Lithuania, Luxembourg, Malta, Norway, Spain[6], Sweden and the United Kingdom.

5.1. A profile of the situation of lone parents

Across European countries, there is a general increase in lone-parent households in both absolute numbers and as a proportion of all households. This is illustrated for the 13 national case studies in Table 5.1(a)-(p.88). In some countries, the growth in lone-parent households has been a trend that began decades ago, traceable to the 1960s in Sweden and the United Kingdom. In other countries, such as Hungary, the trend dates back to the 1980s. In Luxembourg, due to a lack of official data, it is unclear whether the numbers have increased substantially in recent years.

(6) The Spanish expert has provided information on lone parents in the context of a wider trend towards the individualisation of Spanish society, which is also traced through increases in the proportion of the population who are single working-age women, and older women over 65 who live alone.

The increased individualism or 'individualisation thesis' of modernity (Giddens, 1994) is widely held to be a factor contributing to the rise of lone parenthood through a combination of marriage and cohabitation becoming more unstable, births outside of marriage becoming more common and less stigmatised, and increased scope for women to be economically independent. This is emphasised in the Hungarian and UK national reports for example. For the Hungarian expert, individualism in the form of greater female economic and social independence has contributed to the high divorce rate, along with fewer legal obstacles and the decline in influence of the Catholic church. In the United Kingdom, the rising rates of divorce and births outside of marriage are indicative of changing social values and coexist with labour market changes for both sexes: on one hand, women have access to more opportunities for some degree of economic independence via the labour market while, on the other, working class men have fewer opportunities to secure stable and decently-paid jobs to become 'breadwinners' which means there are fewer financial incentives for women to marry them.

Rising rates of divorce are a major factor behind the increase in lone parenthood. This is reported to be the main route into lone parenthood in Lithuania and Luxembourg. In Lithuania, the expert reports that two thirds of divorced couples have children under the age of 18. The divorce rate is also an major factor in Bulgaria and Liechtenstein, where it has increased, and in Hungary, where it has remained stable but at such a high level that 40% of marriages end in divorce.

In Finland and the United Kingdom, divorce is also an important route to lone parenthood but the separation of unmarried cohabiting couples is now a similarly common route given that rates of cohabitation have also risen (both for never married and once married couples). The national experts for Hungary, Liechtenstein, Lithuania, Luxembourg and Norway also note that the rising incidence of cohabitation and 'unmarried mothers' means that a growing proportion of lone-parent households emerge from non-marital relationship breakdown. In Sweden, divorce and cohabitee separation are reported as together being an important cause of the increase in lone parenthood, but in Sweden these data are aggregated. In some countries it may also be that cohabiting parents are more likely to separate than married couples. This is the case in Norway for young parent couples aged 20 to 24 years who are four times more likely to separate if they cohabit than if they are married. However, there are no data available to suggest that this applies for all ages or in all national settings.

There is little evidence that 'solo' parenting, that is women having children without either being married or cohabiting, is a major route into lone motherhood. Similarly, while high or rising rates of teenage pregnancy are a focus of public debate in some countries, such as Ireland and the United Kingdom, this particularly vulnerable group of young mothers constitutes only a minority of all lone mothers. In the context of the national debate in Ireland, the expert addresses this issue directly, arguing that the rate of unmarried teenage pregnancies is not high when compared with either the recent past or to other countries. In the United Kingdom, solo parents are disproportionate from economically deprived neighbourhoods or family and the incidence of sole parenting also varies by ethnicity and is highest for Afro-Caribbean mothers.

5.2. The risks of social exclusion and poverty faced by lone parents

The majority of lone parents are women, reflecting the broader structure of gender relations whereby in most households it is mothers who have the primary responsibility for children. It can be seen in Table 5.1(a)-(p.88) that women account for 80% to 95% of all lone-parent households in 11 of the 13 country case studies, dipping to just over three quarters of lone-parent households in Spain and Malta. Lone-parent households are vulnerable to poverty for several reasons. Firstly, there is a financial disadvantage plus the work–family reconciliation pressures of raising children single-handedly compared with the resources available to dual-parent households. Lone parents in the United Kingdom have an employment rate of 56.2%, and although lone fathers have a higher employment rate (67%) than lone mothers, it is low compared with that of partnered fathers, illustrating the difficulties that all lone parents face in participating in the labour market. Secondly, women command lower wages in the labour market compared with men, making it more difficult for them to secure a 'breadwinner' position.

The disadvantaged position of lone parents is evident from the statistical common indicators developed for the EU monitoring of the Social Inclusion Process. Table 5.2 (p.91) shows that, in each country, lone parents have a greater risk of living in poverty compared with other adults.

In the EU Nordic countries (DK, FI, SE) lone parents do not have an at-risk-of-poverty rate far in excess of that for other groups (see Table 5.2-p.91). Hence the 'social democratic' welfare state and employment systems in these countries provide more social integration for lone parents than occurs in other national policy settings (Esping-Andersen, 1990; Lewis 1997). However, despite the relatively favourable situation of lone parents in these countries compared with other national settings, lone parents remain disadvantaged to some extent. When compared with couple families with children within Sweden, single mothers do have a greater risk of poverty. Similarly in Norway, lone parents are more likely than other parents to be sufficiently poor to receive means-tested social assistance. In Finland, single-parent median household income from all sources was EUR 13 900 in 2002 (up 5% since 1990), compared with an average couple-parent household income of EUR 20 000 (up 10% since 1990). An additional finding in Finland is that housing costs make up a higher proportion of income for lone mothers than other groups, reducing their disposable income.

In the other countries, the risk of poverty is significantly higher for lone-parent households compared with other households. The starkest contrast is found in the United Kingdom, where the proportions are 50% and 18% respectively, but a greater risk of poverty is identified for lone parents in Luxembourg and Lithuania, and for lone mothers in Malta. In Spain, the risk of poverty is greater for lone mothers than lone fathers, with the respective at-risk-of-poverty figures being 45.8% and 36%. Similarly in Ireland, the respective figures are 54.7% for lone mothers and 36.7% for lone fathers. Income disadvantages associated with lone parenthood are experienced by men as well as women, but not to as great a degree.

Table 5.1(a): National data on the extent of lone parenthood in the 13 case-study countries

	Number of households (LPHs)	Percentage of LPHs which are headed by a female lone parent	Trend and scale of lone parenthood in relation to national population
BG	290 028	83	Up in the past 15 years 12.24% of all households are lone-parent households
EE	34 500	90	Up In 1990, 10% of births were to a lone mother; in 2003, 15% 27% of households with children < 18 years old are lone-mother households
ES	273 200	77	Up 1991, 134 101 lone-parent households; in 2001, 282 153
FI	85 000	80	Up In 1980, lone-parent households constituted 12% of households with children; in 2002, 20% Lone-parent households constitute 2.8% of all households
HU	470100	88	Up Started to grow in the 1980s 994 170 people live in lone-mother households, constituting almost 10% of the population
IE	117 200	91	Up In 1999, 88 000 lone-parent households; in 2004, 117 200 Female lone parents comprise 3.3% of the population Approximately 12% of all households are lone-parent households
LI	920	95 approx	Up 7.08% of all households are lone-parent households
LT	65 379	93	Up In 12.8% of households with children < 18 years old are lone-parent households 4.5% of the total population live in lone-parent households
LU		85	Probably up In 1985, 6% of households were lone-parent households; in 1999, 7% Alternative data for 2001: lone-parent households represented 1% of all households; 5% of all households with children
MT	3 310	76	No information provided.
NO	116 207	85 approx	Up 15% of all mothers with children aged 0 to 15 years are lone mothers

Table 5.1(a): National data on the extent of lone parenthood in the 13 case-study countries (continued)

	Number of households (LPHs)	Percentage of LPHs which are headed by a female lone parent	Trend and scale of lone parenthood in relation to national population
SE	222 494	82	Up In the mid-1960s: lone-parent households constituted < 10% of all households with children, now: approximately 25%
UK	1 873 000	90	Up Lone-parent households constituted 2% of all households in 1961; 2004: 7% 25% of working-age families with dependent children are headed by a lone parent
EU			4.4% of all households are lone-parent households

Table 5.1(b): Available national data on the extent of lone parenthood in relation to national population

	Number of lone-parent households (LPHs)	Percentage of LPHs which are female headed	Trend and scale of lone parenthood in relation to national population
AT	300 000	78	7% of households are headed by single mothers and 2% by single fathers
BE	163 000	93	11% of all households are lone-parent households
CZ	434 400	88	4.4% of the female population are lone mothers
DE	2 502 000	75	19.7% of families with children are lone-parent households. Lone mothers head 17.0% of all families with children.
DK	131 734	86	Lone-parent households represent 4% of all households with dependent children
EL	56 400	:	Lone-parent households constitute 16.9% of families
FR	1 500,00	86	4% of the total population live in lone-parent households
LV	:	:	5.8% of the female working-age population are lone parents, 1% of the male working-age population are lone parents
NL	:	:	11.5% of all households are lone-parent households
PL	2 030 000	89	19% of all families are lone-parent households
PT	353 971	87	
SI	105 000	86	

No data were provided for CY, IS, IT, RO, SK.

In some countries, the greater risk of poverty faced by lone parents is part of a broader picture whereby dual-parent households containing children are also more at risk of poverty than households without children. This occurs where family policy makes few resource transfers via the tax or benefit system to provide some support for the additional costs which households with children face. So in Hungary, for example, 1996 data showed that the risk of poverty increases markedly if there are three or more children and that lone parents were less likely to be in poverty than nuclear families with young children under four years old.

In many countries the lower income of lone-parent households means that they are more likely to be concentrated in social housing or the rented market rather than to be owner-occupiers. For example, in Spain and Malta, the experts referred to the disproportionately high number of lone parents who rented their accommodation. In Spain, 83% of the population are owner-occupiers, but this figure stands at 66% for lone mothers and 72% for lone fathers. In Malta, 25.5% of the population do not live in homes that they own, but for lone parents the figure is 42.4%. Lone parents may also be particularly exposed to poor quality accommodation associated with their lower income, as noted in the national report for Luxembourg. Hence, the housing tenure of lone parents makes them particularly dependent on government housing policy in relation to the cost and quality of social housing and the private rental market.

In some countries part of the reason why lone parents face a higher risk of poverty is that their employment rate is lower than that for other groups. This applies to the three Nordic countries considered here and the United Kingdom.

In the national reports for Finland and Sweden, this pattern is identified as being a relatively new phenomenon, following recession in the early 1990s (Box 5.1-p.92). The recession resulted in a large fall in the employment rate for all women, but since the mid-1990s it has been couple mothers who have been more likely to be employed, overtaking the lone-mother employment rate and reversing the pre-recession pattern of female employment participation.

Part of the possible explanation for this trend may be found in employer demands for flexible workers, which has been observed in Finland as putting lone mothers

at a disadvantage in the labour market. Moves by the Finnish government to subsidise low-paid employment, and a trend towards the creation of more low-paid jobs in general, could also be seen to discourage lone parents in particular from entering the labour market, as such jobs are unlikely to support household expenditure. A further post-recession change has been identified in Sweden in terms of working hours. The previous tendency for lone mothers working full-time has been eroded while couple mothers' hours have increased. Lone mothers experiencing involuntary part-time work is identified in both Sweden and Norway. In Norway, of those lone mothers who are working part-time, 26% are in involuntary part-time employment. The figure is 10% for couple mothers.

It would appear from the Nordic national reports that lone mothers have experienced a reduced ability following recession, to gain employment and to work the hours that they prefer. However, it is striking that despite reduced lone-mother labour market participation, the risk of poverty for lone parents remains similar to that of other groups within these countries. This suggests that the treatment of lone parents in Nordic social protection systems is superior to that found elsewhere in Europe, and brings into doubt the centrality of employment as a guarantee against poverty.

The only other country from the 13 national case studies where the employment rate of lone mothers is less than that of mothers in couples is the United Kingdom. The employment rate for lone parents in 2005 was 56.2% in the United Kingdom, compared with 71.9% for mothers in a couple. Lone-parent employment remains low in the United Kingdom, but there has been some increase in recent years due to a concerted active labour market programme for lone parents ('New deal for lone parents'). In relation to the minority of lone mothers who are teenagers, a 'care to learn' scheme has been introduced which funds childcare for teenage mothers. The proportion of teenage mothers in education, employment or training has increased from 23.1% in 1997 to 29.7% in 2002-04. Despite the rise in employment rates for lone mothers in the United Kingdom they still face a much higher risk of poverty than other adults there. This signals that the UK benefit system and the job openings which lone mothers are able to secure are insufficient to prevent lone parents facing a much higher poverty risk than the national average, in contrast to the situation for lone parents in Finland and Sweden.

Table 5.2: At-risk-of-poverty rates in EU countries (2001 and 2002)

Country	Men 16+	Women 16+	Lone parents
AT	9	15	23
BE	12	15	25
CY	16	20	41
CZ	6	8	30
DE	9	12	36
DK	11	12	12
EE	17	19	35
EL	19	22	37
ES	16	19	42
FI	10	15	11
FR	14	16	35
HU	8	9	17
IE	18	22	42 (a)
IT	17	19	23
LT	16	16	30
LU	11	11	35 (a)
LV	16	16	35
MT	13	14	59
NL	10	10	45
PL	16	14	24
PT	18	19	39
SE	9	11	13
SI	9	12	17
SK	19	19	40
UK	13	18	50
EU	13	16	34

Note: (a) Small sample size or many missing observations
Sources: For new Member States and EU average: 2002 data except CY (1997), MT (2002) and EU (various years) from European Commission (2005a, Table 8a, p. 190). For EU-15: 2001 data from European Commission (2004a, Tables 1 and 9, pp. 229 and 233).

Luxembourg and Hungary are examples of countries where lone mothers have a higher employment rate than partnered mothers. Luxembourg has high employment rates for all groups, and 2003 data show rates of 81.3% for lone mothers and 59.9% for part-nered mothers. Lone mothers tend to work full-time more than couple mothers (59% compared with 56% of those in work in 2003) but full-time working for both groups of mothers has declined considerably over the past decade (the figures were 82% and 71% in 1992). In both Luxembourg and Hungary, what

could be termed as the greater 'integration' of lone mothers in the labour market does not appear to be an adequate protection against poverty, as in both countries lone parents face a considerably greater risk of poverty than other adults (see Table 5.2).

Where provided, gender disaggregated data on lone-parent employment rates shows fathers to be more likely to be in employment than mothers in Spain (35% compared with 25%), Ireland (54.5% compared with 43.4%) and the United Kingdom

Box 5.1: Trends in lone-mother employment rate in Nordic countries

In **Sweden** in 1980, 87% of lone mothers were in the labour force, compared with 76% of cohabiting mothers. Figures for 2003 show a reversal in the pattern, as for those with children aged under seven years, 63% of single mothers were in employment compared with 78% of mothers living in a couple. For those with a youngest child aged 7 to 16, the figures were 79% and 88%. Similarly in **Finland**, the 1989 employment rate figures were 87.3% for lone mothers and 83.0% for mothers in a couple, but in 2002 the proportions stood at 67.0% and 77.4% respectively. Recent data on **Norway** shows an employment rate for lone mothers of 70% , compared with 81% for couple mothers, placing Norway alongside the other Nordic countries as having a disproportionately low lone-mother employment rate.

Source: national report.

(67% compared with 56.2%). These data suggest that lone mothers face particular problems in accessing paid employment. However, from the previous discussion it is apparent that the relationship between employment rate and risk of poverty is a complex one. It can be said from the national reports that the risk of poverty for lone parents is not reduced by employment per se. Wider issues around the quality of employment and wage levels, and the degree of support through tax/benefit transfers are of crucial importance.

In some countries, one factor which contributes to the vulnerable labour market position of lone parents is that their qualification levels are below the national average. The tendency for lone mothers to be relatively less qualified than the population as a whole was noted in several countries (including Finland, Lithuania, Malta and the United Kingdom). In Spain, lone mothers are reported to have high illiteracy rates (23%) compared with the population as a whole (8%), with lone fathers found to have the highest illiteracy rate of all (30%). The expert from Luxembourg noted that lower levels of education were found among young mothers in general, whether lone mothers or partnered mothers. However, a high level of education cannot itself be seen as a guarantee against poverty for lone mothers, as in Bulgaria 23.5% of lone mothers with a university degree live below the poverty line.

5.3. Limitations in current policy provision from a gender mainstreaming perspective

In some welfare states there are specific financial transfers for lone-parent households through either the tax or benefit system. In many of the post-2004 Member States new benefits have been introduced for lone parents as part of a wider reform of welfare state provision (Fagan and Hebson, 2006). In the 13 country cases considered here there are specific benefits for lone parents in all but Bulgaria, Estonia and Luxembourg.

In recent years, the general direction of lone-parent policy in European countries has been targeted at promoting their employment: the 'adult-worker' model (Lewis 2001). Where some countries used to place reduced job search and job availability requirements on lone parents – particularly when children were young – reforms have placed tighter job search requirements on lone parents, usually accompanied by benefit reforms to 'make work pay'. Lone parents on social assistance in Germany and the Netherlands, for example, now face greater pressure to take jobs (Fagan and Hebson, 2006).

Reforms aimed at increasing employment among lone parents can take the form of a reduction in benefits (a negative incentive) and/or the introduction of new forms of financial support for those entering employment (a positive incentive). In the 13 case-study countries there are examples of both approaches. Recent reforms in Ireland and Norway involve a reduction in lone-parent benefit entitlement, but in Norway positive and negative incentives have been combined to encourage lone parents to enter the labour market (Box 5.2-p.93).

In some countries there are specific active labour market programmes for lone parents. In Malta, lone mothers and pregnant women aged 13 to 18 are included in small-scale projects encouraging employment and/or a return to education. The United Kingdom has a specific ALMP – the new deal for lone parents (NDLP). From its introduction in 1998 until 2003, the NDLP appeared to have been quite successful in that 51% of participant lone parents entered work compared with 27% of non-participants. However, 29% of those placed in jobs returned to out-of-work benefits within 12 months, suggesting problems with childcare and job quality. In recent years, reforms to the NDLP raise two important issues with salience across Europe. Firstly, though participation in the NDLP formally remains voluntary, since 2003 all lone parents making a new or repeat claim for income support (means-tested social assistance) have had to attend a compulsory meeting with a personal adviser where their employment prospects are discussed. This small movement towards compulsion illustrates that the line between positive and negative incentives for labour market participation can become blurred, as the availability of state support to enter the labour market can transform into a pressure to participate. Secondly, the NDLP has been extended in its coverage to those with very young children, raising the issue of whether it is in the best interests of children that an ever-higher proportion of lone parents are in employment.

The above discussion has focused on the relationship between state support for lone parents and labour market participation. There are, though, sources of income for lone-parent households that do not involve an explicit or implicit drive for activation. Rather, the issue with these 'passive' sources of income is whether they adequately cover lone-parent household expenses so that poverty is avoided.

In Sweden and Estonia, special rights exist for the children, rather than the adult, in lone-parent households. In Estonia, the single-parent's child allowance shifted from being an adult to a child entitlement in 2002, while in Sweden an entitlement for children who do not live with both parents was introduced as early as the 1930s. Given that in some European countries lone parents are sometimes attacked as undeserving in pub-

lic debate (for example in the United Kingdom and Ireland), a benefit entitlement instituted as the right of a child may prove to be more enduring.

There are also specific rights for lone-parent households in Hungary to free or subsidised school meals and free textbooks. These rights are seen by the national expert as beneficial for lone parents and a welcome policy development.

In some countries there have been recent reforms designed to increase the financial contribution of absent fathers. In Lithuania, lone mothers have been allocated additional social benefits by the state for heating and water since 2003, but only if the father of the child is identified and he is not able to provide financial support. However, if the father is not identified, the lone mother can be worse off than before the 2003 law, with lone-mother households in Vilnius in this situation having their social benefits reduced by one-third. The aim of this policy is not so much to improve the living standards of lone-mother households but to change behaviour – encouraging both parents to be responsible for a child and discouraging births out of wedlock. Limitations of a policy to make up lone-mother household income through financial support from absent fathers are evident in that lone mothers in Bulgaria lack the funds to complete the necessary judicial procedure. Similarly, the introduction of the UK Child Support Agency in 1993 was plagued by operational problems (computer software problems, staffing shortages and complexity of regulations for assessment) and low compliance (high rates of non-payment and protracted appeals by fathers), which caused problems between estranged parents.

Box 5.2: Negative and positive incentives for lone-parent employment in Ireland and Norway

In **Ireland**, one-parent family payment (OPFP) is distributed according to the number of children in the household. To encourage labour market participation, a lone parent does not lose any entitlement to OPFP up to a certain level of employment income (the 'earnings disregard') but the amount of this disregard is not indexed to earnings and has remained the same since 1997. Between 1994 and 2004, failure to index the OPFP earnings disregard has resulted in a reduction in its value from 94% of the poverty level to 72%. The low level of the earnings disregard limits lone-parent employment options to low-paid and/or part-time work.

In **Norway**, there is a specific 'transitional allowance' for lone parents: a means-tested benefit set at subsistence level. Lone-parent labour market participation has been encouraged through, first, a more lenient income-test in 1990 (a positive incentive) and, then, the 1998 reform, which combined positive incentives through higher benefit rates and increased support for childcare and a negative incentive through a sharp reduction in the period of entitlement from 10 years to three years. The 1998 reform has caused an increase in labour supply, though it has been criticised for increasing lone mother 'time poverty' and the pre-1998 transitional allowance has been argued to allow lone parents to better combine employment, education and benefit (Kjeldstad, 2000, cited in Ellingsæter, 2005).

Source: national reports.

Childcare is a pivotal issue for lone parents. While child-care services have been expanding in some countries stimulated by the Barcelona target, only Belgium, Denmark, France, Iceland and Sweden reach the target of at least 33% of children under three years of age having a childcare place. Regarding the second Barcelona target, that at least 90% of children aged between three years and the mandatory school age should have a childcare place, 10 countries meet the target or score rather close: Belgium, Denmark, France, Germany, Iceland, Italy, the Netherlands, Norway, Spain and Sweden (Plantenga and Remery, 2005, p. v). In Lithuania, provision is anticipated to increase from 65% in 2005 to 87% by 2008 (national expert information). Provision is lowest in Greece, Lithuania, Slovenia and Poland, and supply has fallen in some of the post-socialist countries, including Bulgaria and Hungary (op. cit., pp. v–vi).

Sweden stands out as having a high level of both coverage and affordability. Municipalities now have an obligation to provide a place within three to four months of demand, and unemployed parents as well as employed parents are able to make a request. A high proportion of of children (85 to 95%) have a place. In 2002, a maximum childcare fee was introduced, and the new system ensures that almost all families pay lower fees than previously.

The lack of plentiful and affordable childcare is a problem reported by experts in several countries. The problem is perhaps most acute in Ireland, as there is provision for only 4% of pre-school children, and it is regarded by the expert as the greatest barrier to work, education and training. The Irish Government is moving to increase provision in the most disadvantaged areas, but progress remains slow. In the United Kingdom, the gov-ernment is pursuing a similar policy and, in addition, now provides a subsidy for childcare paid to parents through the childcare element of the working tax credit. Despite a recently announced increase in this subsidy, childcare remains expensive in the United Kingdom.

In Spain and Malta there are no public subsidies for childcare, and coverage in Spain is low, with only 12.1% of 0- to 3-year-olds covered in 2002. The absence of a tradition of employer-provided childcare is reported by experts in Liechtenstein and Malta (but not in in Liechtenstein's public administration since 2002). The government in Liechtenstein meets 50% of the costs of childcare, but it remains expensive and there are waiting lists for nurseries and childcare centres.

Few countries have specific working-time provisions for lone parents in the form of additional leave or rights to working-time adjustments. One interesting exception are the provisions in the Lithuanian labour code (Box 5.4-p.95)

5.4. Concluding assessment: gender mainstreaming the policy direction and priorities for lone parents

The national experts have suggested a range of policies and priorities to aid lone parents in their countries. These suggestions can be divided into three broad types:

- policies to increase the lone-parent employment rate, including benefit incentives and childcare;

- policies to increase lone-parent income from employment, including training initiatives;

Box 5.3: State support for lone parents in Sweden

In Sweden, the welfare system is comprehensive in that all parents receive fixed-rate, non-means-tested benefits such as the child allowance, children's pension allowance and financial aid to children attending gymnasium. Lone-parent households also receive the advanced maintenance allowance, instituted as a right for children, which was introduced to help reduce the reliance of lone parents on means-tested social assistance.

Social transfers and the tax system combined provided lone mothers with an average disposable income of 80% of the average cohabiting fathers' income in 2002, despite having a market income of only 54.3%. The transfer and tax system also benefited cohabiting women, but to a lesser degree, boosting their market income of 55.6% to a disposable income of 67.7% of the average for a cohabiting father. Single mothers gain more from the tax and benefit system as they receive more support-related and means-tested benefits. One of the three main goals of the Swedish government is to halve the level of dependence on means-tested financial assistance, and the pursuit of this goal can be anticipated to have a negative impact on the incomes of single mothers who are not in employment.

Source: national report.

policies to increase lone-parent income from benefits; these policies can be divided between those that increase benefits for just lone parents and those that increase benefits for a wider group of which lone parents are a part (e.g. all parents).

In the national reports from Liechtenstein, Lithuania, Norway and Sweden there is an emphasis on the necessity to increase the lone-mother employment rate. This is put most explicitly by the Swedish expert who regards the key issue as the employment rate and degree of involuntary part-time working among lone mothers. The Norwegian expert emphasises the need for more focus on the demand side, as employer attitude may be a major obstacle to lone mothers' access to jobs. Similarly in Finland, employer demands for greater labour flexibility are seen as disadvantageous to lone mothers.

For Ireland, Malta and Spain the experts suggest changes to the tax-benefit system to create better incentives and support for lone parents to participate in the labour market. The experts do not recommend cuts in benefits to force participation, but rather that benefit entitlement for lone parents should continue once they are in employment, at least up until they reach a higher level of employment income. In Liechtenstein, the expert suggests that lone parents could benefit from involvement in active labour market programmes. One of the suggestions made in the UK national report, which already has substantial in-work benefits for parents in the form of tax credits and a specific ALMP for lone parents, is that the tax credit system should be simplified to make it easier for lone parents to access the package of available state support when entering employment. The need for improvements in the quantity, quality and affordability of childcare are highlighted by most national reports as being necessary to increase lone-parent labour market participation.

In Norway, the relatively high level of poverty among out-of-work lone-mother households, and a favourable national labour market context with relatively high wage levels, leads the expert to argue that a mother's employ-

---

Box 5.4: The Lithuanian labour code and the rights of lone parents

The labour code establishes rights specifically for employed lone parents with a child under 14 (or under 16 if the child has limited functional capacity) to work part-time hours if they choose and to 35 days' leave per year rather than the standard minimum of 28 days.

Source: national report.

---

ment is the best insurance against low income. However, there is also evidence of considerable in-work poverty in some countries, with 20% of employed lone parents in Finland living in poverty in 2000. For Luxembourg, the expert identifies poor quality lone-parent employment rather than a low employment rate as the key problem. A need to improve labour market incomes of lone mothers through policies such as special training provision is identified in Estonia, Ireland and Malta. For Bulgaria, the expert suggests greater regulation of the labour market so that better pay and conditions can be accrued.

Two of the experts argue that there is a need for new or increased benefits specifically aimed at lone parents. The Spanish expert argues for a national social assistance benefit, housing benefit and support with childcare aimed at lone mothers to alleviate their poverty, in conjunction with policies to change incentives and increase employment rates seen as the more important 'preventative' measures. For Bulgaria, the expert argues that it is not appropriate to treat lone mothers alongside other groups that have a relatively high risk of poverty, and suggests preferential treatment for lone mothers through higher levels of child benefit, prioritisation in the distribution of kindergarten places and lower childcare fees. In other countries, experts suggest increases in general child-related benefits that would increase lone-parent incomes (such as child benefit in the United Kingdom, payable to all parents).

6. The intersection of gender and ethnicity in social exclusion – the Roma

A recent European Commission report (2004b) reviewed the situation of the Roma in 11 Member States (BG, CZ, EL, ES, FR, HU, IE, PO, RO, SK, UK). It concluded that there is a lack of systematic data on the socioeconomic situation of the Roma in most countries, but that

> 'the scarce data that does exist points to very dramatic gaps between the situation of the Roma and non-Roma throughout Europe in fields relevant to EU social inclusion policy'.

(European Commission, 2004b, p. 17)

The report noted that the pattern of inequality and disadvantage identified was to a large extent common to almost all Member States. It also noted that a gender-based analysis is mostly weak or absent in the studies and statistical series which do exist but the few studies which are available demonstrate that Roma women face even more problems than Roma men in accessing education, employment, health and other services; and that they thus face additional or 'double' discrimination compared with women of the majority community (European Commission, 2004b).

In this chapter, we focus on the gender issues in relation to the disadvantages faced by Roma women and men, drawing on national information provided by the national experts for eight countries (BG, CY, CZ, EL, HU, SI, SK, RO). The national experts note that statistical data or systematic research on the socioeconomic situation of the Roma is very patchy, and a gender breakdown is almost entirely non-existent. They draw on the limited national information which is available from official sources and on research studies undertaken by NGOs and academics. The latter are often detailed case studies of particular local areas or particular aspects of the Roma's situation.

6.1. A brief profile of the situation of the Roma and the EU legal and policy framework

Following enlargement, the Roma, Gypsy and Traveller[7] communities – or the 'Roma' for brevity – now constitute the largest ethnic minority group within the EU (European Commission, 2004b). The Roma and related communities are diverse, and the diversity is multi-dimensional, involving differences of language and dialect, history, culture, religion[8], social class and education.

It is estimated that there are possibly over 10 million Roma in Europe as a whole, and that around one and a half million Roma joined the EU when the 10 new Member States acceded to the Union in May 2004 (European Commission, 2004b). Precise demographic data are not available because many governments do not identify Roma as a separate ethnic category and many of the Roma are reluctant to identify themselves as such for official purposes due to widespread distrust of national governments rooted in their experience of widespread persecution, discrimination and racism, and forced assimilation programmes (see Box 6.1-p.99). This leads to widespread under-counting in official censuses when there are attempts to enumerate the Roma (Box 6.2-p.99).

Another problem with establishing precise population estimates is that cross-border movements can produce marked changes in the numbers resident in a country in a given year, notably a major influx into western Europe since the late 1990s due to a combination of deteriorating economic conditions and heightened persecution in a number of central and east European countries. The available national estimates are presented in Table 6.1 (p.101). These show that there is a Roma population living in most of the

---

(7)   The term Traveller is adopted by various groups commonly thought of as being linked to Gypsy communities, whether or not they are/were nomadic. The term is used particularly in Ireland and the United Kingdom. The Roma communities also include groups which refer to themselves using other nomenclature, for example the Manouches and the Sinti (European Commission, 2004, p. 1).

(8)   Roma in Europe tend to belong to either one of the Christian churches or (predominantly in the southern Balkans) to be Muslim.

30 European countries listed, and it is particularly sizeable in some central and east European countries (BG, CZ, HU, PL, RO, SL). The size of the population is growing in some countries, for example in Greece, largely through immigration. In Hungary, the Roma are growing in absolute and relative terms due to population decline in the non-Roma, even though birth rates are also declining among the Roma.

Hence the status of the Roma as an ethnic minority group has only been officially acknowledged in some countries in recent years, and even in those countries where this status is recognised there is little if any systematic monitoring of the socioeconomic situation of the Roma or social inclusion policy impact assessment. The Roma are diverse; some are settled and some nomadic; some are much more integrated into non-Roma society than others. However, the overriding situation of the Roma in both new and older Member States is marked by pronounced discrimination and severe social exclusion in relation to all areas of life: employment, public services (education, social protection, healthcare, housing, etc.), the judicial system and as consumers of market-based goods and services (shops, leisure services, transport, etc.). We detail the different dimensions of the social exclusion of the Roma across Europe in Sections 6.2 and 6.3 (see Appendix 3 for a holistic summary of the coexistence of these different dimensions in one national setting: the example of the Czech Republic).

In many of the post-communist countries the economic and political crisis produced a major deterioration in the socioeconomic situation of the Roma, for according to the Czech national expert, the transformation to a market system further marginalised those who were already on the margins of society, particularly those, like the Roma, who lacked education and other forms of capital (Box 6.3-p.102). The heightened poverty and marginalisation of the Roma forced many to fall back on traditional separatist survival strategies. Finally, many of the Roma now face the problem of statelessness, which is a particular problem in the Czech Republic following the division of the Czech and Slovak Republics[9]. In Slovenia, only a minority of the Roma have citizenship (the autochronous Roma, estimated at 6 264 in total).

Additional issues in relation to asylum and immigration are faced by those who try to enter EU states from non-EU countries. For example, the limited and deteriorating economic opportunities in Romania provoked the Roma to try and migrate to west European countries. In Slovakia there was a mass departure of the Roma in 1997, destined for the United Kingdom, and again in 1999 to Finland. In Greece, the size of the Roma community has increased since the beginning of the 1990s as many Roma fled Albania and the former Yugoslavia.

Recent development in the EU legal framework and related policy measures signal some important first steps to redress the social exclusion of the Roma. Racism and race discrimination is now illegal in the EU following the adoption of a series of anti-discrimination directives (the race directive and the framework employment directive)[10]. These measures should now have been transposed into law in all Member States[11] and prohibit direct and indirect discrimination in employment, training, education, social protection and access to goods and services (including housing and healthcare). This is particularly important for those Member States where national legislation was lacking or only addressed certain fields. A range of other relevant developments in relation to human rights and resources targeted at the needs of the Roma is underway with the Council of Europe, the UNDP, the OSCE and the World Bank (see European Commission, 2004b, p.16).

This new EU legal framework is a significant development with the potential to provide major improvements in the situation of minority groups such as the Roma. However, evaluations of the actual impact and adequacy of this legal framework are not yet available (European Commission, 2004b), and the evidence from the history of the EU legal framework on sex discrimination strongly suggests that discrimination can

(9)   The majority of the Roma living in the Czech Republic today are originally from Slovakia or are members of the originally nomadic Olah or Vlachiko in the historial aftermath of the genocide of the Holocaust. In the former Czechoslovakia there was forced dispersal from Slovakia to the Czech regions. After the division of the Czech and Slovak republics at the end of 1992, the Roma on Czech territory had difficulty obtaining citizenship because of their original place of birth. Many others were excluded because they had a criminal record, even when this was for a minor offence (national report).

(10)   Council Directive 2000/43/EC implementing the principle of equal treatment between persons irrespective of racial or ethnic origin (OJ L 180, 19.7. 2000); Council Directive 2000/78/EC establishing a general framework for equal treatment in employment and occupation (OJ L 303, 2.12.2000); as well as the more established set of Council directives on equal treatment for women and men. In addition, a revised Article 29 of the Treaty establishing the European Community (TEC) increases the powers of police and judicial authorities to cooperate on matters related to, among other things, 'preventing and combating racism and xenophobia'.

(11)   The deadline for transposition of the race directive into domestic law was 2003 for old Member States and the date of accession for new Member States.

Box 6.1: The history and culture of the Roma population in Europe

The historical origins of the Roma are not well documented but the consensus is that the Romani people are descended from groups who left the Indian subcontinent towards the end of the first millennium C.E. The Roma history in Europe is marked by persecution, slavery and genocide, including the Romani Holocaust during World War II. In the post-war period the Romani suffered from government measures to promote forcible settlement and assimilation in central and eastern Europe under state socialism, which included practices such as forced sterilisation and the removal of children for placement with non-Romani families or in state institutions. Similar practices took place in the early post-World War II period in some western European countries as well.

Post-1989 there has been an outbreak of intense anti-Romani sentiment across Europe, producing heightened systematic persecution and racist attacks in many countries, including Albania, Bulgaria, Germany, Hungary, Poland, Romania, Russia, Slovakia, Ukraine and Yugoslavia. This includes the ethnic cleansing in Kosovo in 1999 where an estimated four-fifths of the pre-bombing Romani population (probably around 120 000 persons) are either displaced or in exile. In some countries, such as the Czech Republic and Slovakia, violence against Roma remains at alarming levels. Public officials have usually failed, or been slow, to condemn anti-Romani violence. In western Europe anti-Romani settlement has frequently broken out following the arrival of Roma from eastern Europe, often followed by collective expulsions and other racially discriminatory measures by public authorities. Opinion polls conducted in the Czech Republic and in Germany, for example, show that anti-Romani sentiment is widespread.

The Romani language is spoken by millions of Europeans, making it one of the principal minority languages of Europe. It is an Indic language, closely related to modern Hindi, with many dialects. In addition, some Romani groups speak other minority lanuagages, some of which are particular to Roma and other groups perceived as 'Gypsies'.

The Roma cultivate a strong communal solidarity through close and extended family bonds and adherence to cultural traditions, which in some communities include adherence to autonomous systems of justice and 'pollution taboos' which discourage contact with the non-Roma communities. Such strategies are commonly deployed by marginalised groups to maintain identity in the face of oppression and pressures for cultural assimilation.

Source: European Commission (2004b).

Box 6.2: Under-counting of the Roma in official census

The Roma became a focus of public debate in CZ and SK from 1989 onwards in connection with preparation for accession to the EU. One of the conditions for membership was the human right of individuals to declare themselves as a member of a minority group if they so choose. In this context the Roma minority was officially recognised as a national minority in the **Czech Republic**. Similarly in **Slovakia**, it became possible for individuals to declare their Roma ethnic identity on the 1991 census for the first time in 60 years, and in the 2001 census for **Hungary** there were optional questions about ethnicity, including self-identity as a Roma, and native language. However, the proportion of the Roma who declare themselves as such in the official census are much lower than estimates of the actual size of the community in the Czech and Slovak Republics, and in many other countries (see Table 6.1-p.101). In **Slovenia**, the official census figures reported in the table conflict with the register of 2 246 Roma in receipt of social support in one region alone (Dolenjska).

In **Greece,** the vast majority of Roma did not have citizenship until the mid-1970s. The only Roma who did belonged to the Muslim minority of Thrace (which was recognised by the 1923 Lausanne Treaty on the exchange of Greek and Turkish populations), who have a different language and religion to the rest of the Roma in Greece. The Greek state currently considers the Roma to be a group with 'cultural specificities' but does not recognise them as a minority group. The size of the Roma community has increased since the beginning of the 1990s due to migration of many Roma fleeing from Albania and the former Yugoslavia. Those who are registered on arrival as immigrants are recorded according to their nationality and not as Roma.

In **Cyprus,** estimates of the size of the Roma population are poor, but there is also additional confusion as to who they are due to political reasons. Most who live in Cyprus are concentrated in the western part of the

Box 6.2: Under-counting of the Roma in official census (continued)

island (mostly in Limassol and Paphos), mainly in the Turkish Cypriot sector, speak Turkish and some prefer to identify themselves as Turkish Cypriots in the context of widespread discrimination against the Roma. The exact numbers are unknown and compounded by nomadic movements, including to and from the Turkish-occupied north.

Source: national reports.

exist long after a legal framework of protection is established. Furthermore, these legal tools are being introduced into a situation where the problems faced by the Roma are enormous, and where additional measures are needed to protect the basic human rights of this minority group. The situation of the Roma is 'approaching a human rights emergency' in many parts of Europe, particularly in the new Member States, which has provoked a 'flight' of the Roma seeking asylum in western Europe. The situation in Slovakia is particularly severe (European Commission, 2004b, pp. 13 and 15).[12]

There are a number of related developments to finance measures to address the situation of the Roma in the EU. Under the accession process, progress was required on human rights for the Roma, supported by a range of infrastructure and public awareness programmes to improve the situation of the Roma funded by the PHARE programme. The current Community Action Programme to combat discrimination (2000–06)[13] is designed to support and complement the implementation of the new anti-discrimination legal framework through information exchange, including examples of best practice. One of the priorities of the programme was transnational actions targeted at integration of the Roma into education and employment. Elements of the EU Structural Funds also have particular relevance for the Roma populations, particularly the European Regional Development Fund (ERDF), the European Social Fund (ESF), and the Cohesion Fund[14] (see European Commission, 2004b, pp. 14–15). For example, the ESF has financed an initiative on employment and training for Roma in Spain, for fighting labour market discrimination in Germany and for school desegregation in Bulgaria (European Commission, 2004b, pp. 14, 20 and 23). There have also been a limited number of projects financed by the Education and Culture DG that address the particular educational needs of the Roma and there

is some scope for the new Community Action Programme in public health (2003–08) to target the needs of minority and migrant populations (European Commission, 2004b, p. 15).

However, much still remains to be done to improve the situation of the Roma. For example, recent assessments of the PHARE programmes on the Roma concluded that the issues facing the Roma are now securing a higher political priority in the EU Member States as a result of this initiative but the scope and scale of initiatives are too small in relation to the scale of the problem (European Commission, 2004b, pp. 15–16). Yet, despite the gravity of the situation of the Roma concerning their very low employment rate and educational attainment, they are not identified as a target group for measures to raise the employment rate or skills profile of the workforce. The integration of the Roma was explicitly identified in the 2004 recommendations only in relation to the Czech Republic and Slovakia, two of the Member States where there has been a prominent public debate on this topic (European Commission, 2004b, p. 14). Yet similar priority in relation to the EES is also needed in other countries with a large and excluded Roma population. Under the social inclusion policy framework there is more mention of the Roma as a disadvantaged group which Member States should consider for priority and targeted action, and Member States are also encouraged to consult with NGOs and related bodies, and this too provides a potential avenue for promoting the interests of the Roma. However, there is no obligation on Member States to treat the Roma as a distinct target group in the preparation of their National Action Plans.

6.2. The socioeconomic situation of the Roma

The social exclusion of the Roma is multifaceted. Both in absolute terms and relative to the living conditions of the

(12) For example, the European Parliament rejected proposals that the monitoring of the human rights of the Roma in Slovakia should be monitored post-accession (European Commission, 2004, p. 13).

(13) The focus was discrimination on the grounds of racial or ethnic origin, religion or belief, disability, age or sexual orientation.

(14) The Cohesion Fund is for Member States whose GDP is less than 90 % of the EU average. In the period 2007–13, this will cover all 10 new Member States plus Greece and Portugal. Ireland and Spain will no longer qualify (European Commission, 2004, p. 14).

Table 6.1: National estimates of the Roma population

AT	15 000 to 20 000 in the mid-1990s according to Machiels (2002).
BE	10 000 to 15 000 (0.1% of the national population).
CY	One estimate is 700 persons (0.001% of the population in government-controlled part of Cyprus).
CZ	Census for 2001: 32 903 (0.3% of the population), of which 48.7% are women. However, the real number is estimated at 160 000 to 200 000 (which would equate to between 1.5% and 1.9% of the population). Machiels (2002) estimated the number might have been as high as 300 000 in the mid-1990s and Barany (1998) estimated that, in the mid-1990s, 2.7% of the population were Roma.
DE	Machiels (2002) estimated it at 85 000 to 120 000 in the mid-1990s.
DK	2 000 (0.0003% of the national population). Machiels (2002) cites higher estimates for the mid-1990s in the range 2 500 to 4 500.
EE	No data provided.
EL	250 000 to 300 000. This implies an increase since earlier estimates of 140 000 to 200 000, made for the mid-1990s by Machiels (2002).
ES	90 000 to 100 000 (2.2 to 2.4% of the national population). An earlier estimate for the mid-1990s put the figure as high as 500 000 to 600 000 (Machiels 2002).
FI	Machiels (2002) estimated 5 000 to 8 000 in the mid-1990s.
FR	250 000 to 300 000.
HU	The Roma are the biggest minority group in Hungary, estimated in representative surveys at 570 000 in total (balanced gender ratio) (6% of the national population), up from 320 000 in 1971. A lower number is recorded in the 2001 population census, based on optional self-assessment. Machiels (2002) estimates that the number was 800 000 in the mid-1990s based on different sources, but this might be an inflated estimate according to the national expert in the EGGSIE network.
IE	20 000 to 27 000 in the mid-1990s according to Machiels (2002).
IT	85 000 to 120 000 in the mid-1990s according to Machiels (2002).
LT	Official census data for 2001: 2 571 (0.07% of the national population).
LU	200 to 500 in 1994 (0.05 to 0.12% of the national population).
LV	No data provided.
MT	No data provided.
NL	30 000 to 40 000 in the mid-1990s according to Machiels (2002).
PL	Census for 2002: 12 900, other sources estimate 20 000 (both estimates are less than 0.5% of the population). Estimates for the mid-1990's were that there were 15 000 to 60 000 Roma in Poland (Machiels 2002), equating to 0.1% of the national population according to Barany (1998).
PT	40 000. This implies a fall since the mid-1990's estimates of 50 000 to 100 000 (Machiels 2002).
SI	Census for 2002: 3 246; however, other estimates are 7 000 to 10 000 (i.e. up to 0.005% of the national population).
SK	Census for 2001: 90 000, but experts estimate the true figure is almost four times as high at around 350 000 (49.8% are women). Machiels (2002) estimated 458 000 to 520 000 in the mid-1990s.
SE	Machiels (2002) estimated 15 000 to 20 000 in the mid-1990s.
UK	200 000 to 300 000 (less than 0.005% of the national population). Machiels (2002) estimated 80 000 to 100 000 in the mid-1990s.
LI	No data provided.
BG	371 356 (49.7% are women) and 4.5% of all women in Bulgaria are Roma.

Table 6.1: National estimates of the Roma population (continued)

	Machiels (2002) estimated 500 000 to 800 000 in the mid-1990s, which according to Barany (1998) equated to 8.4% of the national population at that time.
IS	No data provided.
NO	No data provided.
RO	Self-identification = 2.5% of the national population. Another estimate is 6.7% of the national population. The Roma are the second largest ethnic group after the Hungarian minority (who make up 6.6% of the Romanian population). Machiels (2002) estimated 1 400 000 to 2 500 000 in the mid-1990s, which Barany estimated was 9.5% of the national population at that time. The 2004 country report for a European Commission study estimated 1.8 million to 2.5 million.

Source: the data are from the national expert reports, supplemented by data from Machiels (2002) and Barany (1998).

Box 6.3: The deterioration of the socioeconomic situation of the Roma in the transformation from state socialism to market economies

The socioeconomic situation of the Roma has deteriorated both in absolute terms and relative to the standard of living of the rest of the population in the **Czech Republic**. In **Slovakia**, low-qualified jobs were reasonably rewarded under socialism and offered some guaranteed living conditions for the Roma, but this has been stripped away. Instead, the market transformation produced extreme territorial marginalisation, so that some areas now suffer from an unemployment rate close to 100% , and it is in these deprived areas where the Roma are often concentrated. The national report for **Bulgaria** notes that the Roma faced more negative repercussions of the social and economic restructuring in the period since 1990 than any other ethnic group. Some of the changes in the Roma's way of life, which had started to change under state socialism, in part through government compulsion via assimilation policies, were reversed. In particular, educational attainment had improved for the Roma in some countries, but this trend stalled or reversed in the aftermath of the transition. Likewise, in some communities there has been a resurgence of traditional family practices, indicated by marriages and motherhood taking place at younger ages. In **Hungary**, the employment rates of Roma men and women rose during the 1970s in connection with the demand for unskilled labour in heavy industry under socialism, but they suffered particularly from job losses under the transition due to a combination of poor education levels, regional concentration in disadvantaged areas and discrimination. In **Romania**, the Roma were not recognised as a specific ethnic minority group under socialism but they suffered disproportionately under the economic crisis from the mid-1970s onwards, as hidden unemployment emerged, discrimination increased and they were increasingly marginalised in education and health services. Literacy and educational attainment fell among the Roma, and fertility increased (in the context of an aggressive government pro-natalist policy and limited availability of contraception).

Source: national reports.

non-Roma population in the country of residence, the national reports for the eight countries in this study (BG, CY, CZ, EL, HU, SK, SL, RO) report the following conditions, which echo the picture portrayed in other reviews of national studies (European Commission, 2004b).

- **Extreme poverty**, including persistent inter-generational poverty. In many countries, the degree of poverty faced is much more severe than for other groups in the society. For Hungary, the national expert emphasises that the Roma are over-represented among the poor but that the problem of poverty extends beyond the Roma population and is widespread across the general population.

- The exposure to poverty is often compounded by a **regional concentration** of the Roma in economically deprived and/or remote areas (e.g. CY, HU, RO, SK).

- **Poor housing** conditions, often in segregated or 'ghettoised' settlements with poor public health provisions.

- **Poor health** due to poverty-related factors (poor nutrition, housing and settlement conditions, alcohol and substance abuse) compounded by inadequate access to health services (lack of insurance/official papers, discrimination and exclusionary treatment by health workers and other health service users, lack of information and health education, physical remoteness).

- High rates of **child and adult mortality, low life expectancy.**

- High rates of **institutionalised care of Roma children** in some countries (e.g. CZ, HU, RO, SK).

- **Segregated and inferior education**, including a concentration of Roma children in schools for those identified as having low achievement or behavioural problems.

- **Low educational attainment** in both mainstream and specialist schools and high rates of irregular attendance and school drop-out.

- **Language barriers** (e.g. CY, EL, SK, SI).

- **High unemployment** rates and **poor employment opportunities**, which are mainly insecure or poorly rewarded and heavily concentrated in the informal economy.

- High rates of **crime** (largely theft).

- A pattern of economic survival, which the Romania expert refers to as **'marginal survival strategies'**, encompassing **high dependency on social welfare systems**, where these can be accessed, supplemented, where there are opportunities, by **economic activity, which is concentrated in poorly-rewarded work (some of which is illegal) in informal and subsistence sectors.**

- Exposure to **widespread social stigma and negative stereotyping** by the non-Roma.

- **Discrimination, racism and exclusionary treatment** (racist attacks, police surveillance, hostile treatment) in the labour market and civil society more generally, for example when attempting to use health or social services or in shops or on public transport.

- A **widespread distrust and suspicion** of officialdom and the non-Roma, including resistance to social inclusion or integration policies where this is at the cost of assimilation through the erosion of Roma culture.

- **Resignation, low morale** and little sense that educational advancement or employment is possible in the climate of social exclusion and discrimination.

- Lack of appropriate **documentation** for accessing equal treatment in the legal system and public services provided by municipalities and the national state (e.g. marriage papers when traditional Roma marriages are not recognised can reduce the protection accorded to women and to children deemed be born outside of marriage). In the most severe cases this amounts to **statelessness**, which is widespread for example for the Roma in the Czech Republic (see Section 5.1).

These conditions are experienced by both sexes, yet gender-based differences in family and economic roles mean that women and men face different forms and degrees of poverty and exclusion. However, a gender-based analysis is under-developed in policy debates. For example, as the Greek national expert notes, quoting from a recent report monitoring the situation of women:

> *'Unfortunately the gender dimension of the discrimination Roma women face is often underplayed or not noticed, due to a racial perception of the discrimination Roma face in general, which is more obvious'*
>
> (Greek Helsinki Monitor and World Organisation Against Torture, 2002).

6.3. The demographic profile and family situation of Roma women

In traditional Roma culture, family ties play a pivotal role in maintaining community solidarity. The cultural norms and practices in relation to the family are patriarchal and organised around separate gender roles. Detailed ethnographic fieldwork documents how men have the main decision-making authority and represent the Roma community in public, while women's main responsibility is family care work in their roles as daughters, wives and mothers. Women's ability to participate in public or political life is heavily constrained by traditional Roma social norms, and often by direct instruction from male family members. The higher status accorded to men begins from birth, with boys accorded a more important position in the family than girls (Štrukelj, 2004, summarised by the Slovenian national expert).

Box 6.4: The family and demographic profile of the Roma

The demographic profile of the Roma population is much younger than that of non-Roma populations.

In the **Czech Republic**, qualified estimates suggest that the Roma population has an age profile where the proportion aged 0 to 14 years is twice the rate of the majority population, while the proportion aged over 50 years is up to three times lower.

In **Romania**, the average age of marriage and first birth fell to an even younger age during the economic crisis and transition, as traditional practices were strengthened as a refuge from heightened economic and political uncertainty. Over the 1990s, the proportion of Roma who were married before 18 years rose from 44.6% to 52% , and the percentage of women giving birth before 18 years rose from 30.6% to 37%. More than 30% of Roma households have six or more children and 46% have five or more (compared with national rates of 5% and 14%). One third of the Roma population are aged 0 to 14 years and only 4.3% are aged over 65 years.

In **Bulgaria**, about 80% of the Roma get married while still a minor. This is followed by early and numerous births: the birth rate of the Roma in Bulgaria is 26.7 per 1 000 compared with 13 per 1 000 for those in Turkey, 6.9 per 1 000 for those in Bulgaria and a national average of 8.5 per 1 000. Of the adult population (aged 15 years and older), 43% of Roma women are in the 15- to 29-year-old age band. Similarly, in **Hungary**, 46% of Roma women are aged under 20 years and only 21% are over 40 years old. In **Slovenia**, 40% of the Roma are aged under 15 years and only 1.7% are aged over 65 years (compared with 17.3% and 13% respectively for the non-Roma majority).

According to data collected during a vaccination programme among Roma children in **Greece**, the average age of marriage was 14 years for a girl and 17 years for a boy. In **Cyprus**, Roma girls are typically married by 14 or 15 years old.

Source: national reports.

Marriages occur at a young age, and are rarely formalised according to the official state requirements of the non-Roma society. Marriage at a young age is encouraged by parents, and traditionally involves a financial exchange with female virginity considered a prerequisite for marriage. Marriages are considered binding and divorce/separation is rare and socially unacceptable. Women become pregnant at a young age and bear a large number of children and, on average, the Roma have larger families than the non-Roma majority (see Box 6.4). Use of contraception is low and the ability of women to access such services is often controlled by the attitudes of their husbands.

There are indications in some of the post-communist Member States that the economic crisis and transition period fuelled a resurgence of traditional family practices as a refuge from the increased economic and political uncertainty the Roma were experiencing. For example, in Romania, marriages and first births started to occur at younger ages for the Roma during this period. The high fertility rates in Hungary are now declining and a slight reduction is also forecast in the trends for Slovakia.

The impoverished living conditions of the Roma means that the higher fertility rate coexists with high rates of child and adult mortality and lower life expectancy compared with the rates for the non-Roma population. Hence the age profile of the Roma is very young (see Box 6.4).

There is also some evidence that the gender profile of the Roma population may differ from that of the non-Roma in some countries, associated with gender-based differences in mortality. In Slovakia, there are more men than women in the Roma population, in contrast to the standard gender demographic profile of the non-Roma population. The limited evidence available suggests this is associated with much higher mortality rates of Roma women in the younger and middle (child-bearing) years. The Slovenian national expert notes that Roma men outnumber Roma women in many of the countries of south-western Europe, but that Slovenia is an exception.

6.4. Gender inequalities and the situation of women in the Roma community

From a gender mainstreaming perspective, the particular problems faced by women within the Roma community are the following:

(a) **Traditional family roles for women create add-itional mechanisms of exclusion from public and political life**

The family-based position of women is even more pronounced in Roma than in non-Roma societies. For example, in the case of Cyprus, Roma mothers typically focus their efforts on getting their daughters married, typically by 14 or 15 years old, and their sons into jobs. It is also common in Cyprus for husbands to discourage or forbid their wives to undertake employment.

One result of the traditional family roles in Roma culture is that women are even more excluded from political and civic life than Roma men. This also means women have less information and awareness about the existing gender equality measures in mainstream society and face additional obstacles in accessing such provisions than non-Roma women (Czech national report).

(b) **Health risks, including those related to Roma women's experience of early and many pregnancies**

The health risks faced by the Roma are more severe than non-Roma society (Box 6.5). In addition, Roma women have particular health risks connected to early and repeated pregnancies, compounded by their poverty and poor access to health services. This contributes to reducing the life expectancy of Roma women. As well as health risks, early and numerous

---

Box 6.5: The health inequalities experienced by the Roma

The Roma population are exposed to particular health risks and have reduced life expectancies due to a combination of poverty, poor housing and slum settlements, and discriminatory treatment in access to health services. For example, 10 years ago the life expectancy of Roma in the **Czech Republic** was 12 years fewer than the national average. There are high rates of communicable diseases (e.g. tuberculosis, hepatitis), particularly for those living in slum settlements. These public health risks are widespread for the Roma in most of the new Member States, but this disadvantage is also found in the pre-2004 Member States. For example, in **Spain**, the Roma have higher rates of hepatitis and lower vaccination coverage generally (European Commission, 2004b, pp. 27–28).

The Roma's marginalisation, poor socioeconomic circumstances and poor access to information, education and health services make the Roma vulnerable to other health risks including HIV/AIDS, STD and drug abuse. For example, drug abuse is increasing in some Roma communities, and some Roma women and teenagers are propelled into the sex industry by poverty, unemployment and discrimination. However, there are no concrete data on these health issues so the problem is that either the risks are ignored or negative and inaccurate stereotypes are developed which further fuel the scapegoating and social exclusion of the Roma (European Commission 2004b, pp. 27–28).

Most Roma in **Greece** lack health insurance. They can access the national health system as a needy category, but many lack the necessary identity papers. A recent study has shown the main reason the Roma do not visit hospitals is widespread distrust of the health services and officials, unfriendly reception and prejudice from hospital workers, and an ignorance of their social rights. The particular implications for women's reproductive health is that they have very limited knowledge or use of contraception and related family planning services. Very few use prenatal services. A recent study found that although nearly all give birth in hospitals (96%), only a third had received any medical monitoring during their pregnancy, with low awareness of screening services (cervical cancer, breast cancer).

In **Romania**, access to medical services are difficult for the Roma due to a combination of their geographical isolation, lack of official documents and health insurance, and discriminatory practices by health providers. The Roma usage of family planning services is very low as a result, which is compounded by some aspects of traditional Roma culture which discourages the use of contraception. In Romania, infant mortality rate for the Roma is four times higher than the national average. A very high percentage of pregnant Roma women are not covered by the healthcare insurance system, and the proportion of pregnant Roma women who do not undergo a prenatal medical examination is higher than that for Romanian women in general (30.8% compared with 11.4%). It is young mothers who are the least likely to access this service – one-third of the Roma mothers who do not receive any prenatal healthchecks are under 18 years of age. Similar problems are also reported in the national report for **Hungary**.

Source: national reports and European Commission (2004b).

Box 6.6: The poor housing conditions of the Roma

Throughout Europe the Roma, Gypsy and Traveller communities live in substandard accommodation in segregated and 'ghettoised' settlements with inadequate infrastructure and services, and are exposed to threats of eviction and rejection by neighbouring non-Roma communities. Sites for nomadic Travellers are often inadequate or non-existent. Many settlements are in hazardous environments with health and safety risks, due to exposure to chemical and gas leaks, risks of explosion or subsidence. For example, information for the **Czech Republic**, **Slokavia**, **Romania** and **Greece** shows that many major Roma settlements and sites are in or near mines and dumps. Legal sites for nomadic Roma are often lacking, or are on marginal land with substandard facilities, with research having shown this to be a problem in several countries, for example **Ireland**, **Greece**, the **United Kingdom** and **France**. As a result, the Roma can be caught in a situation of trespass and repeat evictions, which is both traumatic and can fuel resentment, negative stereotypes and racism between Roma and non-Roma. When the Roma attempt to purchase land and procure public utilities, their efforts are often blocked (European Commission 2004b, p. 30).

In **Greece,** a nation-wide survey in 2002 found that 50% of Greek Roma have lived in the same place for over 20 years. However, those living in tents and basic sheds in 79 segregated settlements on the periphery of urban areas are the largest and most disadvantaged group. These Roma face a high-risk of eviction and deprivation of basic human and social rights; thus they face problems of survival in addition to those of racial discrimination and social marginalisation. Twenty-four of these settlements have been officially designated as squalid by the Greek Ministry of Health and Welfare because they have no access to running water, sanitation or electricity and/or are located in sites unfit for habitation due to their location near rubbish dumps, in former river beds, etc.

The situation is similar in **Slovenia**, where the Roma mostly live in separate settlements on the edges of non-Roma urban areas and villages. More than 60% of Roma households have unsuitable, substandard housing; many are illegal and lack electricity, water and sanitation. Approximately half of Roma families live in shacks without electricity or running water.

In **Slovakia**, a recent survey, carried out by the Office of the SR Government Plenipotentiary for Roma Communities and co-funded by the World Bank, estimates half of the estimated 320 000 Roma in Slovakia live in about 780 segregated settlements with extremely low standards of living. This includes 149 segregated settlements on the periphery of towns or villages without running water, where sewage or sanitation services are rare and where more than 20% of the dwellings are illegal. The material living standards of Roma in such segregated settlements are much worse than those of the 'integrated' Roma.

In **Romania**, there is growing homelessness for the Roma due to a multitude of economic and political causes: restitution of nationalised buildings to their former owners, no social housing provided for evicted tenants, inability to pay housing costs in the economic disruption of the transition, and explosion of fraud, particularly in the early years of transition. Only 3% of the Romanian population do not own their own home, compared with 21% for the Roma. One-quarter do not have documents attesting ownership of their house/land which exposes them to eviction when ownership is disputed. The Roma are often segregated on the outskirts of urban areas or in remote regions. Roma housing is typically overcrowded (a rate of 80% of Roma households, which is twice the national average) and lacking in basic utilities.

In **Bulgaria**, only 25% of Roma families have electricity, water supply and central sewerage, compared with 71.7% of Bulgarians.

In **Cyprus**, the Roma lack adequate housing, and much of it is substandard and lacks basic services such as electricity and water and sanitation. Overcrowding is common, ventilation is poor and humid, and furniture is insufficient.

Source: national reports and European Commission (2004b).

births contribute to the exclusion of Roma women from education and labour market advancement, which is discussed separately below.

The large families of the Roma are not simply a result of 'traditional culture'; they also result from a lack of opportunity to access contraception and family planning services. For example, in Romania survey data reveals that the desired family size reported by the Roma is similar to the national average and notably lower than the Roma average family size. The Romanian national expert argues that this discrepancy is due to a lack of birth control services for the Roma.

(c) The legacy of forced sterilisation under some previous government policies

Sterilisation programmes for Roma women were government policy in the former Czechoslovakia in the 1970s and 1980s, and in Hungary and other central European countries. These programmes encompassed sterilisation without consent or full information and, sometimes, with financial inducements to comply. The programmes have stopped but are still recent history and part of women's experiences. For example the sterilisation programmes were only abolished in law in 1990 in Slovakia, and in the Czech Republic the programmes did not cease until the middle of the 1990s. There has been no justice, compensation or public apology yet for the women who experienced forced sterilisation, and a judgement on the legal complaint that was lodged by Czech and Slovak public prosecutors on behalf of sterilised Roma women in both republics was postponed (European Commission, 2004b). In addition, this previous exposure to programmes of forced sterilisation may create problems in securing Roma women and men's acceptance and use of family planning and reproductive health services, and this should be taken into account in policy designed and targeted at the Romas' needs.

(d) Poor housing conditions and a heavy domestic workload

The housing conditions of the Roma are extremely poor and insecure across Europe (see Box 6.6-p.106), and Roma women are no more disadvantaged than Roma men with regard to lack of access to decent housing conditions. However, the gender division of labour means that women have the primary responsibility for domestic chores and this workload is heavier for Roma women because their families are larger and they live in homes with few domestic appliances and in settlements which lack basic amenities (running water, heating).

Poor housing is compounded by an exclusion from local services. This can arise through eviction, or simply because municipal authorities refuse to accept the Roma as residents with eligibility to local services. For example, the Greek expert reports that, according to the European Roma Rights Centre (ERRC) and the Greek Helsinki Monitor (2003), a sharp rise in forced evictions and demolitions has been documented and, in a number of municipalities, authorities have refused to register Roma who are resident as resident. This effectively precludes them from access to public services and hence a number of fundamental social and

---

Box 6.7: The educational exclusion of the Roma

Many Roma housing settlements are heavily segregated away from the non-Roma population (see discussion of housing). The itinerant movement of some groups of the Roma, in some countries, and language barriers also present particular needs for education provision. However, education policy also contributes to this segregation. In some countries, for example **Denmark**, this is because educational authorities have in recent years made targeted provisions for Roma children to address their particular needs. The problem is that in many countries the education segregation of Roma children is all too often associated with inferior and 'ghettoised' provision and poor educational outcomes. For example, one country which does monitor educational achievement by ethnicity is the **United Kingdom**, and this monitoring reveals that Roma children have a very low educational achievement compared with other ethnic groups (European Commission 2004b, pp. 18–20).

Research in the **Czech Republic**, **Slovakia**, **Hungary** and **Bulgaria** reveals that Romani children are heavily concentrated into remedial schools, and those that are in mainstream schools are heavily segregated into substandard schools with inferior buildings, material resources and teaching provision. In **Bulgaria**, the segregation is so pronounced that there are 'Gypsy schools' located in or near Roma quarters. There have been some government initiatives in all these countries in recent years to address this segregation; however, progress has been limited. For example, follow-up research in the Czech Republic showed that policies had had little impact to date and segregation was still high. Data for **Germany** show that only 50% of Roma children attend school and those that do are over-represented in schools for under-achievers, which in some regions reaches a rate of 80% of all Roma children enrolled in education. Educational segregation of Roma children is also reported to be pronounced and increasing in **Spain**, and to exist in **Denmark, France** and the **United Kingdom** (European Commission 2004b, pp. 18–19).

In some countries, for example **Hungary**, education levels for the Roma had started to increase under state communism, partly through compulsion from the governments' assimilation policies. However, the increase was insufficient to protect the Roma from the extreme economic vulnerabilities they were exposed to in the economic crisis.

Box 6.7: The educational exclusion of the Roma (continued)

In **Greece**, most Roma children either do not enrol in school, or attend irregularly and drop out at an early age. Only a minority reach mandatory secondary-level school, and 60% are illiterate. A number of factors contribute to this poor education. School access is difficult, due to the physical remoteness of many settlements, which is compounded by municipal exclusionary practices (refusing to register students or to provide transport); and racism from teachers, and pupils and their parents is common. In addition, a travelling way of life, including forced relocations due to expulsion, makes it difficult for children to integrate.

In **Romania**, the participation rate in pre-school education for the Roma is four times lower than the average national rate. The Roma have the lowest education levels in Romania: attendance at elementary and secondary level school is 25% and 30% lower than the national rate respectively. Nearly one in five (17%) of Roma children aged 7 to 16 years have never had any formal education and over one-third of the Roma people (38.6%) are functionally illiterate. Roma children are concentrated in poorly resourced schools (as are other poor children in Romania), where they experience an inferior educational environment. Schools where Roma children predominate have much lower achievement rates.

Only 3% of the Roma in **Slovenia** have occupational or secondary school-level education and 80% of the unemployed Roma do not have primary school-level education. In **Cyprus**, the Roma have a high rate of illiteracy and most only have elementary school education and are highly marginalised in education, employment and public life.

Source: national reports and European Commission (2004b).

economic rights. This makes it even more difficult for Roma women to access health and education for themselves and, in their domestic role as custodians, for their children and other relatives.

(e) Low educational attainment

The Roma have markedly lower rates of education participation and achievement, including a high illiteracy rate. Educational achievement by ethnic group is only monitored in a few Member States, and is particularly rare for the Roma (European Commission, 2004b). The evidence that is available reveals very low achievement and widespread racial segregation of Roma children in the education system. Hence the shortfall from the Lisbon European Council targets for education and training by 2010[15] is particularly great for the Roma. However, the indicators developed for monitoring progress does not include an ethnic breakdown, so this aspect of the exclusion of the Roma is in danger of being overlooked. Various processes contribute to the low educational attainment of the Roma: segregated and remote settlements, nomadic ways of life, language barriers, and education policies which segregate Roma children

into education which is all too often 'ghettoised' and has substandard resource levels (see Box 6.7).

This educational disadvantage is even more pronounced for Roma women. The emphasis on women's domestic roles in Roma culture – with the widespread practice of early motherhood and many pregnancies – is accompanied by a widely held view that education is not important for young girls. For example, the illiteracy rate among Roma women in Bulgaria is 17% , three times as high as for Roma men. This pattern persists among the younger generations of Roma. The Roma community is the only ethnic community in Bulgaria where the educational level of women is lower than that of men.

In Romania, school attendance dropped sharply after 1989 and the transition period but the trend has been reversed in recent years as a result of sustained intervention. Participation is growing for both sexes at all levels of education, according to official records, although rates are still much lower than the national average (and the under-estimation of the Roma population may underestimate the scale of the problem). Interestingly, it seems from official records that the participation in schools of Roma girls is beginning to

(15)   These include: (1) an EU average rate of no more than 10% early school leavers; (2) the percentage of 15-year-old low achievers in reading literacy should have decreased by at least 20 % in comparison with those in the year 2000; (3) at least 85% of 22-year-olds in the EU should have completed upper secondary education; (4) the total number of graduates in mathematics, science and technology in the EU should increase by at least 15 % and at the same time the level of gender imbalance should decrease; (5) the EU average level of participation in lifelong learning should be at least 12.5 % of the adult working population (25 to 64 age group). *Source*: Commission of the European Communities (2004), cited in European Commission (2004).

surpass that of boys, which suggests that the detail of the educational programmes have managed to redress the problem of lower participation rates for Roma girls, found in many other countries.

It is common knowledge in development programmes with poor and excluded communities that poor education levels and high fertility rates are mutually reinforcing for women. This can be illustrated by data for Hungary: the average fertility rate of a Roma woman with elementary schooling is 2.7, falling to 1.61 for those with secondary school education. This is a result of various factors, whereby school access is partly dependent on financial consideration, which in turn curtail labour market opportunities and reinforce poverty. The combination of poverty, poor education and high fertility traps women into poor economic conditions where the lack of education obstructs women's access to information about their rights and opportunities and limits their employment prospects.

Another related problem is that the poor educational levels of women contribute to the inter-generational transfer of educational disadvantage, since it can have a negative impact on the educational aspirations and achievements of their children.

(f) Labour market disadvantage

The Roma have very high unemployment rates, which reach 80% in some of the new Member States, for example 88% in Slovakia and 50–80% in the Czech Republic (see Box 6.8-p.110). The economic situation is very precarious in the post-2004 Member States as well. For example, in Spain, half of the working-age Roma are estimated to lack a stable or legal job (European Commission, 2004b).

There is widespread labour market exclusion of the Roma. This is acute where the Roma lack the necessary citizenship or residency papers, which is widespread in the Czech Republic. Discrimination by employers and training providers, as well as ineligibility for active labour market measures where this is contingent on a work history record or tied to benefit eligibility, operate to exclude the Roma. As well as facing widespread discrimination, the low qualification levels held by the Roma mean that they are constrained to low-paid and insecure work. The options open to Roma women are even more constrained given the combination of the traditional cultural emphasis on their family roles and their lower educational opportunities. In the case of Cyprus, the national expert notes that Roma women face language as well as education barriers in the labour market, for most do not speak Greek, and that NGOs observe that it is common for husbands to discourage or forbid their wives from undertaking employment.

There are few available gender breakdowns of unemployment and employment conditions for the Roma; however, the evidence which is available signals pronounced gender inequalities. For example, in the Czech Republic 90% of the unemployed Roma are women (European Commission, 2004b, p. 23). The national reports for Bulgaria and Hungary also provide statistical data: in Bulgaria it is estimated that 80% of Roma women are unemployed and 66% have never held a paid job, in contrast to 34% of Roma men who have never held a paid job. In Hungary, the employment rate for Roma women is 16% compared with 29% for Roma men, with both rates significantly lower than those for the non-Roma population (57% and 63% respectively).

Often women rely on a patchwork of three or four jobs in the 'grey' or informal economy, where typical activities include door-to-door selling, domestic work, agricultural work and traditional handicrafts. These jobs lack social protection and place the women in situations where they are vulnerable to low pay and exploitation. Their precarious labour market position and extreme poverty increases the risk that the Roma are drawn into prostitution (see below) and theft as one component of 'marginal survival strategies'.

In Romania, among the Roma, women are even less likely than men to have professional/vocational training. Among the Roma identified in the 2002 census, women were three times less likely to be employed than men. Their much lower employment rate is mirrored by high inactivity rates; although recorded unemployment rates were much lower than for Roma men. Those Roma women who were employed worked mainly in agriculture and processing industries; family work and self-employment was common.

Roma women who are household heads due to single parenthood, widowhood, or an escape from domestic violence face particularly acute problems when trying to secure the economic well-being of their household.

(g) Dependency on social welfare benefits

The high unemployment rates of the Roma are accompanied by high levels of dependency on social welfare

Box 6.8: National data on the unemployment and poverty of the Roma

In the **Czech Republic**, research among the Roma has confirmed that the Roma experience the non-Roma majority society as alien, external, unfriendly and threatening. The Roma have a risk of poverty which is twice that of the majority society. Unemployment rates are very high, at 50% or more. Three-quarters of the unemployed are long-term unemployed and in 40% of families at least one parent is unemployed; in one-third of families at least one parent is in receipt of a disability pension. At the end of the 1990s, the Czech Ministry of Labour and Social Affairs estimated that about 47% of the Roma population of working age were financially dependent on public resources. Overall, the majority of Roma families are dependent on social benefits, which means incomes hover around the official minimum income, which is below the poverty line.

In **Slovakia**, the Roma have high and vastly disproportionate rates of unemployment, estimated at 88% in a recent study (European Commission, 2004b). The national report records that the Roma account for 30% of the long-term unemployed; rising to 52% of all those unemployed for four years or more. An estimated 80% of the Roma population is dependent on social benefits, according to the Ministry of Labour, Social Affairs and Employment. The reform of social welfare in 2004 introduced more stringent conditions for entitlements and a reduction in benefit levels, which hit large families particularly hard and dramatically reduced the living standards of the Roma.

In **Bulgaria**, the employment rate for the Roma is much lower than that of Bulgarians or the Turks, which is the other major ethnic group. Unemployment rates are very high for the Roma, and even more so for Roma women. It is estimated that 80% of Roma women are unemployed and 66% have never held a paid job, in contrast to 34% of Roma men. Only 7.5% of Roma have permanent jobs, 34% depend entirely on social benefits and 25% rely on the income of other household members. The proportion of the Roma who live in poverty is estimated at 62%, compared with 21% of the Turk ethnic group and 6% of Bulgarians.

In **Greece**, only about 40% of the Roma are employed and child labour is commonplace. The employment rate for women is much lower than that for men. In urban areas women usually work informally as street vendors, fortune-tellers and beggars, or help their husbands in petty trade. Roma men also work in the informal sector; typically in unskilled manual jobs, in petty trade or in clandestine activities.

In **Hungary**, the employment rate of the Roma population declined over the 1970s and 1980s, with a particularly sharp fall from the end of the 1980s. The employment rate of working-age Roma men and women in 1987 was 74.4% and 49.3% respectively; by 1993 this had fallen to 29% for Roma working-age men (compared with 63% for non-Roma men) and 16.3% for Roma women (compared with 56.9% for non-Roma women). These extreme disparities persist to this day. In 2003, the employment rate for Roma women was 2.6% for those aged 15 to 19 years, around 14% for those in their twenties and just over 20% for Roma women in their thirties and forties through to mid-fifties. The Roma have higher poverty rates and exposure to low income. This can be illustrated by the following comparison: the mean average gross monthly earnings in Hungary is HUF 157 500 (EUR 390), yet 62% of Roma households have a per capita income of less than HUF 19 999 (EUR 80).

In **Cyprus**, unemployment rates for the Roma are higher than for the majority population, with employed Roma men largely found in temporary jobs while very few Roma women are employed.

In **Romania**, very few of the Roma are registered as officially unemployed, but the true level is almost certainly much higher. Data from 1998 records that only 47% of the Roma were employed compared with the national rate of 61.7%. In the 2002 census, the Roma minority had the highest inactivity rate and the lowest employment rate. Only 27.5% of Roma hold a salaried position, which is less than half the national rate. Most work on their own account (71.7%), commonly as day labourers in agriculture and other casual jobs in the informal economy. Long periods of unemployment are common. In 2004, three-quarters of the Roma population were living in poverty: three times the rate of poverty for the national average (74.3% compared with 18.7%). The risk of severe poverty is five times higher than the national average. The Roma are heavily dependent on welfare benefits (e.g. half obtain between a quarter and two-thirds of their household income from child allowances), and this dependency appears to have increased for wages accounting for only 13% of the average household income in Roma families, which is half of what it was at the beginning of the transition period. Subjective self-assessment data record that two-thirds of the Roma think they lack even the bare necessities for life compared with 31% of the overall popu-

---

Box 6.8: National data on the unemployment and poverty of the Roma (continued)

lation, and this perception of impoverishment rose during the 1990s. Almost half live in rural areas, and suffer the additional marginalisation of the peripheral, rural parts of the economy.

In **Slovenia**, a combination of low education levels and widespread discrimination makes the Roma extremely vulnerable to labour market marginalisation. There are no official Slovene data, but unemployment rates are estimated at 87%. Most of the employed Roma hold temporary and unskilled posts, and they are often the first to lose their jobs when economic conditions deteriorate. Fieldwork research has revealed widespread employment discrimination. The implementation of policies and programmes which aim to improve the employment situation of the Roma is undermined by the poor economic climate. Because of their precarious position, the Roma are eligible for various forms of social assistance, and their widespread reliance on social welfare causes problems: it can contribute to a demoralisation and reduce motivation for active labour market participation; and it can fuel racial prejudice and conflict with the majority population.

Source: national reports.

Box 6.9: Problems of documentation and access to social welfare and other public services

In **Slovakia**, a common problem is that the Roma lack a residence permit for the place where they are actually resident, and this means they are excluded from public services. In the **Czech Republic**, **Hungary** and **Slovakia** there are documented examples of local officials removing Roma from the municipal register of permanent residents, even if they were born or long-term resident in the municipality (European Commission 2004, p. 32).

In the context of the break-up of Czechoslovakia the problem of statelessness became acute, and the Roma constituted the vast majority of those excluded as stateless by the **Czech Republic**. Long-term residents in **Germany**[16] still only hold a temporary status called 'tolerated' ('duldung') which must be renewed frequently and which can include restrictions on freedom of movement, access to employment and various forms of social assistance. Documentation problems also face the Roma in **Greece** and **Austria**.

In **Romania**, there are an estimated 46 500 people without ID papers, most are Roma. This means they are excluded and cannot access social assistance, insurance or legal employment.

Source: national reports, supplemented by European Commission (2004b).

---

benefits (see Box 6.8). In some countries, this dependency stems in part from state policy towards the integration of the Roma. For example, the Slovakian national expert emphasises that, under the communism state, paternalism through social welfare payments was an integral part of state policy targeted at the assimilation of the Roma as a means of challenging the traditional Roma system of family solidarity and autonomy.

While many Roma rely on social welfare, they often experience negative treatment and discrimination when accessing welfare payments, particularly when applying for discretionary means-tested support. Additional difficulties are faced by Travellers due to their nomadic residency. For example, in France there is widespread assumption by social welfare officers that the Roma are working illegally or informally and this is used in means-tested assessments (European Commission, 2004b, p.

31). Often the Roma lack the appropriate documentation (including birth and marriage certificates, residence permits, identification documents), which creates severe problems in accessing social services and in some cases results in 'statelessness'. In some situations, the lack of documentation can result from direct action by municipal authorities to exclude the Roma (see Box 6.9)

While Roma men and women both face these problems in accessing social welfare, there may be additional hurdles for women. The inferior employment situation of Roma women also means they are even less likely to have an independent entitlement to unemployment insurance-based benefits. Another factor is that traditional Roma marriages are rarely recognised in official law and this can cause major disadvantages for spouse-based eligibility for pensions and other benefits, spouse visiting rights in prisons and hospitals, etc. Finally, where

---

(16) Citizenship laws in Germany were until 1999 based solely on descent and included no provision for the acquisition of citizenship through birth on German territory (European Commission, 2004, p. 32).

welfare support is being reduced this can create additional pressures on Roma women in their domestic roles if they have to make the household budget stretch further. They may also face even greater difficulties in accessing active labour market programmes unless there are specific measures targeted at Roma women.

Recent welfare reforms in some of the Member States have made it more difficult for the Roma to access welfare benefits, and here too there are negative gender impacts. Many European countries are reforming welfare support to 'make work pay' by tightening the eligibility conditions and requirements for job search or participation in training programmes. Often these reforms have negative impacts on women due to a lack of gender mainstreaming in policy design (for more detail see Fagan and Hebson 2006, Rubery et al. 2004). In some of the new Member States, welfare support has been reduced but in an economic context of high unemployment and very few opportunities for employment as a legacy of the economic transition from state socialism (Box 6.10-p.114).

(h) Prostitution and trafficking

In some countries – notably Bulgaria, the Czech Republic and Slovakia – poverty, unemployment and discrimination has fuelled the prostitution and trafficking of women, in which Roma women and teenagers are one of the vulnerable groups (European Commission, 2004b, p. 27–28). The Czech national report notes that one qualified estimate is that one in three prostitutes in Prague are Roma women. In Bulgaria, Roma women are also propelled towards prostitution by the combination of high illiteracy rates and poor employment prospects. These trends are driven by extreme poverty and deteriorating circumstances in particular countries and are not a generalised phenomenon across Europe, for traditional Roma culture forbids prostitution (Silvera, 2005).

(i) Domestic violence

The full extent of domestic violence is underestimated in all societies but it is pervasive – it is found in families from all ethnic groups and in affluent as well as low-income households. The available evidence suggests that the overwhelming majority of domestic violence is perpetuated by men on women and their children.[17] For the Roma communities, several aspects of their situation present a package of factors which can combine to heighten the risk of domestic violence. These include the material and psychological hardship of living in conditions of poverty and social exclusion, the additional pressures of economic turbulence and disruption, the stress of teenage marriage and parenthood, and a family system which has traditionally bestowed authority and higher social status upon men.

According to the Greek National Observatory for Combating Violence against Women, physical abuse and domestic violence against Roma women is frequent and widely sanctioned as a 'normal' part of behaviour by fathers and husbands. The result is that many Roma women have learnt to expect this as part of their life from early childhood (national report). Similarly the national report for Cyprus notes that a high incidence of domestic violence in Roma families is noted in a range of sources, from NGOs working with Romas through to academic research.

Leaving a situation of domestic violence is difficult for all women, but Roma women face additional barriers. Many women who experience domestic violence have learned to 'accept' it as part of their lives, as something which they deserve; and this socialisation may be more pervasive in communities where traditional male authority within the family is still widespread, such as among the Roma. There are other structural problems which may create a particularly severe trap for Roma women if the only way of escaping is to seek assistance outside of the Roma community: here distrust and negative experiences of governmental authorities or non-Roma NGOs, possibly combined with language barriers, future uncertainty and the potential rupture of family ties, create high barriers for Roma women to overcome.

6.5. Concluding assessment of the policy direction and priorities for reducing the disadvantage of Roma women

The Roma community in Europe is larger than the national population of some Member States and faces some of the most extreme forms of social exclusion and poverty in relation to all aspects of life: political participation and civil rights, health, housing, education, labour market disadvantage, and social welfare. Our discussion has identified gender inequalities which run through all these aspects and how the intersection of ethnicity and gender

---

(17) It is likely that the under-reporting of domestic violence may be even greater for men than for women, because it is even less acceptable for men to admit that they are being beaten by a female or male partner as it undermines social norms about masculinity and men's physical strength and ability to defend themselves.

compounds the disadvantage faced by Roma women. The reduction of the disadvantage of Roma women requires a gender mainstreaming of all social inclusion policies for the Roma (education, unemployment, poverty, anti-racism legislation and campaigns including measures to stop discrimination by municipal authorities, etc), with targeted provisions for Roma women as one component. There is little positive progress to report on gender mainstreaming so far, for as a recent European Commission report on the situation of the Roma notes:

> 'Most government policies on Roma are silent on the issue of gender equality, or include only inadequate provisions. Where gender matters are addressed in policies, they are frequently confined to issues related to marriage, the use of contraception or parental responsibility.'

(European Commission, 2004b, p. 35)

Gender mainstreaming of the recently launched international 'Decade of Roma inclusion 2005–15'[18] is also very precarious, uneven across the different signatories[19] and in places contradictory (Perić, 2005; Bogdanić, 2005). The fact that these criticisms are being published on a link to the official website is a small sign that some positive developments may be secured in the longer run if the issues raised are taken up in the central initiatives and this action plan is modified as it unfolds. However, there is also the risk that such criticism will remain ignored in the context of criticisms about the philosophy and focus of the programme that are being raised in a number of quarters, including some Roma organisations such as the Dženo Association (www.dzeno.cz). The national experts for Bulgaria and Romania also emphasise that the limited government budgets made available for these national programmes in their countries limits their efficacy.

The national expert reports for this study note that a number of policy initiatives for the Roma have been introduced or extended in their countries and, for the new Member States, this includes a particularly intensive period of government action during the pre-accession period, in response to external political pressures from the EU and other international bodies. Their conclusions echo that of another recent review (European Commis-

sion, 2004b): firstly, that a more coordinated, comprehensive policy programme is required that addresses the various domains of exclusion (health, housing, education, employment, legal services, racism) together; and, secondly, that extensive consultation and involvement of the Roma in the policy design and delivery is a key ingredient for the success of programmes.

The national reports in this study provide additional messages after gender mainstreaming the analysis. One is that the consultation and involvement has to be designed to reach Roma women as well as men. The second is that measures for women have to extend beyond a focus on mothers, as a means for improving the situation of Roma children, and have to address the education, health and economic needs of women themselves as a particular priority for gender mainstreaming. Given the young age profile of the Roma, young women are identified as a particular target for gender mainstreaming policies. With a gender mainstreaming focus, it is evident that many of the objectives concerned with raising women's employment and education can be interpreted as a direct challenge to some traditional Roma values concerning appropriate gender roles. Hence, there may be strong suspicion and resistance to such programmes from some Roma groups, even though adherence to such traditional values and attitudes vary between different groups within the Roma, as is the case in any population. One part of the solution is to be found in investing energy in improving consultation and involvement with the different interest groups within the Roma community.

For example, in Slovenia there was an initiative to consult and involve Roma women as a small element of a wider series of government programmes for the Roma ('Roma women can do it' – E Romane Džuvlja Saj). This was the only element of the programme which was concerned with gender mainstreaming. As a result of the consultation, the Roma women identified their priorities in order to enable them to participate more fully in public and political life: legal recognition of Roma settlements, improved settlement infrastructure (water, electricity, sanitation), education, information services and outreach, and measures to improve communication within Roma communities (e.g. between NGOs and other influential Roma 'opinion leaders') and between Roma and non-Roma women. The other conclusion of the series of con-

---

(18) This is sponsored by the World Bank and the George Soros Open Society Institute and brings together governments and Roma leaders from eight central and east European countries (www.soros.org/initiatives/roma/news).

(19) For example, the national expert report for Slovakia states that gender mainstreaming is completely absent from the action plan for the Roma Decade. Gender issues in relation to specific social groups are only beginning to be addressed in the Czech Republic, which includes a government agreement signed in 2004 to include the issue of gender inequalities within the Roma as one of the priorities for state subsidies of NGO programmes. Similarly the Slovenian NAP/inclusion is one of the minority where a gender perspective is developed in relation to disadvantaged groups.

sultation meetings was that measures were also needed to inform Roma men about the value of gender equality policies and related measures to enhance women's opportunities to participate in public and political life.

A final consideration is that statistical indicators are important for advancing gender mainstreaming as a means for identifying and monitoring gender inequalities within ethnic groups. Currently there is a lack of data monitoring the situation of the Roma and other ethnic groups in many European countries, including the eight countries whose national reports are discussed here. In the particular case of Cyprus this would require drawing a distinction between the Roma and non-Roma within the Turkish Cypriot ethnic minority group. The development of statistical monitoring of the situation of the Roma is a politically sensitive task in many countries, not least because of Roma concerns as to how this information might be used. This political sensitivity about monitoring means that there is less detailed information available now than there used to be in some of the Member States, such as Slovakia (national expert report). This lack of information is double-edged. It can offer some means of civil liberties and protection from surveillance and persecution. However, lack of information also means policies cannot be evaluated, and it also means there is no evidence to counter racism, negative stereotypes and discrimination.[20] The key point here is that any efforts which are made to expand statistical monitoring according to ethnic group in politically sensitive climates must include a gender-based breakdown as a necessary tool for gender mainstreaming.

Box 6.10: Recent reforms to 'make work pay' have had negative effects on the Roma

In **Slovakia**, the 2004 benefit reforms to 'make work pay' reduced assistance for low-income families, including reduced supplements for large families. This reform disproportionately impacted on Roma, given their above average number of children. However, the loss of welfare support cannot easily be offset by efforts to increase earnings – few job openings exist and there are not enough places on active programmes which have the added bonus of an activation allowance. The openings for employment or on active labour market programmes are in particularly short supply in deprived regions where the Roma are concentrated. The reforms led to numerous protests and unrest which were particularly severe in the deprived regions where the protests were reportedly accompanied by lootings and raids on shops, and where the police and army were called in to restore order. Later that year the government revised cash benefits, improved the rates for the activation allowance and introduced subsidies for school meals and equipment for low-income families.

Similarly, in the **Czech Republic**, the new active employment policy does not provide measures that are capable of addressing the low employment rate of Roma women. The tighter eligibility conditions for social benefits and the reduced period of support mean there is less support available, yet their job search efforts are confounded by widespread employer discrimination.

In **Bulgaria,** the Roma are included in the social assistance scheme and literacy programmes and they are entitled to participate in all active labour market policy measures. There is no ethnic monitoring of participation, but it is known that the Roma are well represented among those registered on the 'From social benefits to employment' labour market programme, which is targeted at the long-term unemployed and others who are on social assistance. Participants have employment placements and training for up to a three-year maximum, at minimum wage rates with related health and insurance benefits. The problem is that social assistance is means-tested and adjusted according to family size, and for many Roma they are financially better off on social assistance than on the minimum wage. Furthermore, it is possible to supplement social assistance by breaking the rules and working in the 'shadow economy' (begging, scrap collection, door-to-door selling, subsistence farming), but this is more difficult to combine with an employment or training placement. Hence there is an incentive for the Roma to avoid the active labour market programme and to remain on social assistance, and in connection with this there has been a marked increase in the proportion of Roma who have become registered as disabled to secure social assistance. As a result the social assistance benefit assessments procedures and regulations have been tightened up.

Source: national reports.

---

(20)   For example, in Slovakia there is no systematic evidence to compare the economic situation (unemployment rates, participation rates in labour market programmes, receipt of unemployment benefits and other social transfers) or other aspects of living conditions (health risks, patterns of crime, etc.) between the Roma and the non-Roma. This lack of information can fuel racist stereotypes and hinder appropriate policy design.

7. Immigrants and migrants

In this chapter we bring a gender mainstreaming perspective to the risks of social exclusion of immigrants and recent migrants drawing on information provided by the national experts for 12 countries (AT, BE, CY, DE, DK, FR, IS, IT, LV, NL, NO, PT).

Details of the numbers of immigrant and migrant women in each of the 12 national case studies, and a brief outline of their circumstances, are presented in Box 7.1. Immigrant/migrant women account for between 5 and 9% of the female population in most of the 12 country case studies, rising to approximately 19% of the female population in the Netherlands. The lowest rates are in Iceland and Portugal.

Table 7.1 (p.118) shows that immigrant/migrant populations are growing in most of the 12 countries in this comparison, except for Belgium (no trend data for Latvia). This is a product of a generally widespread pattern of political and economic insta-

bility in origin countries in conjunction with some nationally specific events such as: German unification or the opening of the 'green line' border between north and south Cyprus; major construction projects in Iceland; and changes to procedural measures for documentation and/or immigration law which facilitated entry or family reunification of migrants (BE, IT). In some countries, such as Germany, and in others with a colonial history, such as France and the United Kingdom, this trend is part of a long history of immigration; in many others it is a fairly new phenomenon. For example, the increasing arrival of non-EU nationals to the Nordic countries presents new challenges regarding social inclusion and gender equality in what were formerly very homogenous societies. Other countries, such as Portugal and Italy, have changed in recent decades from being countries which mainly exported labour to countries which are now major destinations for migrants.

Box 7.1. Profile of the number of immigrant and migrant women

Austria

In 2003, there were 759 567 immigrants (EU citizens and other nationals) living in Austria: 9.4% of the total population. Of these, 362 681 were women (8.7% of all women). The Public Employment Service records for 2003 show that there were 220 000 immigrants employed under employment permits and approximately 168 000 without permits. Of the number employed under permits, approximately 80 500 were women. Since 1995, the number of women employed with employment permits has fallen while the number employed without permits has risen sharply. These changes, however, cannot be ascribed to a more liberal employment policy on foreigners – on the contrary, in recent years, this has become ever more restrictive – but to a change in the population of immigrants: the ratio of immigrants from the European Economic Area who do not require permits under the law on the employment of foreigners has risen and the ratio of 'third state' citizens has fallen.

Belgium

Immigrant/migrant women account for 8% of the total female population in Belgium. Although the majority of these women belong to the EU, many non-EU nationals are also present in the population. Between 1990 and 2001, 357 080 foreigners acquired Belgian nationality, among which 63% were Moroccans or Turks. It is these non-EU migrants that are the most vulnerable. Figures show that they ask for naturalisation more often than EU nationals, and that they face a greater risk of unemployment or inactivity and hence poverty.

Cyprus

Foreign workers comprised 12.9% of the employed labour force in 2003. According to the Ministry of the Interior, there are currently 17 995 legally employed female migrant domestic workers in Cyprus. The majority are from Sri Lanka (7 802) and the Philippines (5 761), and from Bulgaria (1 661), India (672) and Romania (569); others are from China, Georgia, Russia, and Indonesia.

Box 7.1. Profile of the number of immigrant and migrant women (continued)

Denmark

In 2004, immigrant women from western and non-western countries comprised 2.2% and 4.1% of the Danish population in Denmark, respectively. Non-western migrants are mainly from Turkey, Pakistan and the former Yugoslavia and comprise an even higher percentage of the age group in their core working years (25 to 50 years).

France

Here, the definition of an immigrant is a person, who was not born in France but lives there, and has foreign nationality or has acquired French nationality. Women account for just under half (47%) of the 4.3 million foreigners in France. In 1999, 8.6% of the economically active population were foreign (2 294 000 persons), up slightly compared with 1990 (8.4%). No gender breakdown is provided in the national report.

Germany

In Germany, there are around 7.3 million inhabitants who have a foreign passport and are defined as 'non-Germans' on this basis. This concerns 8.9% of the overall female population. In addition, there are around 2 million people who have immigrated within the past 15 years from east European countries and who are defined as having a German background and therefore German nationality. The situation of this latter group of migrants is less well documented than that for other migrants, as they are recorded as German in official statistics, which also applies for those migrants that subsequently obtain German nationality (around 140 000 per year). Immigrants here originate from a number of different ethnic groups in southern Europe, Turkey, the Soviet Union, the former Yugoslavia, other east European countries and Asia. They are concentrated in certain regions, mainly in urban regions and in the west.

Iceland

An estimated 5 000 foreign workers are now active in the Icelandic labour market, a figure which accounts for around 3% of the working-age population in Iceland (aged 16 to 74 years, no data breakdown is provided in the national report). In 2004, 3 524 citizens from the EU-15 were registered in Iceland. In recent years, the largest groups of people coming to Iceland on the basis of temporary work permits have been from Poland, the Philippines and Thailand. Recently, most of the work permits issued by the Director of Labour were to people working as cleaners (13%), in fish processing plants (23%), in other factory work (14%) and as dancers (10%).

Italy

Around 5% of the population in Italy are immigrants. With a net migration rate equal to 2.07 migrants per 1 000 inhabitants (2005 estimate), Italy is at the moment one of the EU countries with the highest migration rate. According to the most recent estimates, almost 3 million immigrants live legally in Italy, while the figure for undocumented immigrants varies from 800 000 to 2 million. By way of comparison, 56 179 foreigners were counted in the 1971 census. It is estimated that the combined presence of legal, illegal, semi-legal and seasonal immigrants may exceed 10% of the labour force. Italy periodically legalises unauthorised foreigners. Estimates by gender are not available but the proportion of immigrants that are women is high and appears to be increasing.

Latvia

The data available are very limited. In 1992, non-Latvians accounted for 52% of the population. There is no information available for recent immigrants or a gender breakdown.

The Netherlands

In 2004, 3 088 152 immigrants (western and non-western immigrants) were living in the Netherlands, about half of whom are women (an estimated 1.55 million). This represents almost 19% of both the total population and the female population in the Netherlands. Aside from chain migration (the process by which family members moved to the Netherlands in order to be with husbands/fathers who were working there), the number of non-western migrants has increased because of the higher natural growth rate. The fertility rate of non-western immigrant women lies above that of other women in the Netherlands, which is especially true for Moroccan and Turkish

Box 7.1. Profile of the number of immigrant and migrant women (continued)

women. A relatively high natural growth stems from the fact that women in the fertile age group cover a relatively large share of total non-western migrants.

Norway

There are 148 600 immigrant women, constituting 6.5% of all women in Norway. They have a younger age profile than Norwegian women: 80% are aged less than 50 years and 54% of them are aged between 20 and 49 years. Most of the first-generation women have only been resident in Norway for a short duration: 50% have lived there less than 10 years, while 24% have been resident for 20 years or longer. Most (84%) of the first generation female immigrants moved to Norway themselves as adults; only 16% were born in Norway to two foreign-born parents. Around one-third of all immigrant women in Norway live in Oslo.

Portugal

Immigrants now represent 4.3% of the population in Portugal, of which around half are women. In 2003, 13 752 people applied for residence in Portugal, 52.9% of whom were women. In 2004, 45% of all foreign residents in Portugal were women. The majority of immigrant women move to Portugal from African countries, especially those that have Portuguese as their official language. There are also significant numbers of women that originate from central and eastern Europe.

Source: national reports.

The policy response by national governments to current trends in immigration and migrant workers are mixed. In some of the country case studies, notably those of Portugal, France and the Netherlands, there are new policy initiatives which aim to improve the particular situations of female immigrant and migrant workers. In Portugal the national expert reports that there is new concern by the government to reform the situation of immigrants. This includes a new law on nationality which will mainly benefit younger generations, and one which will improve the benefit entitlements of those migrants, mostly women, who only hold a 'permit of permanency' rather than a residence permit (see Section 7.1(a)). An increasing number of political documents in Portugal mention the need to develop policies targeted at assisting immigrant women, although the number of concrete measures is rather limited so far[21]. In France, immigrant women and 'second and subsequent generation' women born into immigrant families are a policy target group; with the problem of the 'twofold discrimination' of women from ethnic minority origin identified as a particular issue in the previous NAP social inclusion; although this emphasis is not mentioned in the most recent NAP. This policy focus has been accompanied by a body of recent research which provides new and rich sources of information about this 'at-risk' group in France. Similarly, the Dutch government has set up the PAVEM committee as a focus for policy development and new measures to address the situation of immigrant/migrant women.

Migrant women are also an explicit target group for some measures in Germany and Denmark, while in Italy they have benefited from a recent registration scheme. The German case study focuses upon migrant women and young school leavers with a migrant background because both groups face severe exclusion processes and represent sizeable portions of the urban population. Their particular problems are acknowledged to some extent in the NAP social inclusion where several programmes and targeted initiatives are listed. In Denmark, migrant and refugee women are identified as a particular target group for various new measures to tackle gender inequalities in the social integration of ethnic minority groups. The initiatives discussed include information campaigns targeted at first-generation immigrant women about their rights, plus a range of training and employment

---

(21) In the Portuguese NAP/social inclusion, the concrete measures concern some limited information campaigns and research activities, such as the production of leaflets on healthcare and two conferences focusing on the situation of migrant women and on genital mutilation; but overall there is very little gender mainstreaming of policies targeted at migrant people. Migrant women are identified as a particular target group in the National Action Plan for gender equality, and in the National Action Plan against domestic violence.

Table 7.1: Summary of the trends in immigrant/migrant women in each country

	Trend	Main reason
AT	**Increasing:** The proportion of women fell slightly between 1981 and 1991 from 44.4% to 43.4%, and by 2003 there were still more men than women among the immigrant population.	Primarily due to the new and overwhelmingly male immigration from central and east European countries.
BE	**Broadly stable:** The number of foreigners was more or less stable during the 1990s – a slight increase between 1989 and 1994 was followed by a decline to 860 287 foreigners in 2004. Over this period (1989–2004) the female proportion rose from 46% to 48.5% of all foreigners.	One possible reason for this trend is that in 2000 the Nationality Code was revised and the procedure of naturalisation was accelerated (a non-Belgian can acquire the Belgian nationality through naturalisation if she/he has lived at least three years in the country as their permanent principal residence).
CY	**Increasing:** Cyprus is becoming more attractive to prospective migrants, asylum seekers, and refugees. The number of immigrant women recruited into Cyprus as domestic workers has increased greatly over the past decade.	One reason is Cyprus's recent European Union membership and geographical location. Another is that the green line between the north and south regions of the area has been opened and, as a result, undocumented immigrants can arrive from the illegal entry point in the north and easily cross into the south.
DE	**Increasing:** There is a long history of migration into Germany, especially since the 1960s, and including second and third-generation migrants. There has been a marked increase since unification. Approximately 140 000 migrants per year receive German nationality.	Political unification and the collapse of communism.
DK	**Increasing:** The number of immigrants has more than doubled in the past 25 years. In 2004, the majority of immigrants originated from non-western countries.	Since 1973, most immigrants from non-western countries have come because of problems in their country of origin or because of family reunions. Most do not have Danish employment opportunities as a reason for their stay. Immigrant women form the majority for families reunited to refugees, and this is also the case for families united from most non-western countries.
FR	**Increasing:** The proportion of immigrant women in France continues to increase. Women constituted 38.3% of immigrants in 1954 and 46.9% in 1999.	This is mainly the result of women increasingly immigrating for economic reasons. Chinese women, for example, are increasingly leaving their husbands and children at home in order to look for work in France, while their husbands remain in the home country.
IS	**Increasing:** There has been a recent increase in the numbers of immigrant workers in Iceland which began in 1997. In 2003, 3.1% of the population (10 636 individuals) had foreign citizenship, rising to 3.6% in 2004.	The increase from 1997 occurred when employers intensified their search for foreign workers from east European countries, such as Poland, to meet growing demands in the construction sector. In 2003, work started on the state-owned power plant (Karahnjukar). The workforce was expected to be 20% foreign, but became higher; in January 2004 40% of the workers were foreign.
IT	**Increasing:** In the 1971 census, 156 179 foreigners were counted and this number has risen to almost 3 million immigrants living legally in Italy according to the most recent estimates. Estimates for illegal immigrants vary from 800 000 to 2 million. The number of legal immigrants grew considerably in 2003, approximately 350 000 applicants were	The regularisation scheme enacted at the end of 2002 allowed the regularisation of over 700 000 previously unregistered foreign workers (the second largest ever legalisation in the world). Also, in 1998, a new immigration law introduced a clear right to family reunification and sponsored migration for employment search.

Table 7.1: Summary of the trends in immigrant/migrant women in each country (continued)

	Trend	Main reason
	female migrants, employed mainly by Italian families for domestic work and personal care.	
LV	No data were available.	No data were available.
NL	**Increasing:** The number of female immigrants from non-western countries has been increasing since 1972.	Chain migration was the main cause of the increasing share of non-western immigrant women between 1972 and 2004.
NO	**Increasing:** The number of immigrant women is increasing. This increase includes women originating from Asia, the number of whom rose from 41 200 in 1997 to 54 400 in 2001.	The prospects of better living conditions and job prospects attract migrants. Another part of the reason for the increase is the higher fertility rates of foreign-born parents compared with fertility rates for Norwegians.
PT	**Increasing:** There has been a significant increase in immigration over the past decade; more than tripling in the period 1992 to 2004.	

Source: national reports.

measures where a particular target concerns migrant and refugee women, including migrant women entering for the reason of family reunion. However, as we see below, this coexists with reforms to social assistance (*En ny chance til alle*) that may have a particularly negative impact on benefits received by female immigrants, and this potentially negative gender impact was not assessed in the NAP. In Italy, the latest ad hoc registration scheme in 2003 extended rights to undocumented workers, half of which were women employed informally as domestic workers.

In contrast the situation of migrant women attracts little or no attention in policy debates in three of the countries discussed in this chapter (AT, CY, LT). The national expert for Cyprus notes that immigrant and migrant women are one of the most invisible groups in national debates about employment and social inclusion, despite their very excluded and vulnerable situation. In Latvia, policy for migrants and non-Latvians lacks a gender perspective. In Austria, the particular situation facing migrant women is rarely addressed or acknowledged in public policy debates, including the recent reform of employment legislation for foreign workers.

7.1. Main forms of disadvantage faced by immigrant/migrant women

Migrants typically move from poorer to more affluent countries to secure a better standard of living. The extreme situation is refugees who are compelled to migrate to flee political and economic problems and persecution. Human trafficking and migrant sex workers are a particular form of migrant labour which is addressed separately in Chapter 8.

Immigrant and migrant workers often have limited labour market opportunities in their host countries. Typically they are recruited to fill vacancies in low-paid and unskilled jobs; some of which are in the informal economy. Migrants who are undocumented are even more constrained in the range of jobs open to them.

Migrants are disadvantaged by a combination of factors: language barriers, poor education or qualifications which are not recognised in the destination country; race discrimination and xenophobia; a legal status which rests precariously on temporary rights to stay and work and secures them fewer rights than those of nationals. The undocumented workers who are illegal migrants have an even more precarious position.

Not all migrants are disadvantaged; those who originate from countries with similar or higher living standards to those of the destination country face little disadvantage (particularly if they share the same colour skin and cultural background). Thus, in general, within the EU it is migrants from Africa, Asia and Latin America, Turkey and more recently from the central European countries (non-EU as well as EU members) who are most disadvantaged and at risk of social exclusion and living in relative poverty in their host country.

The Dutch national experts argue that immigrants face two main forms of potential disadvantage: structural and socio-cultural integration. The former includes access to education, employment, income and economic independence and this depends partly on the resources which the migrant arrives with (e.g. language, qualifications) and partly on the institutions of the receiving country (anti-discrimination legislation, training systems, eligibility in welfare systems, etc.). Socio-cultural integration encompasses differences of religion and social values, including gender roles within the family, and how the receiving country responds to differences (e.g. extent and form of policies concerning multiculturalism).

All migrants risk facing these disadvantages; but women can face additional forms of disadvantage. They may enter as economically dependent spouses and this route may limit their independent rights to take employment or secure social welfare. They may come from a cultural background where women have limited educational opportunities and where it is less acceptable for women to be in employment compared with the values and practices of the host population. They have to contend with sex discrimination as well as other discriminatory treatment and racism faced by migrants.

(a) Documentation and status

Access to documentation which provides a legal right to stay and to take employment is a basic condition for social integration, and provides a greater degree of protection for 'documented' compared with illegal or 'undocumented' migrants. Examples from five of the national reports (AT, DK, IS, IT, PT) illustrate how the detail of national policies can operate in ways that make it more difficult for female immigrant/migrant workers to secure these rights. Austria and Portugal are examples of where the permit system establishes groups of migrants with different sets of rights and where women are less able to secure the better status (Box 7.2-p.121). In Portugal immigrant/migrant women are more likely to acquire a 'permit of perma-

nency', which accords them fewer rights than a residence permit. In Austria, growing numbers of immigrant women are employed as domestic workers but this sector is not covered by short-term 'key worker' employment permits or commuter agreements. The consequence is that many immigrant women can only carry out work in this sector 'informally'.

The status assigned to married women who arrive to join spouses under immigration provisions for family unification can be such that women are defined as economic dependents with no rights to seek employment, which has the effect of enforcing their economic dependence on a spouse. This is the case in Austria, where married women arriving to be reunited with a spouse are only entitled to receive a 'residency permit for all purposes other than economic activity', according to an annual quota. Only after four years can the woman apply for a 'residency permit for all purposes including economic activity'. Usually, however, the employment permit necessary for taking up work is only issued after an eight-year stay in Austria. Married women are thus economically completely dependent on their husbands for a very long period. In addition, immigrant women can only claim a limited amount of the welfare benefits available to Austrian women, dependent on the length and type of their residency. In Iceland, recent reforms have improved the legal footing and social protection of migrants, including better access to temporary work permits for close family members. However, temporary work permits for all migrants are granted to the employer and not the individual and follow a similar principle to the Austrian 'key worker' permits. This limits the opportunities for migrants to seek alternative employment. In Denmark, migrant women who enter for the reason of family reunion are ineligible to claim the migrant introductory benefits and hence are economically dependent upon their family until they secure employment; however, to help mitigate this financial dependency, migrant and refugee women are a particular target group for various training and employment measures.[22]

Italy is a country where many migrants gain employment before their documentation. The overwhelming majority of migrant workers enter Italy legally (for tourism, to visit relatives, or on student visas) on short-

---

(22) The Danish National Action Plan also mentions an initiative to limit forced marriages, which is targeted at young immigrants. While this may provide some positive protection for young women and young men, it might also have some negative effects depending on how it is enforced in the opinion of the Danish expert. This is because in practice it can be difficult to identify between an arranged marriage entered into voluntarily and a forced marriage; another issue is that the provision also makes it impossible for young people to marry persons from outside the EU and Nordic countries and still live in Denmark.

Box 7.2: Documentation and status of immigrant women

In **Portugal,** a 'permit of permanency' is required to stay and work legally. This can only be obtained by possession of a work contract provided by an employer. This 'permit of permanency' provides far fewer rights than a residence permit. It is often non-married migrant women that in general only receive this 'permit of permanency'. Although the Portuguese government has placed a limit of 8 500 of these permits to be issued each year, only 641 were given in 2004. The Director of Services of Foreigners and Frontiers in Portugal was reported as saying in a recent interview that this policy is inefficient and needs to be reformed.[23]

In **Austria**, the 2003 law on the employment of foreigners specifies three types of employment permit for immigrants from countries not in the European Economic Area: *Beschäftigungsbewilligung, Arbeitserlaubnis* and *Befreiungsschein*.

The *Beschäftigungsbewilligung* is a permit limited to a particular workplace and a particular activity, and is usually issued for one year for 'key workers'. It is only granted if, among other things, no Austrian worker is available, if the annual quota has not yet been exhausted and if there is a finite period of stay. The restrictive legislation means that at the moment new immigration is practically only still possible for 'key workers', for example those with an occupational qualification or skills that are in demand and with a wage of 60% of the highest social security contributions basis (approximately EUR 2 070 in 2004).

Immigrants who have already been employed in Austria for one year have the right to apply for an *Arbeitserlaubnis*. This entitles them to take up any employment in a particular federal province and is issued for a period of two years.

The *Befreiungsschein* is issued for five years and is valid for the whole country. In order to receive a *Befreiungsschein*, an employment period in Austria of at least five years or at least five years' marriage to an Austrian must be proven.

The key worker regulation is particularly disadvantageous to women.

In **Iceland**, a new Act on the Employment Rights of foreign nationals came into force in January 2003, the purpose of which was to secure the legal status of foreigners coming to work in Iceland. Some of these new provisions required employers to provide sickness insurance for employees until they became entitled to insurance under the Social Security Act. In addition to this, they also provide for the possibility of granting a temporary work permit for close family members of foreigners. However, it does not address the criticisms made by the United Nations Human Rights Committee that Iceland's practice of granting temporary work permits to employers and not the particular immigrant worker limits the opportunities of immigrant workers to change their employer.

Source: national report.

term visas but without a work permit. It is common for new immigrants to overstay their short-term visas without a proper residence permit and look for employment. The vast majority find their first job in the underground economy, where jobs are fairly easy to obtain and there is little competition from native workers. Hence, migrants are able to live and earn an income without a residence permit while waiting for a regularisation programme. The relationship between residence and working status in Italy is complex. A residence permit for work purposes is usually granted on a temporary basis – one or two years – and renewal is conditional on holding a regular job or proof of sufficient income. Although opportunities are repeatedly provided for unregistered migrants to regulate their positions, relapsing into illegality is quite common, e.g. after expiry of the residence permit, job loss, or conclusion of a short-term contract. Thus, an immigrant worker may have neither a residence permit nor a regular job, or s/he may have a residence permit and

(23) A new decree was passed in February 2006 (lei No 41/2006), after this report was written, which improves the situation of immigrants with a 'permit of permanency' (i.e. mainly women) by giving them the right to receive the family allowance and 'social insertion' income that migrants with a residence permit were already entitled to.

a regular job, or may find her/himself in a mixed situation. While some migrants move from illegal to legal status in residency and work, others frequently change their position, shifting back and forth. In the most recent regularisation scheme, in 2003, approximately half of the 700 000 applicants for registration were female migrants employed by Italian families for domestic work and personal care (elderly care).

(b) Employment and unemployment rates

Male migrants typically have higher activity rates than non-migrant males, in part because of a younger age profile and a smaller proportion of older persons. Unemployment rates are also usually higher; the exception is in countries where the majority of migrants are regulated via work permits and migrant unemployment is 'exported' through obligations to exit the country when their employment and work permit ends.

For migrant women, economic activity rates are often lower than those of non-migrant women; but not always. For women, the dynamics of the country of origin play an influential role: cultural factors, such as those concerning women's traditional economic roles, their qualification levels and whether women arrive as dependent family members (wives, daughters) or as independent (single) economic migrants, and the economic period in which the migrants arrive. All of these have influences which shape the labour market integration of migrant women also shape the experiences of second and subsequent generations of women. This can be seen, for example, in the labour market patterns of women according to ethnic origin in the United Kingdom whereby women of black Afro-Caribbean ethnic status have the highest economic activity, particularly when measured in terms of full-time employment rates; part-time employment is primarily a feature of the activity profile for the ethnic majority white women, while female activity rates vary markedly between the different ethnic minority Asian groups (Dale and Holdsworth 1998).

(c) Job quality and working conditions of migrants

The poor labour market conditions for immigrants and migrants are a major cause of their disadvantaged economic and social position in the country they are working in. Those who manage to secure employment are disproportionately concentrated in precarious and low-paid jobs and in the informal economy, for labour markets are heavily segregated by race and migrant/non-migrant status as well as by gender.

Those who secure jobs alongside non-migrant workers in better paid parts of the economy are often employed on inferior terms to those of comparable non-migrant workers (on finite permits, or with lower bonus schemes and other benefits). For example, in Iceland, the unions argue that foreign workers on temporary work permits are paid lower rates than Icelanders in comparable jobs. They are vulnerable to job loss when the economy enters recession, and many immigrant workers on work permits state that they are not able to make full use of their skills in the jobs which are open to them.

Immigrant/migrant women are even more segregated into a narrow range of low-paid and largely female-dominated jobs than non-migrant women. They are largely concentrated in personal services and sales and particularly in cleaning and domestic service (Box 7.4-p.125).

Part of the reason for the inferior labour market position for most groups of immigrant/migrant women is that they have lower educational qualifications, or their qualifications are not recognised in the host country. However, they are also exposed to structural processes of discrimination and segregation, so that those who are qualified are also subject to labour market marginalisation and exclusion. For example, most migrant women come to Portugal seeking employment to provide for their family. They have higher average educational qualifications than the Portuguese population and are overqualified for the jobs they occupy, obtaining more precarious working conditions and lower salaries than the Portuguese workforce. Many immigrant women have pay which is lower than the statutory minimum and/or work hours in excess of the legal limit, and occupational insecurity is common as a result of working in the informal job sector. Often, they lack an employment contract, which impedes them from gaining a resident's permit, and prevents them from legalising their presence in Portugal. These processes of discrimination and segregation have been exposed by research on recruitment in Belgium, France and Norway for example (Box 7.5-p.126). The Dutch national report emphasises that workplace diversity policies to remove discriminatory practices and negative images about the employability of immigrant women are an important part of the package of measures required to reduce the social exclusion of this group of women.

Box 7.3: Labour market problems faced by immigrant women

In **Belgium,** the employment rates of foreign women are lower than those for foreign men, and the unemployment gap observed between nationals and non-EU nationals is more pronounced for women than men. Women from non-EU countries have very high inactivity and unemployment rates. Although the foreign female activity rate has risen much more rapidly than for Belgian women, their unemployment rate has remained stable at a high 30 to 33% level.

In **Denmark**, immigrant women from non-western countries have the lowest economic activity rate. The overall activity rate in 2004 for all immigrants was 60.3% for men and 46% for women. This is much lower than the activity rate for native Danes (81.2% for men and 75.4% for women) and the gap is greatest for women.

- The lowest of these rates is found in female immigrants with origin in Iraq (15%), Lebanon (21%), and Somalia (14%), while the rate for males from these countries was more than twice that reported for women. Female immigrants from these countries are also the most likely group to become dependent on the welfare state.

- A very high percentage of immigrants from non-western countries in the age group 16 to 66 years are unemployed. This seems to be a growing tendency for female immigrants from non-western countries with one out of four of these women being unemployed and more than one third (37.3%) being dependent on state benefit in some form. The corresponding proportion for native Danish women is 7.3%.

In **France**, there was for a long time a problem of immigrant women being 'invisible' in general and in particular regarding economic activity. Bringing families together was the only justification for their presence in France, as mothers or wives. However, the image of immigrant mothers with large families and low economic activity rates is now partly out of date. The economic activity rate of immigrant women in France is 57.1%, which is significantly lower than that for immigrant men and for all women (63.1%) but far from being marginal or secondary.

- The pattern varies according to country of origin, for example the economic activity rate of women born in Portugal and south-east Asia is as high as or even higher than that of women born in France. Similarly, economic activity rates of Chinese women who arrive in France at a young age and often alone are high, whereas that of sub-Saharan African women is low. Women from the Maghreb still have a high rate of economic inactivity and long periods of unemployment, and they occupy part-time jobs more often.

- Immigrant women, just as women in general, are more affected by unemployment: the unemployment rate of immigrant women is 25% , while that of immigrant men is 20%. The rate is lower for immigrants who have taken on French nationality, but still higher than the national average.

- The unemployment rate of non-EU women foreigners is three times higher than that of French and other European women.

In the **Netherlands**, non-western immigrant women are a disadvantaged group. Their labour market participation rates have been increasing over the past few years, but in general the participation rates are still lower than those of Dutch nationals. Employment rates are low. Since 2002, the unemployment rate for non-western migrants has been rising and in 2004 it reached a level of 16% , which was over three times as high as the unemployment level for people in the Netherlands (5%). For non-western immigrant women, unemployment rose from 9% in 2001 to 14% in 2003. They also have a high risk of becoming inactive due to disability. This lack of labour market integration means they often have low income levels.

Non-western immigrant women in the Netherlands are generally less prepared for employment, because of a low level of education and insufficient Dutch language fluency. Traditional ideas about women's family roles can also hamper their labour market participation (whether held by women or by the men in their family). Their integration is also impeded by cultural stereotypes, racism and employment discrimination.

In 2004, 53% of all non-western immigrant women were in an underprivileged position: they have not finished a senior secondary vocational education, do not have a job and are not economically independent. This is especially true of Turkish and Moroccan women. Single mothers from Suriname and the Antilles also form a vulnerable group.

Box 7.3: Labour market problems faced by immigrant women (continued)

The national report for **Portugal** states that the main form of disadvantage for immigrant women is lack of access to the labour market. In 2001, the unemployment rate for this group of women was 14.4%. Nearly half of migrant women were employed (47.7%), another third were supported by their family (36.8%) and only 3.9% were claiming unemployment or other forms of social welfare.

Source: national reports.

A common theme of many of the 12 national case studies is the growing number of migrant women employed as domestic workers in private households providing care services and housework. Many are employed informally and so lack access to any employment rights which documented migrant workers may have. Research shows that families recruit migrant workers informally because they are unable or unwilling to pay the higher costs of recruiting regular labour or because of a freeze on residence permits and/or out of bureaucratic difficulties. This form of employment has mushroomed in Italy, which now has the largest proportion of domestic and personal care workers in the national economy in western Europe. Most are migrant women, often employed without a regular contract. This growing demand for care workers in private households has emerged in a specific political, economic, cultural–social and institutional context. The presence of a large underground economy operating outside of the scope of legal regulation is a structural feature of the Italian labour market. This makes it possible to live and work in shifting relations of legality and illegality. This is true in general for migrants in Italy, and in particular for female migrants employed by Italian families. The growing demand of households for domestic workers is in the context of an ageing population and a welfare state system which provides few elderly care services to assist families.

Work in the care sector in Italy may compare very favourably to alternative opportunities back in the home country of immigrants and also within Italy. Interviews with female immigrant workers in this sector have disclosed that their wage is between seven (Romania) and 15 times (Moldavia) more than what they could have earned, or what their husbands earned, back home. However, the sector is extremely under-regulated and working conditions can differ greatly, varying with the type of contract (or agreement), the geographical context, and personal characteristics of the worker (nationality, religion, language). Despite this, much of the work remains informal and as such does not afford immigrant workers the employment rights they are due. Exploitation of foreign workers, and the particular vulnerability of migrant domestic workers, was also a concern in the Cyprus report. According to the Nicosia District Labour Office, 540 female migrant domestic workers complained to the Cypriot authority about contract violations in 2004.

The working conditions of migrant women may compare favourably with the poor alternatives on offer in their origin country, and on this basis migrant women may largely accept the conditions under which they work. For example, research in Norway has found that despite their poor working conditions many migrant women expressed satisfaction with their job. However, this does not justify the poor working conditions under which they work in more affluent countries. Furthermore, the host society is not simply a passive host or 'receiver', the structural features create processes of marginalisation which reinforce and exacerbate the vulnerability of migrant workers. This is illustrated vividly in the Austrian national report, which quotes the conclusions of Erna Appelt (2003) based on her interviews with immigrant women, where she states:

> *'From an occupational point of view, it is above all the lack of recognition of education, the hurdles to naturalisation and the de-qualification that make the lives of immigrant women more difficult and which they experience as being particularly oppressive. Many interviewees complained that they are employed well below their qualification and have little chance of changing this. The lack of occupational advice and the non-existent promotion opportunities discourage many and represent a further barrier to integration.'*

Box 7.4: The segregated employment patterns of immigrant/migrant women

In **Belgium**, the majority of women who are non-EU nationals are concentrated in two main occupations: service workers and shop and market sales workers, and sales and services elementary occupations.

In **France**, immigrant women occupy low-skilled jobs, often in services to individuals (home helps, caretakers, cleaners, etc.). Undeclared work is more frequent: 15% of immigrant women, compared with 10% of immigrant men (especially in domestic service).

In **Norway**, immigrant women are predominantly employed in low-paid, labour-intensive sectors such as unqualified care work and cleaning.

In **Italy**, the jobs undertaken by migrants are in labour-intensive service activities or in manufacturing where international competition rests upon low-wage non-union conditions and unskilled labour. Italy now has the largest proportion of domestic and personal care workers in the national economy in western Europe; most are migrant women who are often employed without a regular contract.

In **Austria**, foreign female workers are concentrated in low-wage sectors, particularly those from non-EU countries. For example, data from 1993 showed that nearly one-third of women from former Yugoslavia and two thirds of Turkish women employed in Austria had income in the lowest income percentile, compared with only 10% of the overall population. In 1998, 18.8% of directly employed foreign women were in the hotel and catering sector and 19.2% in company-related services, indicating an above average concentration in two unattractive economic branches. A growing number of immigrant women are employed as domestic workers but the design of the legislation on the employment of foreign workers means many can only be employed informally.

Domestic work is a common source of employment for migrant women in **Cyprus** as well.

Migrant workers in **Portugal** have more precarious working conditions and lower salaries than the Portuguese workforce. Many migrant women are employed in the informal sector, either with a temporary labour contract or no contract at all, and are vulnerable to dismissal and unable to claim social security benefits. The lack of an employment contract means they are unable to secure a residence permit and hence legal status. A survey in 2002 found that nearly one-third were paid less than the statutory minimum wage and in 2004 nearly one in five worked more than 45 hours per week, exceeding the legal maximum of a 40-hour week.

In some countries migrant women from particular origin countries have higher rates of prostitution than non-migrant women, which is discussed in Chapter 8 of this report.

Source: national reports.

Similarly, the Italian national report emphasises that many of the migrant women, particularly those from eastern Europe, recruited as domestic workers providing care for elderly persons in private households have good qualification levels. Such care work involves dedication, patience, judgment, trustworthiness and so forth; in other words, the work involves a set of skills, yet these are rarely acknowledged or reflected in pay levels. The demands and privatised arrangement of the job can diminish the immigrants' skills and prevent them from moving out of these jobs and becoming more integrated into the Italian labour market. Furthermore, the working hours and household-based nature of the work makes it difficult to participate in Italian society and it may also make it extremely difficult for the immigrant worker to form or care for her own family, especially if the country of origin is too distant for temporary and rotational migration to be possible.

(d) Education and training (including language proficiency) and active labour market programmes

In many of the countries in this study, migrant women are disadvantaged by having lower educational qualifications than the non-migrant population; and for women from some origin countries there is an additional disadvantage of language barriers (Box 7.6- p.127). Portugal is a notable exception in this study,

> ## Box 7.5: Studies of recruitment reveal widespread discrimination against immigrant women
>
> A **Belgian** study presents evidence of discrimination towards immigrant women and men. Based on situation tests (two candidates having the same profile apply for the same job, the only difference between them being their ethnic origin). The research concluded that discrimination of both women and men (mainly at the first contact) was present, but much more often among men than among women.
>
> In **France** some 'testing' experiments (Adias/Paris I), though limited in number, have shown that immigrants, women (*a fortiori*, foreign women), older people and the disabled are excluded from recruitment, right from the outset.
>
> In recent research in **Norway**, immigrant women report experiences of discrimination in their contact with the Employment Office. Regardless of their experience and qualifications, when they approached the Employment Office looking for relevant work they were offered cleaning jobs. One form of discrimination that was noted in the report was that of religious discrimination. This was evident among women wearing religious headscarves. In another study, 20% of the organisations that took part reported that they do not allow religious headscarves to be worn as part of a uniform.
>
> *Source:* national reports.

where migrant women have higher average qualification levels than women who are Portuguese nationals.

Language proficiency courses and active labour market programmes may be less successful at reaching migrant women than migrant men if the programmes are not designed to identify gender differences in training needs and skills. For example, research in the Netherlands suggests that the mandatory integration courses which are obligatory for migrants are not very effective at motivating migrant women to become proficient in Dutch. Targeted job creation programmes may have more impact than general integration courses for addressing the marginalisation of immigrant women. One successful example in the Netherlands was a job creation project in the 1990s, aimed at Moluccan migrants. This project resulted in over 1 200 Moluccan migrants finding employment through an improved matching of job searches with vacancies. Similarly, in Norway, active labour market programmes and training schemes have low expectations concerning immigrant women's employment: there are examples of fewer requirements being placed on immigrant women to participate in training programmes, and the courses offered are less relevant for the labour market than those offered to men. Reforms are needed so that these programmes include a targeted focus on measures to increase immigrant women's participation and completion of qualification programmes, and to ensure that these programmes are of good quality and relevance for their particular needs.

In Germany, a key source of disadvantage for young migrants is their poor integration in the educational system. Successful labour market integration is strongly connected to the level of education and training achieved through either the dual system of vocational training and apprenticeships or the university route. In nearly all vocational groups the proportion of young migrants has declined during the past five years, and their proportion is very small in the newly created occupations like IT specialist and other highly skilled and 'modern' occupations.

In Belgium, the majority of policies aimed at helping immigrants and non-native Belgians are focused on the educational system. All communities responsible for education have set up instruments, such as positive discrimination schools, specific out-of-school programmes for homework, better links between the three different secondary education fields (general, technique and professional) and third-level education, to tackle the educational disadvantage of this population. A major weakness of this approach is that most of these measures are not particularly gender mainstreamed even though research has exposed gender disparities in terms of school achievement in Belgium, and this gender perspective on the problem is relevant for the integration of women from migrant backgrounds.

(e) Welfare and social protection systems

The inferior labour market positions of migrant/immigrant women, compared with those of migrant men and non-migrant women, means they are more exposed to the risk of poverty (Box 7.7-p.128). Many fail to accumulate full entitlements under the social

Box 7.6: Qualification levels and language skills as barriers to the integration of migrant women

In **Belgium**, immigrant/migrant women have lower education levels than Belgian women: 56% of non-EU nationals have only a low qualification level, compared with 51% of other EU nationals and 39% of Belgian women.

In **Germany**, one of the main forms of disadvantage concerns the integration of young migrant people into the educational system. In 2000, the integration of young people in education (schools), vocational training (dual apprenticeship or vocational schools) and universities was highly dependent on nationality and sex. The data suggest a stable proportion of around one-third of all young female migrants in the age group 15 to 20 years do not attend general education, vocational training or higher education in a university. In the age group 15 to 20 years, only 67.5% of migrant women in Germany attend a general school, vocational training or a university, compared with 93.5% of German women of the same age. In the age range 20 to 25 years, 38.8% of German women and only 13.2% of migrant women attended vocational training courses or university.

In **Denmark**, it is estimated that over 50% of female immigrants from non-western countries have no vocational training or education, and less than 50% have occupational experience before arriving in Denmark. Female immigrants from non-western countries have an employment rate lower than 40%.

In **the Netherlands**, the main obstacles to labour market participation and social integration of immigrant women are language skills and level of education.

The main forms of disadvantage faced by immigrant women in **Norway**, especially those of non-western origin, are low educational attainment levels, weaker language skills and fewer formal qualifications.

In **Latvia**, legislation introduced in 1991 requires that everyone who does not have an educational qualification from a Latvian institution must undertake a Latvian language proficiency course. Although the aim is to ensure that all residents in Latvia are capable of speaking the language, it also acts as a barrier for non-Latvians who are seeking immediate employment.

Source: national reports.

protection system, particularly if their employment is largely in the informal sector. Pension rights are often minimal, even for those who have spent a large part of their working life in the host country.

The problems are particularly severe in some countries. Austria is one example where the welfare system largely excludes non-EU migrants from protection. According to Bettina Haidinger (2004:68) immigrants fulfil 'a doubly beneficial function for the Austrian welfare state'. This is because, as non-recipients of welfare-state benefits, they are not a burden on the fiscal system and simultaneously they guarantee the delivery of social services and related activities, based on badly paid and insecure employment conditions which they are forced to take because of their status as immigrants.

Even in welfare systems which are more inclusive, the structure of eligibility presents potential problems for migrant women; particularly those with a limited work history or those who enter as a dependent partner through family reunion. The Dutch system is one such example. For instance, the right to claim unemploy-

ment benefit is only assigned when someone has worked for four years (at least 52 days per year) of the last five years he or she spent in the Netherlands and has been employed for 39 of the last 52 weeks. These requirements may obstruct access to unemployment benefit for immigrant women. Another example is that under the Dutch Exceptional Medical Expenses Act a woman can also only claim compensation for medical expenses 12 months after she has come to the Netherlands. Another issue that negatively impacts on migrant women's rights to social security is the partner-dependent right of residence. Here, a woman who has migrated for the purpose of marriage, or to be reunited with a spouse is entitled to a residence permit for three years on condition that she lives with her partner. After three years, an independent residence permit can be claimed. However, if a relationship comes to an end within the three years, the woman loses her right of residence. In these circumstances she would have to start a new procedure to obtain a residence permit and she may also lose her rights to several social benefits (such as the right to compensation for medical expenses) because she has to pass the waiting time again.

Box 7.7: The greater risks of poverty and reliance on social welfare of women with a migrant background

In **Norway**, in 1999, the average income of first-generation women immigrants was 22% lower than the income of non-immigrant women in Norway. Whereas 79% of the income of immigrant women from Nordic countries comes from paid work this falls to 59% of the income for women who have migrated from third world countries. The latter have a higher rate of reliance on state transfers (which account for 23% of the total income of this group).

In **Denmark**, the average income for immigrants from non-western countries is less than two-thirds of the general average income, the proportion of poverty among immigrants from non-western countries is about three times the general proportion of poverty, and the proportion of immigrants from non-western countries living in welfare residential housing is more the three times the proportion in general. More than 40% of all women in crisis centres are non-natives and half of them are in Denmark by family reunion. Non-native women stay at the centres, on average, almost twice as long as native Danish women, and more often move back to their husbands.

In **Austria,** the risk of poverty for immigrants originating from non-EU countries is approximately four times higher than that of EU and Austrian citizens. This may be an underestimate of the full extent of inequalities for immigrant households as a rule are under-represented in the surveys and administrative data used for these estimates. In 1998, 73.3% of all Austrian households lived in a category A living space (the best category); this was true only for 40.1% of households of immigrants from former Yugoslavia and for 38.6% of Turkish households.

Source: national reports.

Government reforms to 'make work pay' may impact more harshly on migrant recipients than on non-migrant claimants if they have inferior labour market prospects. For example, in Denmark immigrants account for less than 10% of the population but three-quarters of married couples in receipt of cash benefits have an immigrant background. Recent reforms increase the job search requirements for immigrants and a greater element of joint rather than individual financial support. This shift in policy is expected to impact particularly on women by increasing job search requirements and directing financial support through their spouse, yet this is not discussed in the NAP. Furthermore, recent research shows that this reduction in cash benefits has not been compensated for by higher employment. This means that, so far, this reform has not achieved its intended objective of improving the labour market integration of migrants.

Access to childcare is also an important aspect of labour market integration for migrant women who are mothers. This can be a problem for migrant women even in countries with relatively good overall provision, such as Norway. Migrant mothers are less likely to use public childcare than Norwegian mothers, due to problems of accessing the services compounded by their more limited earnings prospects, and these combined factors operate to constrain their labour market integration. Likewise, in Belgium there are policy efforts to improve social diversity by increasing migrant/immigrant families' access to crèches and kindergartens. However, non-EU families still make less use of formal childcare than Belgian families, due to a combination of financial obstacles and cultural differences.

The French NAP/inclusion has a strong focus on addressing the social exclusion of immigrant and ethnic minority groups, which is distinctive in comparison to the low profile given to this issue in many of the NAPs for other countries. However, while many of the reforms are generally positive for migrants[24], a major omission is that the plan lacks any gender mainstreaming analysis of the intersection of gender and origin ('twofold discrimination') even though this was identified as a particular focus for policy in the previous NAP (2001–03). Some proposals which may be particularly beneficial for migrant women have been discussed but as yet have not been implemented; such as positive discrimination (in favour of foreigners) and the introduction of anonymous CVs in order to limit discrimination during recruitment.

(24)   For example, it includes a section on 'integration and territorial equality', which is aimed at the creation of a major public reception service for migrants by merging two existing bodies. The aim of this is to provide for the 100 000 foreigners who come to live in France every year. This new national reception service will be responsible for taking care of all migrants who have a one-year resident's permit, and all health and administrative action concerning short stays. A *contrat d'accueil et d'intégration* — CAI (reception and integration contract) will offer services for foreigners who come to France for more than a year. Such services will include language courses, administrative support and social aid.

Box 7.8: Danish welfare reform to 'make work pay' for migrants – 'A new chance for everybody' (*En ny chance til alle*)

The agenda for the Danish integration of immigrants is largely based on an economic approach, and the key word of the Danish integration policy has been 'self-support'. The government's major overall social inclusion goal is to develop the inclusive labour market as described in the *Flere i arbejde* (More people in work) programme introduced in August 2003. A chapter in the agreement concerns reductions in cash benefits in order to create incentives for entering employment. These financial incentives include further limits on cash benefits in the recent *En ny chance til alle* (A new chance for everybody) agreement between the government, the Social Democrats and the Danish Peoples Party made in June 2005. The agreement implies that persons on cash benefit will have to demonstrate that they are part of the labour force, which means taking part in labour market activity schemes. If one of the spouses in a family, where both receive cash benefit, has not worked at least 300 hours within a period of two years, the person will lose the right to a cash benefit, and the other spouse will receive a family allowance. Both spouses cannot lose the cash benefit at the same time.

This change in policy will have a particular influence on immigrants (as they are, to a higher extent, dependent on cash benefits), and probably most female immigrants, but it is not mentioned or discussed in the latest NAP/inclusion report. A recent report from SFI (the Danish Institute for Social Research) commissioned by the Danish Directorate of Employment concludes that the ceiling on cash benefits has not yet resulted in more cash benefit receivers being employed.

Source: national reports.

7.2. Concluding assessment

Migrant and immigrant women – particularly those from non-western countries – are poorly integrated into the labour market. Most groups of migrant women have lower employment rates than non-migrant women in the host country. Migrant women from some countries have employment rates which are close to or exceed those for non-migrant women, for example single Chinese migrant women in France, but the pay and working conditions of employed migrant women is typically inferior to that of non-migrant women. Yet many of them are performing socially necessary jobs for which the host country is very dependent on their labour, as evidenced by the growing pool of migrant women performing care and domestic work for private households and the concentration of migrant women in sales, cleaning and related jobs.

The labour market disadvantage of migrant and immigrant women is compounded by poor social protection coverage, thus exposing them to greater risks of poverty. Women who arrive as dependents are particularly vulnerable, since their legal rights to enter the labour market may be constrained and any social protection rights they have are largely contingent upon the continuity of their marital relationship; this makes them extremely dependent on one man.

Similarities across the countries included problems of lack of proper access to the labour market and the subsequent protection that this affords employees in terms of work contracts and regulated conditions. This in turn led to problems of high unemployment in this group; again a common problem found across the 12 national reports. In addition to this, some specific problems were also highlighted. For example, it was emphasised in the Danish report that recent policy changes affecting immigrant's rights to state benefits may have serious social and financial ramifications for this group.

Together, the 12 national case studies pointed to the need for measures to improve the employment rights and social protection coverage of migrant workers, underwritten by more effective anti-discrimination legislation. Some countries have introduced new or stronger anti-discrimination legislation which increases the protection that migrants may acquire. For example, Belgium introduced an anti-discrimination law in February 2003 which prohibits discrimination, direct and indirect, based on sex, race, colour, origin, sexual orientation, health, disability, etc. The law charges the Centre for Equal Opportunities and Opposition to Racism with the prevention of and action against these forms of discrimination. There is, however, a risk that the particular problems migrant women face due to the intersectionality of gender and race or origin may not be addressed because of the institutional division of responsibilities whereby sex discrimination remains the provenance of the Institute for Equal Opportunities for Men and Women. This may mean that any weaknesses in the implementation of the legislation are magnified for women if they try to seek redress.

In order to generate a better understanding of the specific needs and disadvantages faced by migrant/immigrant women from different countries of origin and in different destination countries several of the national reports conclude that more research is needed as a basis for gender mainstreaming social inclusion policy.

A summary of the overall conclusions of the 12 country specific reports is provided in Box 7.9.

Box 7.9: Policy priorities identified in the national reports

Austria

The necessary steps to secure an improvement in the working and living conditions of immigrant women in Austria include:

- the abolition of the restrictive or discriminatory regulations governing the access of immigrants to the formal labour market and the social security system, and in particular the length of residency or marriage and access to the formal labour market or rights to welfare-state benefits;

- the creation of a right to residency for women that is independent of their husband;

- minimum employment law standards, independent of legal status, that would protect those workers in jobs such as private housework;

- further research to identify and assess the problems faced by migrant women, which is needed to inform policy.

Belgium

- Further research is necessary to assess the extent, and exact nature of the problems facing this group of women: to expose the extent and form of discrimination in recruitment; patterns of segregation and unemployment; wages and working conditions. Analysis by ethnic origin, not simply nationality, is needed.

- More effective anti-discrimination legislation is needed to address the situation of immigrant and migrant workers.

- Policy work should be undertaken with the social partners to address discriminatory treatment in employment.

Cyprus

One of the main sources of the problem faced by immigrant and migrant women in Cyprus is a lack of social inclusion and integration.

- The NAP update includes a section on refugees and immigrants which focuses on education and providing free Greek lessons to refugees and notes the need to introduce an integrated strategy for the employment of foreign workers, with the participation of all relevant ministries and social partners. However, no details of the implementation of these plans are available.

- There is a lack of policy programme to combat the exclusion of immigrant and migrant women. Basic initiatives which are required include public information leaflets, language courses for refugees, information campaigns to inform migrants and refugees of their rights, and intercultural events.

- Further research is necessary to assess the extent, and exact nature of the problems facing this group of women.

Denmark

- In the NAP/inclusion there is an awareness of ethnic minority women's low labour market participation.

- The emphasis of social inclusion policy for immigrants and migrants is on self-sufficiency through reductions in social welfare under the *En ny chance til alle* agreement. A key challenge for the NAP social inclusion is whether this policy approach will result in social inclusion. There is a risk that the reductions (where the latest may result in approximately 2 500 married families having a considerable drop in income) will instead result in a higher degree of polarisation in Denmark, and ethnicity may become an even more visible polarisation factor.

Box 7.9: Policy priorities identified in the national reports (continued)

France

There are various difficulties faced by women immigrants in France. In order to minimise these and improve integration, several policy directions should be taken.

• Real integration paths should be created that provide free, compulsory language and training courses.

• More effective anti-discrimination legislation should be developed.

• Further research is needed, mainly in the area of employment conditions, in order that the problems faced here can be properly assessed and used to inform policy.

Iceland

Immigrant workers are vulnerable because of their employment conditions.

• Temporary work permits should be issued to the individual instead of to the prospective employer. This would give temporary immigrant workers the opportunity to choose where they work and/or for whom.

• Employers should be required to apply equal pay for immigrants, to remove the situation whereby immigrants are paid at negotiated rates while Icelandic workers have, to a greater extent, been paid additional payments in order to raise their pay above the standard wage rates.

Germany

For a long time, Germany treated migrants as guest workers and lacked a policy on integration for migrants. This still prevails in Germany today. The disadvantages faced by migrants in Germany are widespread, and it is only recently that policy has attempted to follow a more systematic approach. Policy efforts are in the right direction, but are insufficiently developed. Two of the main problems faced by migrants and immigrants are inferior training and inferior employment opportunities.

• Binding anti-discrimination regulations are still absent; they would force a more comprehensive policy both in education, training and labour market integration.

• An antidiscrimination policy programme is needed for the integration of migrants in all parts of society: education and vocational training, employment, lifelong learning, development of a positive understanding and application of multiculturalism.

• Gender mainstreaming needs to be developed in order to expose the particular situation of migrant women more systematically.

Italy

There is clearly an imbalance in the quality of the labour supply (female foreign workers) and the quality of jobs (housework and care work) available in Italy, whereby many migrants have high skill levels which are under-used or under-rewarded.

Latvia

• Language training for non-Latvians would improve the integration opportunities for migrant women.

• More effective implementation of existing policies is needed as a basis for improving the social inclusion of migrant women.

Netherlands

In July 2003 the Dutch government appointed the PaVEM (Participation of Women in Ethnic Minority groups) commission, for two years, with the goal to stimulate participation of immigrant women at all aspects of society. The commission focused on policy measures at the municipal level, with special attention to immigrant women's Dutch language skills, labour market position and their integration in wider society. According to the national plan of action, the lack of Dutch language skills of immigrant women should be significantly reduced by 2010.

Box 7.9: Policy priorities identified in the national reports (continued)

- However, most of the measures put forward by the PaVEM commission focused on immigrant women with a reasonable chance of entering the labour market. In addition to these, supplementary policy measures are needed for those groups of women with fewer opportunities, particularly education and training which combines work and learning (such as traineeships) and government subsidies for employers who hire low-skilled immigrant women.

- Social security facilities in the Netherlands are often not suited for the situation of immigrant women. Limitations in their rights caused by waiting time or occupational history requirements could be solved by making exceptions in legislation in favour of those women.

- More guidance is also needed with respect to the right to a pension benefit for this group of women who often are not aware of the possibilities of the current pension system. At present, ethnic organisations are asked to inform immigrant men and women about their pension rights.

- The Dutch government is exploring the possibility of an extension of the duration of the partner-dependent right of residence from three to five years.

Norway

Studies on skills and employment underscore the need to distinguish between structural, cultural and individual barriers in Norway. This is especially true given that policies still tend to focus on individual barriers in explaining the problems faced by immigrants in the Norwegian labour market.

- More empirical research on this group of disadvantaged women is needed, especially on non-western immigrant women's relations to work and family, so that present stereotypes can be countered.

- The cash-for-care arrangement in Norway has been of particular concern. Parents with children aged one to two years have the right to a monthly cash benefit of around EUR 450 if they do not use publicly subsidised childcare. This arrangement produces disincentives both to immigrant women's participation in the labour market and to immigrant children's use of childcare.

Portugal

Immigrant women face difficulties in gaining employment and typically work in segregated and low-paid jobs.

- There are few effective, concrete policies for the social integration of immigrant women into Portuguese life beyond the recent reform which gives those migrants with a 'permit of permanency' (mainly women) the same right which migrants with a residence permit (mainly men) have to claim family allowance and the 'social insertion' income. A wider set of concrete and gender mainstreamed policies for the social inclusion of migrant women are needed in government policy.

- The legislation which exists to provide immigrants with certain rights and protection against discrimination and exploitation is largely ineffective.

- There is a lack of information or public awareness about the extent of racist and xenophobic crimes; the problem is ignored in public opinion and policy debates.

Source: national reports.

8. Violence and sexual abuse against women – domestic violence, human trafficking and prostitution

In this chapter we focus on the problems of women's exposure to violence and sexual abuse in two domains – domestic violence, and human trafficking and prostitution. In both of these situations the majority of the victims are women, and men constitute the majority of the assailants and customers. This dominant gender asymmetry should not, however, be used to ignore the plight of the minority of victims who are male: domestic violence reaches young boys as well as some adult males, and disadvantaged young men are at risk of being drawn into prostitution (largely same-sex) through homelessness or drug addiction.

We draw on three national case studies of domestic violence (EL, MT, RO) and seven national case studies on human trafficking and prostitution (BG, CY, LT, MT, NO, PL, RO). Many of the other 30 country reports provided estimates of the scale of these problems in their countries, where such information exists, which is summarised in the Appendix 2 of this report. The scale of both problems is often underestimated, particularly when the estimates are based on statistics of reported crime.

The reasons for under-reporting by victims of domestic violence are various. They may distrust the authorities or think their complaint will not be treated seriously. They may lack a refuge to escape to and live in fear of retribution from their assailant. They may be socially isolated, or feel unable to turn to relatives or friends for support in societies or social circles which stigmatise and exclude those who experience domestic violence. Often they have been reduced through violence to such a poor psychological state that they have come to accept the violence as a normal part of their life which is somehow their fault.

Poverty and indebtedness are major factors propelling women into prostitution, and in relation to human trafficking they are either taken as prisoners or

tricked into travelling to another country on the understanding that they are going for legitimate and decently paid employment. Women caught in prostitution and trafficking are trapped by similar factors to those experienced by victims of domestic violence plus other factors such as being forcibly held against their will, sex slavery, sexually transmitted health risks, widespread drug dependency, and fear of prosecution, including deportation for victims of trafficking.

8.1. Women's exposure to domestic violence

Box 8.1 (p.134) summaries the available national information concerning the problem of domestic violence in the three case studies of Greece, Malta and Romania (see Appendix 2 for available estimates for the other countries in this report). Data on the scale of the problem has only recently become available in Greece, is more limited in Malta and absent in Romania. Data on trends are lacking but the national experts for Malta and Romania argue that the available evidence indicates an increase in the scale of the problem in their countries.

For Romania, the disruption and insecurity of the economic and political transition is argued to be a possible cause of the increased violence against women. It is triggered by various processes, which include: rising stress and frustration, due to economic depression and high unemployment, which increase family conflicts; the dramatic reduction in police authority during this period; a crisis of trust in the legal system; the sudden sexual liberation of women, which may have produced a denigration of the image and value of women; and the explosion of the sex industry, which may have placed more women at risk.

The Greek national report argues that domestic violence is still ignored in public debates and is not monitored by official statistics. However, growing political visibility of the problem, promoted at EU level, has stimulated the first policy investigations and initiatives, which signal some limited progress. Nonetheless, it is still a hidden problem in Greece; for example, a recent study found that one-third of victims considered themselves to be the guilty party and the cause of the violent behaviour of their husband or partner, and none of this group had contacted any public agencies for support. Similarly in Malta, in recent years awareness of the problem is growing within government and non-government organisations, including the Catholic Church, and some services have been developed. In contrast, the invisibility of domestic violence is pronounced in Romania.

Box 8.1: Estimates of the scale of domestic violence – the examples of Greece, Malta and Romania

Greece

A nationwide sample survey conducted by the Research Centre for Gender Equality Issues (KETHI) during 2002–03 found that 56% of women aged 18 to 60 years had experienced verbal and/or psychological violence on a frequent or occasional basis. In addition, 3.6% had often or sometimes suffered physical abuse, and 3.5% were often or sometimes forced to have non-consenting sex by their spouse or partner. Domestic abuse is often a long-term experience: 56% of the victims interviewed declared having been abused for 10 years and over.

A high proportion of the women had witnessed (13.3%), or suffered (11.2%), violent incidents as children, the most frequent perpetrator being the father. This exposure as a child increases the risk of repeat experiences as an adult. More than one in four (29.2%) of those who had suffered domestic violence as children were now living with a violent husband or partner and were being abused; the respective rate was 26.3% for women who had witnessed violence among their parents.

A recent study of 385 abused women who had contacted the reception centres in Athens and Piraeus, found that over half (56%) of the women had experienced the first incidence of domestic violence after marriage. A large proportion of them were unemployed (57%), with a low or medium education attainment level (43% and 32% respectively). Incest rape is another problem which is under-reported and inadequately addressed in the judicial system: in a sample of 312 judicial decisions in Athens on rape cases that were tried between 1980 and 1993 only 17 cases of incest rape were adjudicated.

Malta

The Ghabex Women's Shelter, which provides assistance to abused women and children, has revealed that 800 cases of domestic violence are reported each year. Of these, 550 are new cases, while the remaining 250 are relapses. This suggests exposure to domestic violence is spreading.

Domestic violence services: These were established in 1994 to help and support adults and child victims. In the seven years since the service was set up it has received 2 526 referrals from all areas of Malta, of which 38% were self-referrals and 20% were primary source referrals from non-governmental shelter services. They are predominantly women (> 96%), largely from younger age groups (18 to 25 years and 26 to 35 years). The type of abuse presented by the service users was predominantly physical and emotional (46%), followed by physical abuse only (16%), and emotional abuse only (15%).

Emergency shelter services: In October 2000, the emergency shelter service of APPOGG (known as L-Ghabex) was opened for women suffering domestic violence. In its first year, 98 women and their children made use of the emergency residential facilities.

Family therapy services: APPOGG also provides a family therapy service to victims of domestic violence, which includes psychological support services.

Perpetrators services: These were set up in 1999 to provide professional therapy to the perpetrators of domestic violence. Therapy groups, individual sessions, and a long-term open-ended support group are available. The aim of the service is to address abusive beliefs and behaviour and to promote awareness and responsibility. Since its inception up until 2001, the service provided help for 91 men.

Box 8.1: Estimates of the scale of domestic violence – the examples of Greece, Malta and Romania (continued)

Romania

Domestic violence is largely hidden, with little visibility in public debate, and there are no data on the types of violence or frequency, or social attitudes towards it. Studies from the 1960s and 1970s show that most cases of female manslaughter are committed by husbands, partners or other male family members and that nearly 800 women experienced rape, including gang rape, in a six-month period. Wives accounted for 40% of the victims of homicides within families in the period 1996 to early 1997. Reports of domestic violence and rape appear to be increasing. In traditional Romanian society, domestic violence has always been seen as a legitimate way of exerting male authority in the family, and this tolerance used to be supported in various degrees by legitimacy both inside and outside the family unit. However, during the past two centuries a culture has emerged which encompasses a blend of modern elements with elements of a romanticised view of women, where she is seen as one who is delicate and requires protection.

Source: national reports.

The problems faced by women who experience domestic violence are largely similar in the three country case studies, as in other countries. Greece is an example of a country where there is little national research on domestic violence and where the national expert argues that more research is needed to collect national information to supplement what is known from studies in other countries. The problems are various and cumulative: victims suffer psychological as well as physical damage, which produces an erosion of self-esteem and confidence. This psychological damage limits their ability to seek help and is often compounded by their social isolation. It also impacts negatively on concentration and performance in employment, which can lead to job loss or exits. Many stay because they see no alternative – they lack the economic means to escape or fear that their assailant will pursue and find them. Additional institutional obstacles exist where public policy does not provide means of support and escape, because the problem is not recognised in legislation or police procedures, and where support services (e.g. counselling, refuges and resettlement) are lacking or inadequate.

In Malta, an additional particular problem is that divorce is not permitted and legal separation or annulment can take years to decide and can be expensive (although the law does provide for mediation prior to separation, through which the parties may reconcile or be assisted in reaching an amicable agreement). Therefore, it is difficult to leave a violent marriage. The Romanian national report provided fairly extensive details on the disadvantages faced by women facing domestic violence; these are summarised in Box 8.2 (p.136).

Each of the three national case studies highlights similar types of failing in policy provision (see Box 8.3-p.137). Public awareness of the problem is low. Legislation on domestic violence is absent or inadequate, making it difficult for women to press charges against their partners. For example, marital rape is not a crime in Greece, while in Romania it falls under the general provision of rape but in practice is rarely reported. The police are poorly equipped to deal with domestic violence due to the limitations of the legal framework and a lack of training. The infrastructure to support victims, such as help lines, emergency housing, counselling and legal services, is also inadequate in Greece and Malta and entirely lacking in Romania.

In all three countries there has been new legislation or policy programmes established in the past few years (Box 8.3-p.137). In Greece, after the failure of policy initiatives in 1997 and 2000, there is now a National Observatory for Combating Violence against Women (established in 2003) and a comprehensive policy programme planned for 2005–06 by the General Secretariat for Equality. However, the Greek national expert argues that more commitment is needed from the government, given that a significant part of the population still considers domestic violence to be a private affair and marital rape a non-issue. Furthermore, the existing services are inadequate and limited in geographical reach. A new Domestic Violence Bill is being debated in Malta and has a number of positive measures, having been influenced by the recommendations made by the National Council of Women. The critical issue is whether it will be implemented effectively. New legislation has also been passed in Romania, but it is assessed by the national expert to be seriously

---

Box 8.2: A summary of the main disadvantages faced by women suffering domestic violence in Romania

State policy under socialism: The socialist regime explicitly promotes the principle of total equality of men and women. However, there was no explicit policy orientation or programme to identify and combat domestic violence against women.

Violence against women in the period of transition: Violence against women increased during this period for four main reasons. There was a resurgence of the traditional mentality of the male as being superior which spread from the rural environments through the uncertainties of urbanisation and industrialisation. Violence was also generated by the process of transition from traditional family structures to modern ones, and by processes of social disorganisation, which in Romania was accompanied by alcoholism. Finally, there is a high degree of economic dependency of women on the family; this is heightened in marginalised parts of the economy where employment rates are low for women.

Low public awareness of violence against women: The problem of domestic violence against women is largely underestimated. It is largely seen as a problem that mainly affects marginal aspects of society, such as more rural areas of the country, and to be associated with poverty, lack of education, and social and personal disorganisation. In this sense, domestic violence in Romania is socially stigmatised and there is little recognition that it occurs in all types of households. The solution to the problem is often seen as being one of modernisation, education, and social and personal development. Since 1989, no significant initiatives have been implemented to try and control violence against women.

Source: national report.

---

flawed in the coherence and scope of the design, and its inefficacy is compounded by the lack of institutional support services for victims of domestic violence.

Although general awareness about the problem of domestic violence and the ramifications of this seem to be increasing in the three countries, each of the national experts draws similar conclusions about the need for legal, financial and social services combined with public awareness campaigns.

- Information and education campaigns are needed to increase public awareness that domestic violence exists and is unacceptable, and that services exist to help victims escape and prosecute their assailants.

- There needs to be appropriate legislation, including reforms (in the case of Greece and Romania) and proper implementation (the new legislation in Malta).

- Training is required for key professions (police, judges, medical and social workers).

- Expanded support is required for those leaving situations of domestic violence (free legal services, a network of refuges and temporary accommodation, financial support).

8.2. Human trafficking and prostitution of women

Sex work is a major industry, the scale of which is vastly underestimated. Carrington and Hearn (2003) report that the United Nations estimates trafficking in the global sex industry alone generates from USD 5 billion to USD 7 billion profit annually and that global trafficking has increased substantially over the past decade. They record that estimates of the numbers trafficked globally vary from 700 000 to four million per year; and in Europe between 200 000 and 500 000 women and children are trafficked per year.

Box 8.4 (p.139) summarises the available tentative estimates concerning human trafficking and prostitution for six of the seven national case studies (BG, CY, LT, MT PL, NO; no estimates available for RO). Available estimates for other countries in this study are contained in Appendix 2.

Poverty and indebtedness are major causes of prostitution. Women are more at risk of entering prostitution if they come from poor economic backgrounds, were abused as a child or raised in institutional care, have a drug dependency to finance or are in financial debt with no access to credit. Economic inequalities between countries create migrant flows of prosti-

Box 8.3: Summary of the policy limitations and developments in Greece, Malta and Romania

Greece

There is no special legislation to protect women against domestic violence; only a general provision under civil law and the penal code, on physical injury. Marital rape is not considered a crime. Most women do not press charges against their partners for several reasons: criminal cases take an average of three to five years to complete; there is a limited infrastructure for the support of victims; extra-judicial compromises are encouraged by police officers, judges, and family members; doctors are often reluctant to report incidences of domestic violence in order to avoid involvement in judicial proceedings. There is also a lack of training for law enforcement officials in relation to family based violence. The curriculum of police academics does include some education on family violence or violence against women, but only in the context of theoretical human rights, not an actual legal framework.

There are only two reception centres for abused women; these are operated by the General Secretariat for Equality in Athens and Piraeus and offer legal advice and psychological support but no accommodation. The information and counselling centres of KETHI in Athens, Thessaloniki, Patras, Volos and Heraklion provide legal advice and socio-psychological support. There are currently three **guest houses for abused women**, two situated in Athens, one in Heraklion. A limited number of NGOs and municipalities operate hotlines providing support and advice for women who are victims of violence.

In 1997, the Ministry of the Interior presented a NAP for combating violence against women; it was never implemented. In 2000, the General Secretariat for Equality announced the creation of an inter-ministerial committee whose task was to design a comprehensive policy to combat violence against women. A bill was drafted and submitted to the Minister of the Interior in 2002 but it was never taken to parliament and now remains dormant. In May 2003, the National Observatory for Combating Violence against Women was created. This observatory is comprised of both governmental and non-governmental agencies and organisations. The main actions planned for 2005–06 by the General Secretariat for Equality are:

- the preparation of a new NAP for the prevention and eradication of domestic violence against women by the National Committee for Equality;

- the preparation and promotion of legislation on domestic violence;

- the establishment of special courts to try such cases and the provision of financial support to victims;

- a campaign to raise awareness among the public and relevant authorities and agencies;

- additional resources for the existing reception centres, refuges ('guest houses') and counselling services of the GSE and KETHI, possibly to include the opening of a second refuge in Thessaloniki and to create sections of short-term emergency accommodation.

Malta

At present there is no specific legislation dealing with domestic violence. The new Domestic Violence Bill is widely debated and, according to the National Council of Women (NCW), reflects the increased awareness of domestic violence. Many of the recommendations submitted by the NCW over previous years have been included in the Bill, and the positive developments include:

- relatives and friends of the victim being able to file reports of domestic violence; previously the victim had to be willing to report the offence;

- the establishment of a commission on domestic violence, with the function of advising the government on all aspects of domestic violence and on public education, as well as devising strategies to facilitate the intervention of public and private agencies with respect to victims and perpetrators.

Romania

There was no specific legislation on domestic violence until 2003, when a law for preventing and combating domestic violence was established. In 2004, a new law was passed regarding any type of violence, including murder, assault, domestic violence, rape, child abuse, incest and infanticide. However:

137

Box 8.3: Summary of the policy limitations and developments in Greece, Malta and Romania (continued)

- the legal and police instruments for intervention and punishment remain inadequate;

- the law specifies that a complaint must be made by the victims themselves, but there is no provision made for the protection of victims once the complaint has been registered;

- marital rape is not classed as a form of domestic violence, but falls under the general definition of rape. In legal practice, cases of marital rape are very rarely reported in Romania.

Analysis conducted by the Institute for Research and Crime Prevention (Minister for Internal Affairs) showed that the women filing complaints of domestic violence had already suffered four to five serious cases of violence.

There are no forms of social services provided by either the government or NGOs to support victims of domestic violence: no temporary housing, counselling, protection or security against the violence. Any support which is given is via the extended family. Domestic violence is interpreted in public debates as an individual, isolated problem rather than a social or cultural one.

Since 1995 several international and national workshops organised by international organisations (UNDP, UNICEF, OMS) operating in Romania have focused on the issue of violence against women. The national plan of action for equal opportunities (developed following the Beijing conference) aims to conduct research on the causes and consequences of violence against women, evaluate the existing legislation, organise and expand resources at the national level, elaborate special training programmes for prevention and control of the problem, and undertake public awareness campaigns. However, the programme lacks financial resources; there is no framework of public services to tackle the problem or to provide support to victims.

Source: national reports.

---

tutes, including those who are trafficked; most originate from poor transitional and developing countries destined for more affluent countries.

The collapse of communism has stimulated an increase in prostitution and trafficking across Europe. The conditions fuelling this were the difficult economic conditions facing many women in transition economies, increased high unemployment, cross-border mobility and a booming sex industry in Western market economies. The scale of the problem is enormous, for example at least 1 200 women are estimated to be trafficked out of Lithuania each year, with other estimates putting the figure as high as 15 000; an estimated 10 000 are trafficked out of Poland each year, and add another 10 000 who were trafficked from Bulgaria in 2004 (see Box 8.4-p.139). Estimates are not available for Romania, but here the problem is 'spiralling and is out of control' according to the national expert.

Prostitution existed under communism but it has grown rapidly since the economic and political upheaval of the transition, and this expansion includes increased trafficking of women. In Poland, the expansion of prostitution includes an increase in foreign women being trafficked into the country to work as prostitutes and the conditions under which prostitutes work has deteriorated. Most victims come from small communities in poor regions and poorer countries, have a low level of education and little or no knowledge of the foreign language. Most hope to achieve independence and support for their families through paid work. Since Poland became a member of the EU, trafficking has increased into and from Poland in connection with less stringent border controls, border corruption and falsification of Polish passports to enable non-EU citizens to enter through Poland. Political instability and war in the region has had a major effect on the trade in women in Romania and other countries in the region, as the presence of soldiers and international workers in the Balkan states expanded the market for sex workers. In Romania, the volume of trafficking rose in 1999 as soon as NATO troops arrived in Macedonia. Romania is now a country of origin, transit and destination for trafficked women and children to a wide range of destinations in Europe and the rest of the world[25]. Women who are trafficked through and to

---

(25) The most common destinations are Albania, Belgium, Bosnia and Herzegovina, Cambodia, Canada, the Czech Republic, France, Germany, Greece, Hungary, Israel, Italy, Kosovo, Luxembourg, Macedonia, Montenegro, Poland, Serbia, Ireland, the Netherlands, South Africa, Spain, Turkey, and the United States of America.

Box 8.4: Profile of the extent of trafficking and prostitution of women

There were 117 reported victims of human trafficking in **Cyprus** during 2004, and in **Malta** in 2004–05 20 people appeared in court charged with human trafficking (nine were sentenced, three of whom received a prison term); but both of these statistics probably underestimate the true scale of the problem. Women who are trafficked into Cyprus and Malta come mainly from central and eastern Europe, Ukraine and Russia. There is increasing evidence of Chinese women being trafficked to Cyprus. In Malta, they usually enter on tourist visas and are then trafficked into private homes or street prostitution. In Cyprus, most are recruited as dancers in cabarets, pubs and bars and enter the country on entertainer visas. Official estimates are that around 2 000 foreign women enter Cyprus every year as entertainers, this figure is disproportionate to the number of establishments – in 2002 there were 108 cabarets and nightclubs on the island, each employing between 5 and 15 entertainers.

According to various estimations, there are about 3 000 to 10 000 prostitutes in Lithuania, including between 500 to 3 000 who are legal or illegal immigrant women, mainly from Russia, Ukraine and Belarus. The scope of prostitution and the number of prostitutes in Lithuania is increasing. One indication is that the number of officially fixed sex services increased from 58 in 1994, to 272 in 2000 and 345 in the first half of 2003. According to Europol, every year approximately 1 200 Lithuanian women fall victim to human trafficking or leave the country against their will. Other expert opinions give higher estimates of up to 15 000 women taken each year by various illegal means from Lithuania and forced to become prostitutes in other countries. Official records of trafficking into Germany show that Lithuania is one of the main countries of origin: more of the cases identified in 2000 came from Lithuania than any other country, while in 2001 and 2002 Lithuania was placed third and second in the rank. The picture is even starker when presented relative to the size of the population at risk (women aged 15 to 30 years); here Lithuania has the highest incidence at an estimated 24 victims per 100 000 which is more than three times higher than Bulgaria, which is placed second. It is estimated that around 10 000 women were victims of trafficking in Bulgaria in 2004, and the risk is increasing.

According to Polish police estimates, there are 7 000 prostitutes in **Poland** with around 30% of them of foreign origin. However, other estimates put the figures much higher at 15 000 foreign prostitutes working in Poland. The Foundation La Strada, the most visible NGO dealing with the problem in Poland, estimates that 60% of the foreign women engaged in prostitution in Poland are victims of trafficking. Trafficking has increased since the transition from communism, and again following membership of the EU. It has also been estimated that 10 000 Polish women are trafficked out of the country each year. Between 1995 and 1999 there were 148 trafficking cases in court, increasing to 250 in the past five years. Polish police figures show that during 2004 there were 44 trafficking cases and involving 21 suspects. However, as most cases of trafficking do not surface to any legal or official level it is suspected that the actual numbers of human trafficking are much higher.

An uncertain estimate is that there are 2 500 prostitutes working in **Norway**. The most recent study on trafficking and prostitution was carried out in the capital, Oslo in October 2003. Here it was estimated that 617 women were working as prostitutes, and that around 1 100 women work as prostitutes in a given year. Women from 40 different nationalities worked in three different arenas: massage parlours, advertisements and the street. Overall 67% were of non-Norwegian origin and all migrant prostitutes came from transitional or developing countries in Asia, central and eastern Europe, Latin America and Africa. Norwegian prostitutes operate in all three arenas and are the largest group on the street. Asian women make up half of those in massage parlours and the largest group operating through advertisements. Women from central and eastern Europe account for 17% of the prostitutes and those from South America, Latin America, Africa and other regions another 18%.

Source: national reports.

Romania come from the Ukraine and Moldova. The Bulgarian national report emphasises that women who manage to return to their homeland do not receive protection, financial assistance or opportunities to secure employment, which puts them at risk of further involvement in prostitution and being trafficked.

Data for Lithuania give some indication of the profit to be made from trafficking. In the mid-1990s women were sold abroad for the average price of between USD 5 000 and USD 7 000, which is very profitable in relation to income levels in Lithuania. The legal system does not provide an effective deterrent, for few of the people involved in trafficking (sellers/interme-diaries/buyers) are caught and prosecuted, and those who buy sex services are not punished either. Many Lithuanian women have a very poor knowledge of their legal rights, and patriarchal traditions mean they are widely treated as being inferior to men, as second-class citizens. Fear and shame mean many do not dare apply for help from the authorities even if they are able to.

While central and east European countries are origin countries for human trafficking, the other three national case studies in our study – Cyprus, Malta and Norway – are primarily destination countries. The women come mostly from poor economic backgrounds lured by the hope of securing a better standard of living. Women who are trafficked into Cyprus and Malta come mainly from central and eastern Europe, and the trafficking from China is also increasing. The typical entry route is on tourist visas for Malta and as dancers on entertainer visas for Cyprus, where the number of entertainer visas issued each year greatly exceeds the size of the cabaret/nightclub sector. The Norwegian prostitution market includes Norwegian as well as non-Norwegian women, and all are a marginalised and stigmatised group in Norway. The Norwegian prostitution market is shifting in that a growing proportion of the women involved are migrants from other countries; from central and eastern Europe as well as Africa and Latin America. The situation is quite distinct in northern Norway, with a large presence of Russian prostitutes because of the border proximity. In Oslo, the capital, nearly half of the migrant prostitutes are citizens (48%) and two-thirds are permanent residents (67%); in contradiction to the widely held stereotype that they are on short-stay visas. A large proportion did not migrate with the intention of becoming prostitutes; two-thirds of the migrant women who are permanent residents had been in Norway for more than a year before they sold sex. Some did so because they lost jobs; others had married Norwegians and found it difficult to find employment despite intermediate or high qualifications, in part because they had come straight from school and lacked professional experience. Many said they needed to send money back home to support their family but their Norwegian husband did not help them with this.

Women who are trafficked face similar forms of entrapment and human rights abuse from their traffickers, regardless of the country where the trafficking commences. Traffickers target economically and socially deprived young women. The women who are trafficked from and within central and eastern Europe are usually poorly educated, and many come from deprived regions with high unemployment. A common characteristic is lack of family support and a dysfunctional family background where they have experienced domestic violence, or their parents had divorced, or they were rejected by parents or a boyfriend because they became pregnant. In Bulgaria, a research project with victims of trafficking found that 70% had only primary-level education. Their poor education, limited job employment prospects and the increases in unemployment in Bulgaria made them more open to persuasion to travel abroad on the promise of a better job. In Lithuania, women who are trafficked have a lower education level than the national average for women; for example 36% had less than secondary-level education. More than 70% of the victims of trafficking were in a very bad economic situation prior to departure, half of them were unemployed, and only 14% had temporary work; the rest had short-term contracts or were enrolled in education. A majority of these women (four out of five) came from one-parent families or were brought up by grandparents, other relatives or in public childcare institutions. The young women are lured by deceptive offers of jobs such as household helpers, bar dancers, or waitresses. In many cases, close relatives or friends made such offers. In Romania women are often recruited by friends, relatives, and newspaper advertisements. Most are unaware that they will be working as prostitutes. A minority of them are sold into prostitution by their parents or husbands, or are kidnapped by trafficking rings for domestic as well as international trade. These trafficking rings are mainly operated by Romanians. Most of the women come from the Moldova region, which is very poor and has high unemployment rates.

The methods of control and intimidation deployed by the traffickers are similar across countries. These methods include withholding possessions, travel and identity documents; imprisonment or confining the women to certain areas; beatings and rape; and threatening violence and revenge on family members. The Polish national report documents that traffickers routinely deprive victims of food and water, drug them, torture them, keep all or most of their earnings, and gather information on their families and threaten to harm them. All this contributes to the women remaining financially, physically and emotionally dependent on their captors. The national expert for Cyprus reports that the conditions amount to slavery and abuse of basic human rights, of persistent violence from employers and clients, and living conditions which are overcrowded and lack sanitation. Health problems are pervasive, and include high rates of hepatitis and sexually transmitted diseases, psychological problems, and drug and alcohol dependency.

The situation of victims of trafficking is not helped by their portrayal in the media or their treatment in public opinion. An analysis of 600 press articles in Poland showed that the media contribute to the stigmatisation of victims by presenting them in a light or sensational way, thereby enticing negative attitudes, and sometimes actually publishing photographs of the victims. Victims of trafficking are presented as naïve or materialistic, greedy, and willing to do anything for foreign currency. The media message is that it is individual traits that are the root of the problem, not the wider social conditions and inequalities. In Lithuania, prostitution is widely held in public opinion to be a fault of the individual; a consequence of poor morality and degradation. In this way, prostitutes are stigmatised and isolated and there is little public support pressing for resources to be allocated to address prostitution and trafficking. This stigma can extend to other women from the same ethnic background, regardless of whether or not they are involved in prostitution, and thus fuel racism. For example, in Cyprus many of the prostitutes who have been trafficked in are of Russian origin; the term 'Russian woman' has now become synonymous with prostitute. All Russian women living in Cyprus are often assumed to be prostitutes and face social discrimination, albeit less discrimination than that experienced by women who are or who have been prostitutes.

The final, obvious points to make about the disadvantaged position of women who are prostitutes is that they are not covered by a whole range of social protection measures. They lack social insurance and protection under labour law, health access where this is insurance based and, in the case of migrants, often lack visas or residency papers. Many are caught in illegal and vulnerable circumstances, for in many countries prostitution is illegal; the exceptions in our case studies are Poland where prostitution is legal and Norway where it is decriminalised. Women who escape trafficking risk deportation in many countries and perhaps further abuse and re-trafficking on their return to their origin country.

All the national case studies report a growing public awareness and recognition of prostitution and human trafficking, and some new measures to address the problem (Box 8.5-p.142). There have been major initiatives in Lithuania, Poland and Romania, but so far the impact is limited or hard to judge, given the measures are very recent. In Lithuania, there have been significant policy efforts, but it is insufficient for the scale of the problem, which is still growing, and NGOs criticise the government for the lack of a regular and systematic policy approach. The Polish national report documents new legislation and that trafficking is one of the strategic priorities of the NAP for women 2003–05, as is the piloting of cross-border initiatives with the Czech Republic and IRIS, another partnership initiative funded under the European Social Fund Equal programme. The national expert cautions that it is too early to evaluate these initiatives, for most have only been introduced recently and others have yet to be implemented. In Romania, there is a national taskforce and action plan on trafficking supported by an inter-agency consortium of government agencies and international organisations. New initiatives include a witness protection scheme implemented in 2003, legislation which requires all government agencies to endorse the relevant part of the action plan, and labour market measures targeted at high risk groups to improve their economic situation. However, the impact of the labour market measures is likely to be modest, given the levels of unemployment and poverty it has to contend with.

Norway is largely a destination country and here, too, there is a National Action Plan to tackle trafficking as well as a regional Nordic/Baltic campaign. The action plan has introduced measures to support victims who press charges and helps them to apply for a resident permit so that they escape deportation. There is some recognition that it is necessary to try and reduce the demand for sex services as well as the supply; for Norwegian state employees and the armed forces are now forbidden from purchasing sex services. However, the plan has been criticised because only a small element is directed at the buyers of sex and one suggestion is that criminalising the purchase of sex is an important element to make action plans effective.

In the other three case studies the policy initiatives have been smaller. In Cyprus, there have been some improvements in relation to prosecution and support for victims including residency permits for those willing to testify, but nothing systematic has been done to prevent the trafficking. Initiatives have been even more modest in Malta and Bulgaria. In Malta, the government has signed up to various international conventions and protocols but the development and implementation of measures has been very limited. Relevant legal and support services are also lacking in Bulgaria.

The growing problem of trafficking and prostitution is attracting wider public recognition; research and information is accumulating and there are more national and international initiatives to tackle the problem. Each of the national experts for the case studies draws similar conclusions about the need for

further and more coordinated efforts covering criminal law and the support provided for victims within countries and information exchange and collaboration across countries. The country-specific priorities presented by the national reports are summarised in Box 8.6 (p.145). The common points arising from this assessment are that there is a need for:

- a comprehensive and international network of collaboration across agencies to coordinate efforts in origin and destination countries;

Box 8.5: Recent policy measures to address trafficking and prostitution

Bulgaria

There are a number of weaknesses in Bulgarian family policy and child protection. A number of revisions in the legislation relating to family and children were made in recent years to provide more protection for children from violence and to try and strengthen support for families; however, the practical implementation of the legislation is not effective. There is a lack of legal, health or information support services for victims of trafficking; and protection under the social assistance system is inadequate.

Cyprus

The US embassy report and World Forum for Religions and Cultures Conference on Trafficking in Persons (27-28 June 2005) stated that the Cypriot government must increase its efforts to fight trafficking and prostitution and must work with local NGOs in three main areas to help combat this problem: prosecution, protection and prevention. In terms of prosecution, much progress has been made. For example, in 2004 police made 194 arrests in 91 trafficking-related cases and charged 20 people with trafficking offences and sexual exploitation. Police also make regular visits to cabarets and interview women privately. In terms of protection there has been improvement. The Welfare Department of the Ministry of Labour routinely ensures that victims receive shelter and legal and financial assistance and has issued residence permits in cases where the victim was willing to testify. An interdepartmental committee aimed at addressing issues of prostitution and trafficking was set up in 2004 with the aim of providing a shelter for victims, but this has not yet come into effect. In terms of prevention, pamphlets that contain anti-trafficking information are now routinely distributed to all newly arriving foreign female workers. However, no large-scale public awareness programmes have taken place even though this was an area of concern highlighted by the abovementioned US embassy report.

Lithuania

The problem of trafficking has attracted more attention in recent years from international organisations (IOM), state institutions, NGOs and the general public. There have been some significant policy efforts by the government, but the problem is still increasing and there is still insufficient effort to help victims. Government funding for prevention, investigation, prosecution, and witness protection remains inadequate, and many NGOs complain that state support is irregular and unsystematic.

One of the most urgent problems is that of safety of the victims. The criminal code in Lithuania pays very little attention to the needs and rights of victims; the aggrieved party is viewed primarily as a potential witness. Women who decide to act as a witness against traffickers usually do not receive any protection. It is recommended that the various NGOs which provide social assistance for the victims of trafficking in people/prostitution should extend their activities to ensure the safety of those who become witnesses. Also, the police need to be better educated about the problem, and reforms are needed to develop a more active collaboration between the police and the NGOs to address trafficking and to provide support and security for women who flee their traffickers and turn witness.

Malta

Malta has signed and ratified the UN convention and subsequent protocols on trafficking in human beings, but the implementation of these is very limited and few measures have been introduced to prevent the problem or to support victims.

Box 8.5: Recent policy measures to address trafficking and prostitution (continued)

Norway

In Norway, the selling and buying of sex is not criminalised. Pimping is illegal, as is hiring out premises for prostitution, and it is also illegal to advertise sex services. Since 2002, there has been a Nordic/Baltic campaign against trafficking, organised by the Nordic Council of Ministers. The Norwegian government has a plan of action to tackle trafficking of women and children for the period 2003–05, though a criticism of the plan is that only a small section of it is aimed at buyers of sex in Norway. One of the measures is directed at illegal migrants. In cases where women are ordered to leave the country, if they are suspected victims of trafficking, the case will rest for 45 days. In this period, the victim will receive help and support in pressing charges. The reflection period of 45 days can be prolonged. Also, when the court trial is over, the authorities can consider granting a resident permit. Norwegian state employees travelling on duty are to abstain from buying sexual services, including in their spare time on such assignments. It is now part of the duty of Norwegians in the armed forces to abstain from buying sexual services while operating abroad. It has been suggested that criminalising the buying of sex would help reduce the problem further.

Poland

Prostitution is legal in Poland but trafficking is not. In 2003, Poland implemented the Protocol to Prevent, Suppress and Punish Trafficking in Persons, especially Women and Children, thereby supplementing the UN Convention against Transnational Organised Crime. The Polish criminal code sets sentences as high as 10 years for trafficking, pimping or recruiting into prostitution.

The prevention of human trafficking and exploitation through prostitution is one of the strategic goals of the second phase of the NAP for women 2003–05. Institutions primarily responsible for anti-trafficking actions are the Ministry of the Interior and Administration (MSWiA), the Ministry of Justice (MS), and the Ministry of Foreign Affairs (MSZ) together with the government plenipotentiary for equal status of women and men (PRdsRSKiM) and NGOs. Based on the government's report on the execution of the NAP for women II implementation phase (PRdsRSKiM, 2005), most of the activities directed at combating trafficking in human beings are being carried out. However, it is too early to evaluate their impact because most of the actions and programmes have only recently been implemented or are not yet in place.

Poland, together with the Czech authorities, has developed a model for support/protection of witnesses and victims of trafficking, this model is being tested in some regions of Poland and after modifications it will become standard practice in other regions as well. Contacts have been established in Belarus, Moldova and Ukraine. There are various other projects that Poland is participating in or implementing; one is IRIS – social and occupational reintegration of women victims of trafficking in humans – which started in June 2005 as part of the European Social Fund Equal programme and includes partnerships in Estonia, Germany, Italy, Latvia, Portugal and the United Kingdom. The goals of the programme are: to provide assistance to trafficking victims in (re)entering the labour market; developing a model of socio-occupational reintegration of trafficking victims; raising the level of social awareness of the phenomenon, especially among the groups at higher risk. Other projects deal with: the implementation of anti-trafficking training modules for judges, prosecutors, police and the NGO sector; combating the forced labour outcomes of human trafficking; and research into understanding the demand side of trafficking. Many of these programmes are relatively recent and therefore ongoing and cannot be assessed at this time.

Romania

Prostitution is illegal. Crimes relating to prostitution and trafficking currently carry prison sentences of two to seven years' imprisonment: if the case involves a minor then the sentence is increased to 3 to 10 years. If an organised group is involved, the punishment is increased by another three years. The Romanian government is required to grant special physical, legal and social protection and assistance and physical, psychological and social recovery to victims of trafficking. The law also entitles victims to protection of their privacy and the right to compensation for civil damages. A witness protection law came into effect at the end of January 2003.

A national task force on trafficking and the inter-agency working group on trafficking in human beings include government agencies, international organisations and donors and provides support to the national task force related

---

Box 8.5: Recent policy measures to address trafficking and prostitution (continued)

to legislation, law enforcement procedures and victim-assistance issues. The Ministry of Labour and Social Solidarity is required to design special measures for the integration of persons in high-risk groups, which includes women in very poor areas, into the labour market. There is also a law requiring that all government agencies endorse the relevant portions of the NAP for the combating of trafficking in human beings.

The first NGO to start work with trafficked persons in 1998 was 'reaching out', from Pitesti. This has an ongoing training programme for 10 social workers and small shelters in three towns outside Bucharest which provide basic assistance and support to trafficked persons. Staff here have developed skills and expertise during the course of their work, but they are not in a position to provide long-term help or support without additional training and financial support. These shelters were supported mainly by the Soros Foundation and have not benefited from the funding designated for anti-trafficking activities in the region. Since 2001, IOM has started to build a new network of NGOs. The Famnet coalition of 13 local NGOs is a network for victim assistance and reintegration. Activities include prevention campaigns, a hotline and website for organisations within the network, shelters for trafficked women and children, and reintegration programmes including schooling and job training. Subsequently, around 20 information events on trafficking took place in schools, using videotape and an anti-trafficking manual.

Source: national reports.

- policy coordination and action between the police, border control, social services and other government agencies, and between the government, NGOs and other relevant parts of civil society such as the media;

- the scale of funding for law enforcement and victim support to be significantly increased in some countries, particularly those where the scale of trafficking is huge and rising;

- more research and information to identify high-risk groups and how trafficking operates in different country contexts;

- wider long-term policies to address the poverty and social exclusion problems of high-risk groups and to reduce their vulnerability to being trafficked (education and active labour market programmes, and support through schools and social services for children in dysfunctional families and institutional care);

- the policy approach to be widened to address the demand from (male) consumers and to criminalise those who buy sex.

8.3. Conclusions

Violence and the sexual abuse of women are widespread, yet the scale of the problem is often underestimated in public policy and is rarely a priority objective accompanied by a comprehensive action programme and adequate budget. The gender dimension is rarely acknowledged explicitly and tackled directly – the fundamental problem is that much of the violence and sexual abuse in society is committed by men against women.

Domestic violence occurs in rich as well as poor families. Women's subordinate status in society can make them more exposed to the risk when political and economic insecurities and deteriorating conditions place additional strains on relationships between women and men. To reduce the social exclusion of victims who are living with domestic violence or trying to escape, a range of legal measures and support services are needed. Policy also needs to address men's behaviour and identify intervention and education measures to reduce male violence.

Trafficking and prostitution are fuelled by poor social and economic conditions in societies. Poverty and unemployment combined with inadequate legal, police and social services create conditions in which traffickers can effectively target disadvantaged groups of young women and children where those who are most vulnerable are the poorly educated, living in areas of high unemployment and poverty, and often lacking family ties and support because they come from families where they have been emotionally deprived or abused.

The causes and conditions of domestic violence and human trafficking and prostitution are in many ways similar from country to country, and this is also the case for other forms of violence and subjugation of women which we have not discussed in this chapter. The differences between countries are the strength and breadth of the legal and policy frameworks for prevention and support, the scale of the problem and, in particular, whether it is a country of origin or destination for trafficking. There may also be national differences in the prevalence of domestic violence but the information is not available to make this assessment.

In most of the national case studies, mention is made that legal frameworks and some victim support measures had been introduced or increased, and public awareness of the problems was growing. However, problems of inadequate resources or poor coordination between the police, the judiciary and support agencies persist. One glaring omission is that efforts are largely targeted at supporting the victims and prosecuting the individuals who commit trafficking or

Box 8.6: Country-specific assessments of priorities for action against trafficking

Bulgaria

- More resources and better coordination is needed between the police, schools and the ministries of education and labour policy.

- A wide-reaching and systematic reform to policy is needed to reduce the risk of women entering trafficking and/or prostitution: family policy reform to provide more protection from abuse and violence; measures to tackle poverty; child protection through schools to make early risk assessments; youth policy to address drug problems.

- Collaboration is needed by the government with the relevant NGOs in order to properly assess the needs of those at risk of trafficking and prostitution.

- Coordination and joint effort are needed across countries.

Cyprus

Some progress has been made in recent years in raising public awareness and in the development of new initiatives but the government has still not grasped the extent of the problem. Particular problems include those listed below:

- more effective collaboration is needed by the government with the relevant NGOs in order to properly assess the needs of those at risk of trafficking and prostitution.

- the government has done little to acknowledge or address the role of the consumer of sex services (men) in contributing to the problem.

Lithuania

Preventative policy measures (long- and short-term) are fairly well integrated into the various national programmes and related activities, such as information campaigns, but:

- there is still a lack of direct measures and resources to assist victims (health, housing, alternative employment);

- the poverty and unemployment of vulnerable groups have to be addressed to make it more difficult for traffickers to operate.

Malta

The National Council for Women has been raising awareness and promoting zero tolerance, and is trying to establish a nation-wide campaign involving government, NGOs and the media. It has identified the following points for action:

- a research and information campaign, so that government agencies and the general public have a better understanding of the problem and the types of policies needed;

- legislation reform, to introduce stronger penalties and more effective implementation;

- the development of social support structures, including rehabilitation programmes for women who want to leave prostitution;

- coordinated networking of government and NGOs, so that they work together more effectively.

Box 8.6: Country-specific assessments of priorities for action against trafficking (continued)

Norway

In order to effectively develop and extend existing measures it is important to:

- synthesise what is already known about trafficking and prostitution and the impact of different policy measures; in particular, there is a shortfall in knowledge regarding how trafficking occurs and how to design counter-trafficking measures;

- collect more accurate estimates of the numbers of victims and their country of origin;

- properly identify risk groups and risk situations;

- ensure a policy distinction between 'free' prostitution and trafficking/forced prostitution and the ways, either differently or the same, in which these are dealt with (stigmatisation and criminalisation of prostitutes only works to marginalise them and make them more vulnerable to exploitation);

- make provision for victims of trafficking and prostitution who want to leave Norway to return home; this should not be done on the condition that they testify;

- address the demand for prostitution as well as the supply and, as part of this shift in policy emphasis, an important element would be to criminalise the purchase of sex services.

Poland

Positive policy developments have taken place in recent years across a number of relevant government agencies (social services, the police, border offices) and other parts of civil society (NGOs, the media). However:

- the government still lacks adequate financial budgets to provide support to victims; for example, there is still a shortage of safe places for women despite the government providing a building to an NGO to convert it into a shelter for trafficking victims;

- more emphasis is needed on prevention through better border controls and introducing monitoring and regulating of all agencies involved in national and cross-border job brokerage;

- wider and longer term preventative measures are needed so that the socioeconomic situation of those considered to be at risk of human trafficking is addressed and improved.

Romania

Positive developments have been put in place in recent years. What is needed is an extension and increased funding of the programmes. In particular, funding and training measures for NGOs are needed to build and extend their pioneering work.

Source: national reports.

domestic violence. What is missing is a more systematic policy approach to address men's behaviour and to reduce the scale of the problem – initiatives targeted at men to stop violent and aggressive behaviour in the home and more widely, and to regulate and reduce the male-dominated consumer demand for the sex industry. More broadly, the linkage between these specific policy areas and reducing gender inequalities are not always made in official policy statements. They need to be, for increasing women's independent economic means and social status is a prerequisite for helping women to avoid or escape abusive situations.

9. Conclusions

Throughout this report we have sought to show that gender differences and inequalities are a fundamental feature of social exclusion and poverty. This is hinted at by the higher at-risk-of-poverty rate recorded for women compared with that for men in most countries. However, the common indicators may underestimate the magnitude of women's greater risk of poverty. This is because resources are not always shared equally within households and women are more likely to 'go without' when money is tight. Clear gender differences are also apparent in many of the other EU common indicators on poverty and social exclusion.

A gender-based analysis is essential for understanding the extent and form of social exclusion among disadvantaged groups within the population, for several distinct reasons.

- Certain vulnerable or disadvantaged groups are numerically dominated by one sex. Many are female dominated, for example lone parents or older persons in low-income households, and women and girls constitute the majority of those who are the victims of domestic violence and sex trafficking. Other situations are male dominated, and include ex-prisoners, some types of homelessness (sleeping rough) and patterns of early school leaving or drug abuse in some countries; and men have a lower average life expectancy.

- A gender perspective remains relevant for analysing vulnerable groups where the membership is more evenly split by sex, for example among the Roma, migrants or disabled persons. This is so that salient differences in the causes, extent and form of social exclusion experienced by women and men can be identified.

- Gender relations, or more precisely men's behaviour, is centrally implicated in a number of social problems: most domestic violence is by men on women; trafficking and prostitution is largely organised and used by men; and, overall, most crime is committed by men (with violent crime and major acts of corporate fraud being particularly male dominated).

Gender-based differences in exposure to different dimensions of social exclusion, for example the particular experiences of women and men from ethnic minority groups is sometimes referred to as a 'double disadvantage' for women who face the additional burden of racism as well as gender discrimination. An alternative, and more nuanced analytical tool is the concept of 'intersectionality', which starts from the premise that people live in multiple, layered identities and are members of more than one 'identity community' at the same time. Hence, gender discrimination, racism, class inequalities and other systems of discrimination structure the relative position of women and men, and combine to push some to the extreme margins of society while others are more included. The result is that women from an ethnic minority group have a substantively distinct experience to that of both men from the same minority group and to women of the ethnic majority group. This conceptual approach also acknowledges that an individual can experience both oppression and privilege in society; for example a woman may occupy a high-status professional position yet still be exposed to racism or domestic violence. Thus, through applying the concept of intersectionality, it is possible to both develop a gender mainstreaming perspective on social inclusion policy and inject a greater awareness of inequalities among women into analysis which focuses on exposing the disadvantaged position of women vis-à-vis men in society.

The report focused on a range of disadvantaged groups identified in social inclusion policies to demonstrate how gender mainstreaming – supported by gender impact analysis – is a necessary tool for analysing the causes and dimensions of social exclusion and poverty, for identifying policy priorities, and for policy design, monitoring and evaluation. Separate chapters discussed gender differences in the poverty risks of younger and older people, long-term unemployment and inactivity, lone parents, the Roma, immigrants and migrants, and violence and abuse against women. The selection covers a wide range of disadvantaged situations, but it was not designed to be a comprehensive review. Rather the case-study focuses have been analysed to expose the main issues to consider as a basis for bringing gender main-

---

Box 9.1: Examples of male-dominated disadvantaged groups

The 'erased' in Slovenia: a male-dominated category

The 'erased' are people from other former Yugoslav republics who are not Slovenian citizens. In 1992, over 18 000 such people who did not apply for Slovene citizenship became illegal residents and lost their social rights. The erased typically came to pre-independent Slovenia as economic migrants, employees of the Yugoslav army or as prisoners. In all these groups the vast majority are men. This 'erasure' was driven by nationalist ideology, has been criticised by Amnesty International and has subsequently been ruled to be illegal by the Constitutional Court in 1999 and 2003. The erased have no right to legal employment, education or state benefits including pensions, and have been subject to wider abuses of their human rights. Since 1999, only 4 000 erased people have had their rights restored, and their situation remains a controversial topic of political and public debate.

The socially excluded 'unattached men' in Estonia

Unattached men are those who are not married (or cohabiting) and have not been employed for a long period. They have low levels of educational attainment and skills, and do not fulfil the traditional male role as breadwinner. They are less likely to contact the state employment office than women who are without employment, due to a combination of reasons including a rejection of state programmes and a conviction that they can manage on their own. These men are a particularly excluded group who are prone to crime, alcoholism, drug abuse and depression and homelessness. They rely on their parents (especially mothers) for support; and if this is not forthcoming many become homeless. Targeted activation policies are required to reintegrate these men into Estonian society.

Source: national reports

---

streaming into social inclusion policy design and monitoring. In particular, for future work in this area it should be noted that gender mainstreaming in relation to people with disabilities was only touched on (in Chapter 4). Other topics such as homelessness or a focus on particularly vulnerable groups of men was not attended to; Boxes 9.1 and 9.2 (p.149) give some brief illustration of why the relevance of gender mainstreaming extends to disadvantaged groups other than those discussed in this report.

More specific conclusions are drawn at the end of each chapter; they are not repeated here. We finish with three general points. Firstly, there is a lack of systematic information on gender disparities for some disadvantaged groups in many countries. This needs to be rectified as a basis for developing gender impact analysis and gender mainstreaming. Simply monitoring average gender differences is ineffective for pinpointing the precise causes and for identifying where progress in closing gender gaps is and is not being made. Secondly, gender mainstreaming emphasises the relevance of a lifecourse perspective for social integration policy; for example the lone parents living in poverty today are likely to become the older women who are particularly at risk of poverty in their old age. Thirdly, some of the problems which women face cannot be fully appreciated and addressed without an international focus. Economic inequalities and political instabilities between countries generate cross-border flows of women from poorer to richer countries: migrant women performing domestic labour and related service jobs, and the explosion of trafficking for prostitution; this also includes the particularly vulnerable situation of women of the Roma, where the scale of the problem equates to a medium-size country when assessed from a European rather than national vantage point.

Box 9.2: Homelessness in Lithuania

Homelessness has increased in Lithuania during the economic and political transition as housing costs have risen and shortages of social housing have increased. There is little reliable data on the number of homeless people in Lithuania. Data from the 2001 census provides a figure of 1 250 people, but this is based on a narrow definition excluding those in temporary shelter and is not disaggregated by gender. Local authority data provide a figure of 2 150, of whom 940 are women.

The causes of homelessness are complex, but research shows that over half of homeless people come from troubled family backgrounds and poor childhood experiences. This commonality coexists with gender differences in the route into homelessness. For men, loss of housing is more often the result of dysfunctional family relations, and homeless men are more likely to be dependent on alcohol (42%) or drugs (4%). Homeless women are less likely to be substance abusers (24% abuse alcohol, 2% drugs) and more likely to have become homeless as a consequence of poverty and low educational attainment.

The experience of homelessness is often worse for women than for men, as they find it harder to adapt to their new situation and social status and find themselves in deeper social exclusion than men. Nearly 30% of homeless women reported that they did not have any income in the week prior to the 2003 survey, compared with 19% of men. Another indicator is health disparities: in subjective assessments of their own health status, the figures for homeless men do not deviate from those of all men in Lithuania, but homeless women regard themselves as being in poorer health.

There are considerable differences by age in the sources of income for homeless women. For those under 30, social benefits (35%) and support of relatives/close friends (29%) are most important; for women aged 30 to 49, earnings from informal work (34%) and salvage (32%) are most important; and for those 50 and over, a pension (32%), informal earnings (30%) and charity (20%) are the chief sources.

The NAP social inclusion policy for homelessness is mostly oriented towards preventing people becoming homeless through increasing social housing stock, rather than on alleviating the poverty of those currently homeless. Policies are lacking for the labour market reintegration of the homeless.

Source: national report.

References

A. National reports

Beleva, I. (2005), *Social inclusion, gender and disadvantaged groups – the Bulgarian national report*, European Commission's Expert Group on Gender, Social Inclusion and Employment report for the 'Equality between women and men' Unit, Employment, Social Affairs and Equal Opportunities DG, European Commission.

Barry, U. and Murphy, S. (2005), *An evaluation of the gender dimension to the National Action Plan for social inclusion 2005 – the Irish national report*, European Commission's Expert Group on Gender, Social Inclusion and Employment report for the 'Equality between women and men' Unit, Employment, Social Affairs and Equal Opportunities DG, European Commission.

Borg, R. (2005), *Social inclusion, gender and disadvantaged groups – the Maltese national report*, European Commission's Expert Group on Gender, Social Inclusion and Employment report for the 'Equality between women and men' Unit, Employment, Social Affairs and Equal Opportunities DG, European Commission.

Ellingsæter, A. L. (2005), *Social inclusion, gender and disadvantaged groups – the Norwegian national report*, European Commission's Expert Group on Gender, Social Inclusion and Employment report for the 'Equality between women and men' Unit, Employment, Social Affairs and Equal Opportunities DG, European Commission.

Emerek, R. (2005), *An evaluation of the gender dimension to the National Action Plan for social inclusion 2005 – the Danish national report*, European Commission's Expert Group on Gender, Social Inclusion and Employment report for the 'Equality between women and men' Unit, Employment, Social Affairs and Equal Opportunities DG, European Commission.

Fagan, C., Rubery, J., Urwin, P. and Donnelly, R. (2005), *An evaluation of the gender dimension to the National Action Plan for social inclusion 2005 – the UK national report*, European Commission's Expert Group on Gender, Social Inclusion and Employment report for the 'Equality between women and men' Unit, Employment, Social Affairs and Equal Opportunities DG, European Commission.

Ferreira, V. (2005), *An evaluation of the gender dimension to the National Action Plan for social inclusion 2005 – the Portuguese national report*, European Commission's Expert Group on Gender, Social Inclusion and Employment report for the 'Equality between women and men' Unit, Employment, Social Affairs and Equal Opportunities DG, European Commission.

Kanjuo Mrcěa, A. (2005), *Social inclusion, gender and disadvantaged groups – the Slovene national report*, European Commission's Expert Group on Gender, Social Inclusion and Employment report for the 'Equality between women and men' Unit, Employment, Social Affairs and Equal Opportunities DG, European Commission.

Kanopiene, V. (2005), *Social inclusion, gender and disadvantaged groups – the Lithuanian national report*, European Commission's Expert Group on Gender, Social Inclusion and Employment report for the 'Equality between women and men' Unit, Employment, Social Affairs and Equal Opportunities DG, European Commission.

Karamessini, M. (2005), *An evaluation of the gender dimension to the National Action Plan for social inclusion 2005 – the Greek national report*, European Commission's Expert Group on Gender, Social Inclusion and Employment report for the 'Equality between women and men' Unit, Employment, Social Affairs and Equal Opportunities DG, European Commission.

Křížková, A. (2005), *Social inclusion, gender and disadvantaged groups – the Czech national report*, European Commission's Expert Group on Gender, Social Inclusion and Employment report for the 'Equality between women and men' Unit, Employment, Social Affairs and Equal Opportunities DG, European Commission.

Laas, A. (2005), *Social inclusion, gender and disadvantaged groups – the Estonian national report*, European Commission's Expert Group on Gender, Social Inclusion and Employment report for the 'Equality between women and men' Unit, Employment, Social Affairs and Equal Opportunities DG, European Commission.

Lehto, A. M. (2005), *An evaluation of the gender dimension to the National Action Plan for social inclusion 2005 – the Finnish national report*, European Commission's Expert Group on Gender, Social Inclusion and Employment report for the 'Equality between women and men' Unit, Employment, Social Affairs and Equal Opportunities DG, European Commission.

Maier, F. (2005), *An evaluation of the gender dimension to the National Action Plan for social inclusion 2005 – the German national report*, European Commission's Expert Group on Gender, Social Inclusion and Employment report for the 'Equality between women and men' Unit, Employment, Social Affairs and Equal Opportunities DG, European Commission.

Mairhuber, I. (2005), *An evaluation of the gender dimension to the National Action Plan for social inclusion 2005 – the Austrian national report*, European Commission's Expert Group on Gender, Social Inclusion and Employment report for the 'Equality between women and men' Unit, Employment, Social Affairs and Equal Opportunities DG, European Commission.

Meulders, D. and de Henau, J. (2005), *An evaluation of the gender dimension to the National Action Plan for social inclusion 2005 – the Belgian national report*, European Commission's Expert Group on Gender, Social Inclusion and Employment report for the 'Equality between women and men' Unit, Employment, Social Affairs and Equal Opportunities DG, European Commission.

Moltó, M. L. and Pazos-Morán, M. (2005), *An evaluation of the gender dimension to the National Action Plan for social inclusion 2005 – the Spanish national report*, European Commission's Expert Group on Gender, Social Inclusion and Employment report for the 'Equality between women and men' Unit, Employment, Social Affairs and Equal Opportunities DG, European Commission.

Mósesdóttir, L. (2005), *Social inclusion, gender and disadvantaged groups – the Icelandic national report*, European Commission's Expert Group on Gender, Social Inclusion and Employment report for the 'Equality between women and men' Unit, Employment, Social Affairs and Equal Opportunities DG, European Commission.

Nagy, B. (2005), *Social inclusion, gender and disadvantaged groups – the Hungarian national report*, European Commission's Expert Group on Gender, Social Inclusion and Employment report for the 'Equality between women and men' Unit, Employment, Social Affairs and Equal Opportunities DG, European Commission.

Nyberg, A. (2005), *An evaluation of the gender dimension to the National Action Plan for social inclusion 2005 – the Swedish national report*, European Commission's Expert Group on Gender, Social Inclusion and Employment report for the 'Equality between women and men' Unit, Employment, Social Affairs and Equal Opportunities DG, European Commission.

Panayiotou, A. (2005), *Social inclusion, gender and disadvantaged groups – the Cypriot national report*, European Commission's Expert Group on Gender, Social Inclusion and Employment report for the 'Equality between women and men' Unit, Employment, Social Affairs and Equal Opportunities DG, European Commission.

Papouschek, U. (2005), *Social inclusion, gender and disadvantaged groups – the Liechtenstein national report*, European Commission's Expert Group on Gender, Social Inclusion and Employment report for the 'Equality between women and men' Unit, Employment, Social Affairs and Equal Opportunities DG, European Commission.

Piscova, M. (2005), *Social inclusion, gender and disadvantaged groups – the Slovakian national report*, European Commission's Expert Group on Gender, Social Inclusion and Employment report for the 'Equality between women and men' Unit, Employment, Social Affairs and Equal Opportunities DG, European Commission.

Plantenga, J., Helming, P. and Remery, C. (2005), *An evaluation of the gender dimension to the National Action Plan for social inclusion 2005 – the Dutch national report*, European Commission's Expert Group on Gender, Social Inclusion and Employment report for the 'Equality between women and men' Unit, Employment, Social Affairs and Equal Opportunities DG, European Commission.

Plasman, R. and Sissoko, S. (2005), *An evaluation of the gender dimension to the National Action Plan for social inclusion 2005 – the Luxembourg national report*, European Commission's Expert Group on Gender, Social Inclusion and Employment report for the 'Equality between women and men' Unit, Employment, Social Affairs and Equal Opportunities DG, European Commission.

Plomien, A. (2005), *Social inclusion, gender and disadvantaged groups – the Polish national report*, European Commission's Expert Group on Gender, Social Inclusion and Employment report for the 'Equality between women and men' Unit, Employment, Social Affairs and Equal Opportunities DG, European Commission.

Silvera, R. (2005), *An evaluation of the gender dimension to the National Action Plan for social inclusion 2005 – the French national report*, European Commission's Expert Group on Gender, Social Inclusion and Employment report for the 'Equality between women and men' Unit, Employment, Social Affairs and Equal Opportunities DG, European Commission.

Trapenciere, I. (2005), *Social inclusion, gender and disadvantaged groups – the Latvian national report*, European Commission's Expert Group on Gender, Social Inclusion and Employment report for the 'Equality between women and men' Unit, Employment, Social Affairs and Equal Opportunities DG, European Commission.

Villa, P. (2005), *An evaluation of the gender dimension to the National Action Plan for social inclusion 2005 – the Italian national report*, European Commission's Expert Group on Gender, Social Inclusion and Employment report for the 'Equality between women and men' Unit, Employment, Social Affairs and Equal Opportunities DG, European Commission.

Zamfir, E. (2005), *Social inclusion, gender and disadvantaged groups – the Romanian national report*, European Commission's Expert Group on Gender, Social Inclusion and Employment report for the 'Equality between women and men' Unit, Employment, Social Affairs and Equal Opportunities DG, European Commission.

B.   Additional bibliography

Anxo, D., and Fagan, C. (2005) 'The family, the state and now the market – home care services for the elderly' in G. Bosch and S. Lehndorff (eds.) *Working in the service sector – a tale from different worlds*, Routledge

AWID – Association of for Women's Rights in Development (2004) 'Intersectionality: A Tool for Gender and Economic Justice' *Women's Rights and Economic Change*, no.9, August 2004, http://www.awid.org, accessed November 3rd, 2005

Barany, Z. (1998) 'Ethnic mobilization and the state: the Roma in Eastern Europe' *Ethnic and Racial Studies*, 21, 2, March, pp308-327

Bogdanić, A. (2005) 'The Croatian National Programme for the Roma: An Example of Gender Inequality?' *Monitoring human rights and the rule of law in Europe*, www.eumap.org/journal/features/2005/romadec/Bogdanic.pdf

Bradshaw, J., Finch, N., Kemp, P., Mayhew, E. and Williams, J. (2003) *Gender and poverty in Britain*, Working paper servies, no. 6, Equal Opportunities Commission: Manchester.

Carrington, K., and Hearn, J. (2003) 'Trafficking and the sex industry: from impunity to protection' *Current Issues Brief* Index no 28, 2002-2003, Parliament of Australia Parliamentary Library http://www.aph.gov.au/library/pubs/CIB/2002-03/03cib28.htm#size

Council of the European Union (2002) 'Fight against poverty and social exclusion: common objectives for the second round of the National Action Plans – endorsement' 1416/1/02 REV 1 (SOC 508), Brussels, November

Crisis (1999), *Out of Sight, Out of Mind? The experiences of homeless women*, London: Crisis.

Crisis (2005), *Homeless Women*, London: Crisis http://www.crisis.org.uk/research/fact_files/women.php

Dale, A. and Holdsworth. C. (1998) 'Why don't minority ethnic women in Britain work part-time?' in J. O'Reilly and C. Fagan (eds.) *Part-time Prospects: an international comparison of part-time work in Europe, North America and the Pacific Rim*, Routledge

Equal Opportunities Commission (2003), 'Gender and poverty in Britain', Research key findings, www.eoc.org.uk/research

Esping-Andersen, G. (1990), *Three Worlds of Welfare Capitalism*, Cambridge: Policy Press.

European Commission (2005), *Indicators for monitoring the 2004 Employment Guidelines: 2005 Compendium* 14/10/2005.

European Commission (2005), *Report on social inclusion 2005: An analysis of the National Action Plans on Social Inclusion (2004-2006) submitted by the 10 new Member States,* Luxembourg: Office for Official Publications of the European Union.

European Commission (2004), *Joint report on social inclusion 2004,* Luxembourg: Office for Official Publications of the European Union.

European Commission (2004), *The Situation of Roma in an Enlarged European Union*, Luxembourg: Office for Official Publications of the European Union.

European Commission (2002), *Joint report on social inclusion,* Luxembourg: Office for Official Publications of the European Communities.

Eurostat (2005), 'Euro-zone and EU-25 unemployment stable at 8.9% ', Euro-Indicators News Release, 7 January. http://epp.eurostat.cec.eu.int/cache/ITY_PUBLIC/3-07012005-AP/EN/3-07012005-AP-EN.PDF

Fagan, C. (2001), *Gender, Employment and working-time preferences in Europe*, Luxembourg: Office for Official Publications for the European Communities. www.eurofound.eu.int/publications

Fagan, C. and Burchell, B. (2002), *Gender, Jobs and Working Conditions in Europe*, Luxembourg: Office for Official Publications for the European Communities. www.eurofound.eu.int/publications

Fagan, C., O'Reilly, J and B. Halpin (2005), 'Job opportunities for whom?' *Labour market dynamics and service sector employment growth in Germany and Britain*, Anglo-German Foundation

Fagan, C. and Hebson, G. (2006), *'Making work pay' debates from a gender perspective: a comparative review of some recent policy reforms in thirty European countries*, Luxembourg: Office for Official Publications of the European Communities.
http://europa.eu.int/comm/employment_social/gender_equality/docs/exp_group_report_en.pdf

Francesconi, M., and Gosling, A. (2005), *Career paths of part-time workers*, Equal Opportunities Commission working Paper Series no. 19, www.eoc.org.uk

George, S. (2001), 'Why Intersectionality Works', *Women in Action*, No 2, 2001, http://www.isiswomen.org, accessed November 3rd, 2005

Giddens, A., (1994), 'Living in a Post-Traditional Society', in Beck, U., Giddens, A. and Lash, S. *Reflexive Modernization. Politics, Tradition and Aesthetics in the Modern Social Order*, Cambridge: Polity Press.

Ginn, J., and Arber, S. (1998), 'How does part-time work lead to low pension income?' in J. O'Reilly and C. Fagan (eds.) *Part-time Prospects – an international comparison of part-time work in Europe, North America and the Pacific Rim*, Routledge.

Glendinning, C. and J. Millar (eds.) (1987), *Women and Poverty in Britain,* Brighton: Wheatsheaf.

Glendinning, C. and J. Millar (eds.) (1992), *Women and Poverty in Britain: the 1990s,* London: Harvester Wheatsheaf.

Lewis, J. (2001), 'The decline of the male breadwinner model: implications for work and care', *Social Politics*, Summer, 8, 152-169.

Lewis, J. (ed.) (1997), *Lone Mothers in European Welfare Regimes: Shifting Policy Logics*, London: Jessica Kingsley.

Lewis, J. and Hobson, B. (1997), 'Introduction' in Lewis, J. (ed.) *Lone Mothers in European Welfare Regimes: Shifting Policy Logics*, London: Jessica Kingsley.

Machiels, T. (2002), *Keeping the Distance or Taking the Chances: Roma and Travellers in Western Europe*, published by the European Network Against Racism (ENAR) with the financial support of the European Commission.

Millar, J. and Rowlingson, K. (eds.) (2001), *Lone Parents, Employment and Social Policy: Cross-national comparisons*, Bristol: Policy Press.

OECD (2005), *Pensions at a Glance: Public Policies Across OECD Countries.* OECD Publications.

Perić, T. (2005), 'Addressing gender inequality in the Decade of Roma Inclusion: the case of Serbia' *Monitoring human rights and the rule of law in Europe*, www.eumap.org/journal/features/2005/romadec/peric.pdf.

Plantenga, J., and Remery, C. (2005), *Reconciliation of work and private life: a comparative review of thirty European countries*, Luxembourg: Office for Official Publications of the European Communities, http://europa.eu.int/comm/employment_social/gender_equality/docs/exp_group_report_en.pdf

Rowlingson, K. (2001), 'The social, economic and demographic profile of lone parents', in Millar, J. and Rowlingson, K. (eds.) *Lone Parents, Employment and Social Policy: Cross-national comparisons,* Bristol: Policy Press.

Rubery, J., Smith, M., Figueiredo, H., Fagan, C. and Grimshaw, D. (2003), *Gender Mainstreaming and the European Employment Strategy and Social Inclusion Process,* report for the "Equality between women and men" Unit, DG Employment, Social Affairs, and Equal Opportunities, European Commission, February.

Rubery, J., Grimshaw, D., Smith, M. and Figueiredo, H. (2004), *Gender Mainstreaming and the European Employment Strategy,* Prepared by the co-ordinating team of the EU Expert Group on Gender, Social Inclusion and Employment (EGGSIE) to the "Equality between women and men: Strategy and Programme" Unit, DG Employment, Social Affairs and Equal Opportunities, European Commission, November.

Women and Equality Unit (2004) *Interim Update of Key Indicators of Women's Position in Britain*, December, http://www.womenandequalityunit.gov.uk/research/keyindicators_womens_position_interim_dec04.pdf

Appendices

Appendix 1. The gender and social inclusion work programme 2005–06

Part A. Context and key challenges

Identify the key challenges and recent trends with regard to social inclusion in the Member State, with particular reference to the objective of promoting gender equality. To do this, you may find it helpful to include a summary of basic contextual trends with reference to the available EU harmonised indicators: macro-economic (e.g. economic growth, inflation, employment growth), demographic (e.g. trends in population size, age structure, fertility, migration) and social protection (e.g. trends in expenditure, care services).

The objective of promoting gender equality is usually expressed in terms of reducing gender gaps in the risks of exposure to poverty and social exclusion (outcomes). A GM perspective emphasises that there are two related aspects to tackling gender gaps, and these different aspects may be helpful to think about when preparing this section:

* reducing the impact of the exposure to such risks, for example through carers' benefits, without necessarily tackling the processes which create gender differentiated exposures;

* reducing gender gaps in the risks of exposure to poverty and social exclusion (outcomes) through tackling the processes which situate men and women unequally (unequal treatment in the labour market, unequal division of care responsibilities within families and neighbourhoods).

National data on trends in social inclusion with respect to gender should be provided where possible. You should also refer to the available EU common indicators, particularly where national data do not exist (if you identify problems with the EU indicators in comparison to alternative national sources then it will be helpful to mention these). The relevant EU indicators and sources are presented in the section 'Guidelines for preparing Part A' (see above).

While in most situations the gender gaps mean that women are the disadvantaged group, this is not always the case. Where men are the relatively disadvantaged group, this should also be discussed.

This section of the report should consider the following points, with an emphasis on providing available national data that enhance the picture obtained from the EU indicators and are of particular relevance/priority for the socioeconomic situation and policy debates in your country:

* levels and trends in employment, unemployment and inactivity rates for disadvantage groups by gender;

* indicators of earnings levels (minimum wages; average earnings and gender wage gaps) to provide context to any discussion of income or benefit levels presented in the case studies;

* comparison of poverty rates for different disadvantaged groups (including analysis of the available EU indicators which are relevant for gender mainstreaming social inclusion debates) supplement the information from the EU indicators with national information where the data are available from other surveys or smaller scale studies;

* absolute and relative size of disadvantaged groups of women, according to data availability and policy relevance for unemployment, inactivity, young women (15 to 24 years), older women of working age (55 to 64 years), older women (65 years and over), rates of lone parenthood, the Roma population (with gender

breakdown if relevant), other disadvantaged ethnic minority groups (with gender breakdown if relevant), the size of the rural population (with gender breakdown if relevant), the disabled population by gender, women in trafficking and prostitution, homelessness by gender (please include details of how 'homelessness' is defined and how the data was collected in the sources used), domestic violence by gender (please include details of how 'domestic violence' is defined and how the data were collected in the sources used, for example: are they based on reported crime, and underestimate the true level, or on a national survey which usually reveals a higher rate?).

Based on the above discussion, **national experts for the pre-2004 Member States should select one or two groups** of disadvantaged women for a detailed focus in Part B; the **national experts for the other Member States and non-EU countries should select three or four groups** (the pre-2004 Member States are asked to do fewer case studies because they had the additional work programme for the evaluation of the NAPs/social inclusion implementation reports submitted by their governments in 2005).

- The long-term unemployed and/or inactive women (including issues of hidden unemployment within inactivity)

- Women in the Roma

- Women from other disadvantaged ethnic minority groups resident (with or without citizenship) in the country

- Immigrant/migrant women

- Lone parents

- Young women (15 to 24 years)

- Older women (aged 55+ years)

- Women in rural areas

- Women in trafficking and prostitution

- Women with disabilities

The selection should be made on the basis of two considerations, which you should include in a statement of the rationale for your selection.

1. The importance of the group in your country in terms of size, rapid increase in size and/or severity of deprivation could be one reason.

2. The availability of information, including qualitative information from research reports could also figure. Please note and mention any groups which have particular disadvantaged conditions but where the lack of information prohibits their selection for analysis in Part C;

3. You should select either three groups for a detailed focus (minimum five pages per group = 15 pages in total) **or** four groups, where two are discussed in detail and two are for a shorter discussion (five pages each for groups 1 and 2; 2.5 pages each for groups 3 and 4 = 15 pages in total).

Part B: Case-study focus on disadvantaged groups of women

Some of the groups listed are more difficult to locate secondary source material on than others – because there are limited statistical sources or research reports which focus on the group in question. For these groups you will need to search more widely for information, searching for smaller qualitative or local studies, or contacting relevant NGOs for information. It is important to try and get some information on such groups to raise their visibility in policy debates, **so experts who are required to prepare three or four case studies are asked to include at least one of the more difficult groups to research in their selection, which are indicated by an * in the list below.**

Disadvantaged groups of women

*   The long-term unemployed and/or inactive women (including issues of hidden unemployment within inactivity)
*   Women in the Roma *
*   Women from other disadvantaged ethnic minority groups resident (with or without citizenship) in the country *
*   Immigrant/migrant women *
*   Lone parents
*   Young women (15 to 24 years)
*   Older women (aged 55+ years)
*   Women in rural areas *

Women in trafficking and prostitution *

Case study

For each of the disadvantaged groups, the case study should provide the points indicated below.

B.1. Profile of their situation

Information on the size of the group and whether it is growing or stable; discuss the reasons for these trends, elaborating with reference to relevant studies which exist in your country.

B.2. Main forms of particular disadvantage faced in the labour market and wider society

Analysis of employment patterns, income levels and poverty rates; other indicators of deprivation or well-being should be presented where possible (e.g. education/qualifications, health, housing conditions). The focus of your discussion should be on the issues faced by this particular group rather than a discussion of the issues faced by women in general.

B.3. Limitations in current policy provision

Limitations in the current policy provisions for the disadvantaged group in question in terms of:

(a) access/eligibility problems

(b) content/relevance/level of resourcing of any provision targeted to their situation.

In your discussion you should focus mainly on why provision is inadequate in relation to other more advantaged groups in the society (i.e. a relative 'disadvantaged gap') rather than general arguments about unemployment benefits being too low for all the unemployed.

Note: you are **not** expected to discuss every policy area in detail, but to focus on the ones which are of particular relevance for this disadvantaged group. The policy programmes to consider for their relevance are: active labour market programmes; care services to facilitate employment and job search; education and training (including e-learning and lifelong learning); social protection systems and minimum income guarantees (adequacy of protection from poverty risks compared with other groups who are non-employed); minimum wage protection – if employed are they covered by this safety net, or vulnerable to exclusion (e.g. through informal work, employer non-compliance in the parts of the economy they are typically employed in); housing conditions; health services; other services (e.g. transport, legal services).

B.4. Concluding assessment of the direction that should be developed in policy in order to reduce the disadvantage experienced by this particular group of women

Issues to consider here include:

- Is lack of access to the available employment a problem? ➜ Measures to raise their employment rate (access to active labour market programmes, education, care services, legal services, etc.).

- Is the problem more to do with the poor quality of employment options for this disadvantaged group rather than a low employment rate? ➜ Measures to improve access to good quality employment (not just supply-side, but also protection by existing minimum wage and labour laws in countries where coverage is uneven, perhaps because of the size of the informal economy, prevalence of small firms).

- Is the problem that there is a higher exposure to poverty risks when not employed than for other non-employed groups? ➜ Measures to target benefit development (e.g. additional benefits for lone parents, provision for interrupted work histories which were due to care responsibilities).

- Is the problem that housing, health or other services do not make provision for the special needs of the disadvantaged group (e.g. the particular needs of older women)?

Table A1. The disadvantaged groups which were the focus in the national reports

AT	Immigrant/migrant women
BE	Immigrant/migrant women
BG	Long-term unemployed women, Roma women, single mothers, trafficking and prostitution of women
CY	Roma women, immigrant/migrant women, trafficking and prostitution of women
CZ	The long-term unemployed, Roma women, older women
DE	Immigrant/migrant women – including a focus on young women
DK	Immigrant/migrant women
EE	Lone parents, early school-leavers, unattached men

EL	Roma women, domestic violence
ES	Women in one-adult households – with a focus on lone parents and older women
FI	Lone parents
FR	Immigrant/migrant women
HU	Roma women, lone mothers, inactive women
IE	Lone parents, women with disabilities
IS	Young women (16 to 24 years), older women (55 to 64 years), immigrant/migrant women
IT	Immigrant/migrant women
LI	Lone parents
LT	Lone parents, trafficking and prostitution of women, the homeless
LU	Lone parents
LV	Long-term unemployed women, ethnic minority women, young women, disabled women
MT	The long-term unemployed, lone parents, trafficking and prostitution of women, domestic violence
NL	Immigrant/migrant women
NO	Lone parents, trafficking and prostitution of women, immigrant/migrant women
PL	Long-term unemployed and inactive women, trafficking and prostitution of women, rural women
PT	Immigrant/migrant women
RO	Roma women, trafficking and prostitution, domestic violence
SE	Lone parents
SI	Roma women, women with disabilities, women in rural areas and 'erased' men
SK	The long-term unemployed, Roma women
UK	Lone parents

Table A2. Gender pay gaps as a key source of poverty risks during working age and retirement

A. Gender pay gap: difference between men's and women's average gross hourly earnings (for paid employees at work 15+ hours), 2003

AT	17		IT	6 [(1)]
BE	12 [(1)]		LT	17
CY	25		LU	15
CZ	19		LV	16
DE	23		MT	4
DK	18		NL	18
EE	24		PL	11
EL	11		PT	9
ES	18		SE	16
FI	20		SI	9 [(2)]
FR	12		SK	23
HU	14		UK	22
IE	14		EU	15

(1) 2001 data.
(2) 2002 data.
Source: European Commission (2005), Indicators for monitoring the 2004 employment guidelines: 2005 compendium, Key indicator 28, p. 50.

B. National information on gender pay gaps and trends in income inequalities

AT	Inequality in income distribution has increased in recent decades. The gender pay gap is partly a consequence of women being employed in lower-paid sectors and being more likely to work part-time.
BE	Expert gives gender pay gap figure of 15% for 2002.
BG	In the late 1990s and early 2000s, women earned on average around 75% of male monthly full-time earnings. In some sectors (manufacturing, health and social work, wholesale and retail trade) women had lower earnings than the average in relation to those of men, and in others (hotels and restaurants, real estate) they had better than average. In 2002, the figure was 82% , showing that the gap persists but is declining. Women with a higher level of educational qualification earn an amount closer to that of their male counterparts.
CY	The minimum wage is expected to increase to 46% of the national median wage this year, closer to the target of 50% by 2008. Women earn approximately 73% of male pay for comparable jobs and skills. The gender wage gap is partly due to the sectoral distribution of male and female employees, as research indicates that women with the same education, age and other characteristics earn 25% less than men in the public sector and 40% less in the private sector. This is partly a consequence of women being more likely to be employed on a part-time or temporary basis.
CZ	Women earn around 75% of male average full-time earnings, with those aged 35 to 39 earning only 66.3%, and those aged 20 to 24 earning the highest proportion, at 89.7%. The higher the level of education, the larger the gender pay gap. Among those with a university education, women earn only 67.3% of annual full-time male earnings. The trend between 1995 and 2001 has been one of a widening gender pay gap, linked, according to the expert, to greater individualism and competitiveness in Czech society.
DE	Gender pay gaps are lower in former East Germany than in former West Germany. In 2002, among manufacturing and some service-sector workers, the gender pay gaps were 22.1% in the east and 25.7% in the west. Among salaried employees, the figures were 22.9% in the east and 29.5% in the west.
DK	There is a gender pay gap in Denmark, but there is the highest level of income equality between rich and poor of any EU country. The expert illustrates the compressed wage structure by pointing out that average hourly pay is only twice the level of minimum pay.
EE	Average and minimum wage levels have increased in Estonia in the period 1998–2004 by 77% and 125% respectively. The proportion of households with per capita income equal to the gross minimum wage increased from 28.5% in 2000 to 46% in 2003.
EL	Minimum wage levels are set through collective bargaining, but reflect individual experience, marital status and number of dependent children.
ES	The gender pay gap for 2002 was 19%, with the gap being 18% for full-time and 34% for part-time work.
FI	Over the past 10 years, data have consistently shown women to earn 80% of male earnings. Finland has a low Gini coefficient by international standards, although there was a period of growing income inequality following the recession of the early 1990s and 2000, due to rapid growth in capital income among higher income groups.
FR	Women employees are twice as likely as men to be paid at the level of the minimum wage (SMIC): 20% of women and 10% of men. Data for full-time employees shows a large gender pay gap among executives (23%) and a smaller gap among service and clerical workers (7%).
HU	The monthly minimum wage in Hungary almost doubled in value between 2001 and 2005, one effect of which has been a condensing of wage differentials. A specific minimum wage rate was introduced for people with a degree in the public sector in 2002, which can be expected to have had a beneficial impact on previously badly paid teachers and nurses. On average, women receive 85% of male earnings, but in white-collar jobs the figure is only 64 to 67% , as women are over-represented in routine administrative jobs.
IE	Ireland has an unequal income distribution, with the top income groups having almost five times more income than the lowest income group in 2003. The minimum wage, introduced in 2000, is an important safeguard for the low-paid, but requires stronger and more effective enforcement to protect women and migrant workers in particular.

IS	The gender pay gap fell from 45% in 1992 to 37% in 2002 as women increased their engagement in the labour market, especially in terms of hours. Data on income distribution over the period 1995–2002 shows a mixed story, as the relatively poor among the poor have been increasing at the same time as those who are relatively rich have become more equal.
IT	Labour market earnings stagnated in the period 1993–2003, with no evidence of a rise in income inequality or poverty levels over this period.
LI	There is no published data on income distribution, but there can be assumed to be a gender pay gap as women are more likely to work part-time and are predominantly employed in certain sectors (such as 'home and health'). Women are very much under-represented in senior management positions in public institutions.
LT	Income inequality has remained relatively stable over the past six years, with a Gini coefficient of 0.3 in 2002.
LU	A higher number of men than women receive pay at the level of the statutory minimum wage, but a higher proportion of female employees (22%) than male employees (13%) receive the minimum wage. Women in Luxembourg earn on average 85% of the earnings of their male counterparts, but among civil servants the gender pay gap is in favour of women (103.5%). There is a wage differential between cross-border workers and residents, in favour of residents.
LV	Earnings have increased in the past five years but over a similar period income inequality has also grown.
MT	The expert provides data showing that, early in 2005, women earned on average 85% of male gross annual earnings.
NO	Over a 30-year period from 1973, the gender gap in annual earnings declined from 45% to between 30 and 35%. A significant part of the reduction has been caused by a decline in the gender difference in weekly working hours, and there has been no systematic reduction in the gender difference in hourly wages since 1985. Over a similar time period, income inequality among women has declined dramatically as more women now have an income still few women earning high incomes.
NL	The relative value of the minimum wage fell in the period 1990–2001. Over this time, the median income of the population increased by almost 15%, while the minimum wage increased by only 5%. A higher share of female employees (5.4%) than male employees (3.2%) are paid at the level of the minimum wage.
PL	In the period 1982–91, the gender pay gap was stable and women earned 68% of male wages. On the balance of evidence, it appears that there was a post-transformation drop in the gender pay gap, so female wages reached around 80% of male earnings in 1992, but the bulk of this change occurred in 1989 when state-owned enterprises were reducing their labour costs. Male jobs and wages were cut, and a fraction of well-educated women entered lucrative positions at this time. Since this period, the wage differential has only narrowed at a slow pace if at all, so the 2002 figure was 83%. The 2002 data shows that women earned 78.4% of men's wages in the public sector and 83.6% in the private sector. A minimum wage has been in operation since 1956, and was at the level of 35.3% of average income in 2004. Approximately 4% of workers receive the minimum wage, but the number of people in the low-wage sector is boosted by the grey economy.
PT	Differential minimum wage rates applying to different sectors were unified in 2004 in the 'monthly minimum pay'. Women are more likely than men to be paid at this level; 8.1% of women and 4.3% of men receive the 'monthly minimum pay'. The expert presents figures for 2003 showing a gender gap among full-time workers of 19.4% and an overall gap of 22.7%.
RO	The real value of the minimum wage fell between 1990 and 1999 but has since been increased by more than the expected rate of inflation.
SE	Sweden does not have a statutory minimum wage, but minimums are set through collective agreements. Younger female workers earn a higher percentage of the male hourly rate than do older female workers. The figures are 87 to 92% for the age group 18 to 44, 83 to 85% for those aged 45 to 54, and 73 to 74% for those aged 55 to 64. However, women work shorter hours than men on average, so the gender gap in annual earnings is wider.
SI	Wages are calculated in accordance with collective agreements, and where this level is below the national minimum wage (introduced in 1995) the employer must pay the difference. In 2004, 2.9% of private-sector employees received the minimum wage. In the highly feminised textile industry, this figure reached 11%. The existence of the minimum wage can be seen as improving gender equality among low-paid workers,

	but there are no gender disaggregated data available on minimum wage recipients. Data for 2002 show that women earned 90.47% of male monthly gross earnings, but among those with a university degree the figure was 80.31%.
SK	The minimum wage in Slovakia is at a low level but even so the employers' association has called for its abolition. The gender pay gap is widest in occupations that require high qualification levels, with female wages reaching only 61.9% of the male average. On average, women work only less than one hour less per week than men, so working time differences only account for a small part of the gender gap.
UK	The gender pay gap, measured as the median hourly pay of full-time employees, narrowed in 2003–04 to its lowest level since records began. This may in part reflect the introduction and up-rating of the national minimum wage, which benefits more women than men. However, 1.1% of jobs remain paid at a level below the NMW, disproportionately affecting women (1.4%). Furthermore, when part-time workers are included in statistics, the gender pay gap is wider, as women are more likely to work part-time, and part-time work is more likely to be low paid.

Appendix 2. Available national estimates of the size of some of the main disadvantaged groups of women at risk of poverty and social exclusion

Note: the full source details are in the national reports.

Austria

Available national estimates of the size of some of the main disadvantaged groups of women at risk of poverty and social exclusion in Austria

Unemployed women

4.6% (81 000) of women were unemployed in 2003.

Inactive working-age women

35.8% of women. *Source: 2005 statistical compendium.*

Young women (16 to 24 years)

482 777 women.

Older women aged 55+ years

1 030 817 women.

Lone parents

There were 3 336 700 lone-parent households in Austria in 2002. 7% of households are headed by single mothers and 2% of households are headed by single fathers.

The Roma population

No data provided.

Other disadvantaged ethnic minority groups

No data provided.

Migrants

2003: 759 567 immigrants (9.4% of the population), 9.8% of whom were unemployed.

The rural population

No data provided.

People with disabilities

No data provided on absolute size.

Women in trafficking and prostitution

No data provided.

Homelessness

No data provided.

Domestic violence

No data provided.

Austrian population

No data provided.

Belgium

Available national estimates of the size of some of the main disadvantaged groups of women at risk of poverty and social exclusion in Belgium

Unemployed women

9% (170 695) of women.

Inactive working-age women

43% (1 453 983) of women.

Young women (16 to 24 years)

12% (618 323) of women.

Older women aged 55+ years

Aged 55 to 64 years: 570 829 (11% of women); aged 65+ years: 1 044 113 (20% of women).

Lone parents

163 000 lone-parent households; the majority (93%) are headed by women (126 480 lone mothers and 9 520 lone fathers).

The Roma population

There are estimated to be 10 000 to 15 000 Roma in Belgium (0.1% of the population).

Other disadvantaged ethnic minority groups

No data provided.

Migrants

No data provided.

The rural population

< 100 000 people in Belgium live in rural areas.

People with disabilities

1 138 750 disabled people in Belgium: 593 834 male, 548 580 female.

Women in trafficking and prostitution

An estimated 10 500 and 14 000 women are prostitutes.

Homelessness

More than a third of homeless people are women.

Domestic violence

More than one-third of women in Belgium experience domestic violence.

Population of Belgium

10.4 million: 5.3 million women, 5.1 million men.

Bulgaria

Available national estimates of the size of some of the main disadvantaged groups of women at risk of poverty and social exclusion in Bulgaria

Unemployed women

End 2003: 203 000 (45.2% of all unemployed).

Inactive working-age women

In December 2003, economic *activity* figures were 64.8% (M) and 55.7% (F).

Young women (16 to 24 years)

No data provided.

Older women aged 55+ years

No data provided.

Lone parents

290 028 single parent households (12.24% of all households), 82.83% of single parent households are headed by a female.

Bulgaria (continued)

The Roma population
Approximagely 371 356 Roma, of whom 184 564 (49.7%) are women. 4.5% of all women are Roma.

Other disadvantaged ethnic minority groups
No data provided.

Migrants
No data provided.

The rural population
No data provided.

People with disabilities
No data provided.

Women in trafficking and prostitution
No data provided.

Homelessness
No data provided.

Domestic violence
No data provided.

Population of Bulgaria
Approximately 7.75 million (based on Figure 1).

Cyprus

Available national estimates of the size of some of the main disadvantaged groups of women at risk of poverty and social exclusion in Cyprus

Unemployed women
Recorded total unemployment rate: 4.3% in 2004. The figure is higher for women, at 4.6% in 2003 and 5.4% in 2004.

Inactive working-age women
No data provided.

Young women (16 to 24 years)
No data provided.

Older women aged 55+ years
Approximately 82 500 people over 65, the majority of whom are women.

Lone parents
No data provided.

The Roma population
Data on the Roma are not accurate but one estimate is approximately 700 individuals.

Other disadvantaged ethnic minority groups
There are currently about 10 000 Turkish Cypriots employed in the government-controlled part of Cyprus but it is believed that the number is much higher since most may be employed illegally, especially in low-skill jobs, and are not registered to receive benefits from the Social Insurance Fund. The majority of Turkish Cypriots working in the south are men, mostly in construction and other manual labour type jobs.

Migrants
Foreign workers constituted 12.9% of the employed labour force in 2003.

The rural population
No data provided.

People with disabilities
No data provided.

Women in trafficking and prostitution
Estimated at around 3 000 women (employed legally).

Cyprus (continued)

Homelessness
No data provided.

Domestic violence
No data provided.

Population of Cyprus
688 000 in 2003 in the government-controlled part of Cyprus.

Czech Republic

Available national estimates of the size of some of the main disadvantaged groups of women at risk of poverty and social exclusion in the Czech Republic

Unemployed women
There are 216 900 unemployed women in the Czech Republic. Women constitute 50.5% of all unemployed.

Inactive working-age women
Of 4 496 200 women in the Czech Republic over the age of 15, 2 240 300 (49.8%) are economically inactive.

Young women (16 to 24 years)
Out of a total population of 5 237 100 women in the Czech Republic, young women make up 12.7% , and women aged 15 to 24 make up 14.8% of the economically active population.

Older women aged 55+ years
Out of a total population of 5 237 100 women, 13.4% are women aged 55 to 64 and 16.7% are women over 65. As regards economically active women, 15.5% are aged 55 to 64 and 19.5% are 65 years and over.

Lone parents
Out of a total of 3 983 800 households in the Czech Republic, 434 400 are single-parent families, which equals 10.7% of all households. According to data from the 2001 census, 88% of single-parent nuclear families were headed by women and 12% by men. The absolute number of single-parent families in the Czech Republic is 343 405.

The Roma population
Data from the 2001 census show a Roma population of 32 903, of whom 16 031 (48.72%) are women. On these figures, Roma constitute 0.3% of the population. However, the real number is estimated at 160 000 to 200 000 people.

Other disadvantaged ethnic minority groups
No data provided.

Migrants
No data provided.

The rural population
No data provided.

People with disabilities
A study commissioned by the Ministry of Labour and Social Affairs is currently under way on 'An analysis of the causes of low employment rates among disabled women'. The NAP/inclusion cites figures from 1993 indicating 1 200 000 persons, which is about 10% of the population of the Czech Republic. No reliable sources of statistical data on disabled persons differentiated by gender exist.

Women in trafficking and prostitution
No data provided.

Homelessness
No data provided.

Domestic violence
The International Violence Against Women Survey (IVAWS), conducted in the Czech Republic in 2003, revealed that out of a representative sample of 1 980 women, 38% had at some point in their lives experienced violence within a partner relationship.

Population of the Czech Republic
10 302 215 in the 2001 census.

Denmark

Available national estimates of the size of some of the main disadvantaged groups of women at risk of poverty and social exclusion in Denmark

Unemployed women
There are 100 770 unemployed women of working age in Denmark (1.9% of the working-age population).

Inactive working-age women
There are 476 500 inactive women of working age in Denmark (8.8% of the working-age population).

Young women (16 to 24 years)
There are 261 438 young women in Denmark.

Older women aged 55+ years
There are 398 514 women aged 55 to 66 and 408 458 women aged over 67.

Lone parents
There are 131 734 lone parents in Denmark; 113 734 are women.

The Roma population
There are estimated to be 2 000 Roma in Denmark.

Other disadvantaged ethnic minority groups
Descendants from western countries: 14 885 (7 256 are women).
Descendants from non-western countries: 89 239 (43 670 are women).

Migrants
Migrants from western countries: 113 965 (61 186 are women).
Migrants from non-western countries: 223 837 (111 411 are women).

The rural population
No data provided.

People with disabilities
No data provided.

Women in trafficking and prostitution
7 000 women are estimated to be in prostitution.

Homelessness
No data provided.

Domestic violence
65 000 women have experienced domestic violence.

Population of Denmark
5 397 640 persons: 2 727 505 women, 2 670 135 men

Estonia

Available national estimates of the size of some of the main disadvantaged groups of women at risk of poverty and social exclusion in Estonia

Unemployed women
2004: 11 200 Estonian females; 17 700 non-Estonian women.

Inactive working-age women
2004: 197 400.

Young women (16 to 24 years)
No data provided.

Older women aged 55+ years
No data provided.

Lone parents
According to data from the civil census in 2000, single-parent families form 15% of households (13% are single mothers and 1.4% are single fathers). In 2000, there were 229 932 households with children aged under 25 (the total number of households was 386 970). According to these data, the number of lone parents is about 34 500 in Estonia.

Estonia (continued)

The Roma population

No data provided.

Other disadvantaged ethnic minority groups

No data provided.

Migrants

No data provided.

The rural population

2000 census: 446 841, of whom 230 505 are women.

People with disabilities

In 2004, there were 3 108 disabled women and 3 774 disabled men aged under 63. New rules for determining incapacity benefit eligibility in 2000 have reduced the number of people classified as disabled by over a half.

Women in trafficking and prostitution

An estimated 500 females of Estonian origin are victims of human trafficking annually. Survey evidence claims there are more than 1 000 prostitutes in Tallinn.

Homelessness

No data provided.

Domestic violence

No data provided.

Population of Estonia

2000 census: 1 370 052 of whom 738 201 are women.

Finland

Available national estimates of the size of some of the main disadvantaged groups of women at risk of poverty and social exclusion in Finland

Unemployed women

111 000 (8.9% of women).

Inactive working-age women

In 2004, there were 723 000 inactive women.

Young women (16 to 24 years)

No data provided.

Older women aged 55+ years

No data provided.

Lone parents

2.8% of Finnish households are headed by lone parents, as compared with the European average of 4.4%.

The Roma population

No data provided.

Other disadvantaged ethnic minority groups

No data provided.

Migrants

There are around 100 000 migrants in Finland.

The rural population

No data provided.

People with disabilities

No data provided.

Women in trafficking and prostitution

No data provided.

Homelessness

No data provided

Finland (continued)

Domestic violence

No data provided.

Population of Finland

No data provided.

France

Available national estimates of the size of some of the main disadvantaged groups of women at risk of poverty and social exclusion in France

Unemployed women

In 2004, there were 1.4 million unemployed women, i.e. a women's unemployment rate of 11.1% ; 51.4% of the unemployed were women.

Inactive working-age women

18.4 million women are economically inactive (all ages); 2.5 million women between 20 and 59 years were 'housewives' in 1997 (INSEE, 1998).

Young women (15 to 24 years)

3.8 million, i.e. 12.4% of all women.

Older women aged 55+ years

Older women of working age (55 to 64 years): 3.3 million (10.6% of all women).
Older women 65 years and over: 5.8 million (18.9% of all women).

Lone parents

1.5 million (16.9% of families), of whom 86% are lone mothers.

The Roma population

Between 250 000 and 300 000 (no gender breakdown).

Minority groups

4.3 million foreigners, of whom 46.9% are women.

The rural population

14.3 million in 1999

People with disabilities

5.4 million (estimation), of whom 52.6% are women.

Immigrant population

No data provided.

Women in trafficking and prostitution

There are an estimated 15 000 to 18 000 prostitutes in France, of whom 7 000 are in Paris; 12 000 to 14 000 are on the streets (3 000 to 4 000 are 'underground', i.e. in flats and hotels, etc.); 600 are men, mainly transvestites; 50% are foreigners, and trafficking from eastern Europe is on the increase. (It is estimated that between 250 000 & 500 000 women are concerned by trafficking that passes through France.)

Homelessness

According to the 1999 census, 221 846 people lived in mobile accommodation, a hotel room or makeshift shelter. A third (37%) of the homeless, who use helping services, are women. They rarely sleep in the street, because accommodation institutions concentrate primarily on women and young people. Only 7% of the homeless who live in the street or makeshift shelters are women

Domestic violence

The national survey on violence against women is the first French statistical survey. It concerned 6 970 women between 20 and 59 years. 10% of them – both in couples and separated – said they had been victims of violence: insults (4%); psychological pressure (37%); physical aggression (2.5%); rape and imposed sexual practices (0.9%). Adult women are subjected to most psychological, physical and sexual violence in couples. 'The term "battered wives" does not take into account the real situation concerning marital violence, because moral harassment plays an important role' (Jaspard, 2001). It should be noted that all categories are concerned, even if violence sometimes takes different forms.

Population of France (2004 estimate)

No data provided.

Germany

Available national estimates of the size of some of the main disadvantaged groups of women at risk of poverty and social exclusion in Germany

Unemployed women
In June 2005, the female unemployment rate was 12.2%. The average figure over 2004 was 1 932 451 (10.1%).

Inactive working-age women
9 438 000 women aged 15 to 65: 63% of all inactive people are women; 22.4% of the overall female population.

Young women (16 to 24 years)
The number of young women aged 15 to 25 is 4 647 000 (11% of the overall female population).

Older women aged 55+ years
No data provided.

Lone parents
2 502 000 lone parents of whom 1 884 000 are women (75%); 4.4% of the overall female population are lone parents.

The Roma population
No data provided.

Other disadvantaged ethnic minority groups
No data provided.

Migrants
3 501 000 (47.7% of the foreign population, 8.3% of the overall female population).

The rural population
No data provided.

People with disabilities
No data provided.

Women in trafficking and prostitution
No data provided.

Homelessness
No data provided.

Domestic violence
No data provided.

Population of Germany
No data provided.

Greece

Available national estimates of the size of some of the main disadvantaged groups of women at risk of poverty and social exclusion in Greece

Unemployed women
314 900 persons aged 15 and over, according to the labour force survey 2005 (first quarter).

Inactive working-age women
1 648 100 persons aged 15 to 64, according to the labour force survey 2005 (first quarter).

Young women (15 to 24 years)
745 697 persons aged 15 to 24 years, according to the 2001 population census.

Older women aged 55+ years
633 802 persons, according to the 2001 population census.

Lone parents
61 000 households in 2001: 91% were women (56 400) and of these 73% were aged 25 to 49 years according to the ECHP. Lone-parent households represent 4% of all households with dependent children in Greece against an EU-15 average of 9%.

The Roma population
250 000 to 300 000 persons (2001 integrated plan of action for the social integration of Greek Gypsies). No gender breakdown.

Greece (continued)

Minority groups

There are no available data for the size of **minority groups**. Since 1951 the National Statistical Service of Greece does not record ethnic, religious or linguistic minorities. The Muslims of Thrace is the only **officially recognised** minority through the 1923 Treaty of Lausanne, signed between Greece and Turkey after the 1922 war. According to a governmental estimate, this minority comprises 98 000 persons, out of which 50% are of Turkish origin, 35% are Pomaks (a group speaking a Slavic dialect and having espoused Islam during the Ottoman rule) and 15% are Roma.

Rural population

1 999 000 persons aged 15 years and over, according to the labour force survey 2005 (first quarter).

People with disabilities

Inactive disabled population of working age (15 to 64 years): 408 506 persons with disability or serious health problems, of which 162 799 men and 245 707 women, were recorded by a survey based on data from the labour force survey 2001 (second quarter).

Immigrant population

It rose to 762 191 persons, of whom 415 552 were men and 346 639 women in 2001, according to the population census. At the end of 2004 the number of immigrants was estimated at 1 150 000, including EU and non-EU nationals. They represented 10.3% of the total population.

Women in trafficking and prostitution

There were 19 400 forced and 3 300 non-forced prostitutes in 2000.

Homelessness

There are no official statistics for the number of **homeless**. Research data suggest that the number of roofless people, those in temporary shelters and people rotating between refugee camps, street living and extremely marginal accommodation is approximately 11 000, of whom 3 000 are Greeks and 8 000 aliens (Sapounakis, 2004).

Domestic violence

There are no official statistics on the number of female victims of **domestic violence**. According to the findings of a nation-wide survey conducted in 2002–03 among a representative sample of 1 200 women aged 18 to 60 years, 56% of the women interviewed often or sometimes experienced verbal and/or psychological violence, 3.6% often or sometimes suffer physical abuse and 3.5% are often or sometimes forced into sexual contact by their spouse or partner (Artinopoulou et al. 2003).

Population of Greece (2004 estimate)

Not data provided.

Hungary

Available national estimates of the size of some of the main disadvantaged groups of women at risk of poverty and social exclusion in Hungary

Unemployed women

142 800 (1.42% of the national population).

Inactive working-age women

1 480 000 women of working age (15 to 59 years) are inactive, constituting 15% of the national population. If we use the 15 to 64 age bracket, the ratio increases significantly, as 46% of women aged 15 to 64 are inactive.

Young women (16 to 24 years)

647 400 young women aged 15 to 25 (6.5% of the national population).

Older women aged 55+ years

664 000 women aged 55 to 64 (6.6% of the national population).

Lone parents

3.8% of households, 88% of which are lone mothers (413 700 lone mothers, 56 400 lone fathers).

The Roma population

The Roma are the biggest minority group in Hungary, estimated in representative surveys at 570 000 in total (balanced gender ratio) (6% of the national population), up from 320 000 in 1971. A lower number are recorded in the 2001 population census, based on optional self-assessment

Other disadvantaged ethnic minority groups

No data provided.

Hungary (continued)

Migrants
15 000 to 20 000, approximately 50 to 56% are women.

The rural population
Village inhabitants: women 1 829 000 women, 1 730 000 men.

People with disabilities
Total 577 000: 294 000 women, 283 000 men.
Based on 2000 census.

Women in trafficking and prostitution
No data provided.

Homelessness
No good data available. There are 6 167 shelter accommodation places, but this underestimates homelessness.

Domestic violence
An estimated 1 million women have experienced domestic violence. The national expert reports a lack of extensive research activity in this field.

Population of Hungary
10 116 700 on 1 January 2004.

Iceland

Available national estimates of the size of some of the main disadvantaged groups of women at risk of poverty and social exclusion in Iceland

Unemployed women
Female unemployment rate 2004: 2.5%.

Inactive working-age women
No data provided. NB: the expert gives numbers on unemployment and social assistance receipt rather than on the absolute numbers in the various disadvantaged groups.

Young women (16 to 24 years)
13 000 (17% of the female labour force) in 2004.

Older women aged 55+ years
12 400 (16% of female labour force) in 2004.

Lone parents
11 902 (16.5% of all nuclear families) in 2003.

The Roma population
No data provided.

Other disadvantaged ethnic minority groups
No data provided.

Migrants
Immigrants constitute 1.7% of the total population and 3% of the labour force.

The rural population
No data provided.

People with disabilities
No data provided.

Women in trafficking and prostitution
No data provided.

Homelessness
No data provided.

Domestic violence
No data provided.

Population of Iceland
No data provided.

Ireland

Available national estimates of the size of some of the main disadvantaged groups of women at risk of poverty and social exclusion in Ireland

Unemployed women
In 2004, 3.9% of women were unemployed.

Inactive working-age women
In 2003, the female inactivity rate (aged 16 to 64) was 41.6%.

Young women (16 to 24 years)
2004 estimates show that 315 200 women were aged 15 to 24.

Older women aged 55+ years
2004 estimates show that 442 000 women were aged 55+.

Lone parents
In 2004 there were 117 200 lone parents with children under 20, of whom 106 500 (90.9%) were women. Female lone parents comprise 3.3% of the population.
NB: the Irish expert report provides data on employment rates and at-risk-of-poverty rates for some disadvantaged groups.

The Roma population
No data provided.

Other disadvantaged ethnic minority groups
2002 census data estimates the Traveller population at 0.6% of the population, 0.4% of the female population.

Migrants
Data for 2002 show 5.8% of all persons aged 15+ are non-Irish (5.6% of women) and that over 5% of the female labour force aged 15+ are immigrants.
The number of work permits issued to non-EEA nationals increased from 6 250 in 1999 to 47 551 in 2003, an increase of more than 700% , three-quarters of these in low-paid jobs, for example 25% in the catering sector (Ruhs 2005). Between May 2004 and April 2005 (the year following enlargement) over 85 000 people from the new Member States were allocated personal public service (PPS) numbers, some of whom may have been already living in Ireland. The largest proportion of those applying for PPS numbers were from Poland (over 40 000) followed by Lithuania (18 000) and Latvia (9 000) (Ruhs 2005). Immigration levels are likely to continue to increase over the coming years.

The rural population
Data in appendix concerns employment levels and sectoral distribution in rural areas.

People with disabilities
Over 9% of women over 15 years live with a disability.

Women in trafficking and prostitution
No data provided.

Homelessness
No data provided.

Domestic violence
No data provided.

Population of Ireland
No data provided.

Italy

Available national estimates of the size of some of the main disadvantaged groups of women at risk of poverty and social exclusion in Italy

Unemployed women
Total: 10%
Female unemployment rate in the south of Italy: 20.3% (2005, first quarter)
Youth female unemployment rate in the south of Italy: 47.2% (2005, first quarter)

Inactive working-age women
No data provided.

Italy (continued)

Young women (15 to 24 years)
No data provided.

Older women aged 55+ years
No data provided.

Lone parents
No data provided.

The Roma population
No data provided.

Minority groups
No data provided.

The rural population
No data provided.

People with disabilities
No data provided.

Immigrant population
Estimated 500 000; women constitute a very large share.

Women in trafficking and prostitution
No data provided.

Homelessness
No data provided.

Domestic violence
No data provided.

Population of Italy
No data provided.

Latvia

Available national estimates of the size of some of the main disadvantaged groups of women at risk of poverty and social exclusion in Latvia

Unemployed women
The unemployment rate of women was 10.7% in 2003.

Inactive working-age women
Female activity rate: 64.7% in 2003.
Inactive people who want to find a job: 10.2% of men, 14.5% of women.
In the second quarter of 2005, 19.8% of women were inactive (p. 77).

Young women (16 to 24 years)
15.1% of the total population are aged 15 to 24.

Older women aged 55+ years
17.9% of the total population are aged 50 to 64; 15.9% are over 65.

Lone parents
4% of the total population live in single-parent households.

The Roma population
No data provided.

Other disadvantaged ethnic minority groups
No data provided.

Migrants
No data provided.

The rural population
No data provided.

Latvia (continued)

People with disabilities
No data provided.

Women in trafficking and prostitution
No data provided.

Homelessness
No data provided.

Domestic violence
No data provided.

Population of Latvia
2.32 million at the end of 2004.

Liechtenstein

Available national estimates of the size of some of the main disadvantaged groups of women at risk of poverty and social exclusion in Liechtenstein

Unemployed women
June 2005: 360 (a 3% unemployment rate).

Inactive working-age women
No data provided.

Young women (16 to 24 years)
No data provided.

Older women aged 55+ years
No data provided.

Lone parents
920 (7.08%) of 13 000 households are single-parent households. Approximately 95% are headed by women.

The Roma population
No data provided.

Other disadvantaged ethnic minority groups
No data provided.

Migrants
About 13 400 people (45% of all employees), commute to work in Liechtenstein on a daily basis.

The rural population
No data provided.

People with disabilities
No data provided.

Women in trafficking and prostitution
There have been no cases of trafficking in women reported in Liechtenstein since 1999. As regards prostitution, from 1999 until 2002 Liechtenstein provided mutual legal assistance in three cases, two requests for assistance originating in Switzerland and one in Austria. This is the only information available on women in trafficking and prostitution.

Homelessness
No data provided.

Domestic violence
29% of women questioned have already experienced violence on one or several occasions.

Population of Liechtenstein
Approximately 34 300.

Lithuania

Available national estimates of the size of some of the main disadvantaged groups of women at risk of poverty and social exclusion in Lithuania

Unemployed women
93 800 (50.9% of the unemployed).

Inactive working-age women
The total number of inactive women in 2004 aged 15+ was 744 500 (61.2% of the total number of inactive people).

Young women (16 to 24 years)
At the beginning of 2005, the total number of females aged 15 to 24 was 257 821; during the past year it has decreased by 615. This age group makes up 14.1% of the total female population.

Older women aged 55+ years
At the beginning of 2005, the total number of females aged 55 to 64 was 201 228 (11% of the total female population). The total number of females aged 65+ was 339 887 (18.6% of the total female population).

Lone parents
Single parents make up 4.5% of the total population. The 2001 population census data record the total number of one-parent families as 65 379. These families make up 12.8% of households with children under 18. Lone mothers with children (total number of households 60 998) make up 93% of lone-parent families.

The Roma population
According to the 2001 population census data, the total number of Roma population was 2 571 (0.07% of the total population).

Other disadvantaged ethnic minority groups
According to the 2001 Population census data, the total number of Poles was 234 989 (6.74% of the total population); Russians 219 789 (6.31%), Belarusians 42 866 (1.23%); Ukrainians 22 488 (0.65%); Jews 4 007 (0.12%); Germans 3 243 (0.09%); Tatars 3 235 (0.09%).

Migrants
No data provided under this heading. See data on other disavantaged ethnic minority groups.

The rural population
At the beginning of 2005 the total number of rural inhabitants was 1 143 900, of whom 589 700 (51.6 %) were women. The rural population makes up 33.4% of the total population, and has even increased during the transitional period (it was 32.3% in 1989).

People with disabilities
According to the 2001 population census, the total number of disabled persons was 262 900, of whom 138 700 (52.8%) were women.

Women in trafficking and prostitution
According to various estimations there are 3 000 to 10 000+ prostitutes in Lithuania. According to Europol, every year approximately 1 200 Lithuanian women fall victim to human trafficking or leave the country against their will.

Homelessness
According to the 2001 population census data, 1 250 Lithuanian inhabitants were considered homeless, 25% of whom were women. A narrow definition is used, so these statistics are likely to underestimate the phenomenon.

Domestic violence
Official statistics only record domestic violence when the victim files a complaint. According to the latest survey evidence, 63.5% of Lithuanian women have experienced (on at least one occasion) physical violence, sexual harassment or 'threatening behaviour'. The expert also presents data on rape.

Lithuania population
At the start of 2004, the total population was 3.4 million.

Luxembourg

Available national estimates of the size of some of the main disadvantaged groups of women at risk of poverty and social exclusion in Luxembourg

Unemployed women
4.6% of working-age women are unemployed.

Luxembourg (continued)

Inactive working-age women
45.5% of working-age women are inactive.

Young women (16 to 24 years)
13% of the population (439 539).

Older women aged 55+ years
Aged 55 to 64 years: 10% ; aged 65+ years: 14%..

Lone parents
The proportion of lone-parent households stands at around 7%. More than 80% of these households are headed by women (80% in 1985, 85% in 1999).

The Roma population
According to Machiels (2002), there was estimated to be between 200 and 500 Roma in Luxembourg in 1994 (0.05 to 0.12% of the resident population).

Other disadvantaged ethnic minority groups
No data provided.

Migrants
No data provided.

The rural population
Agriculture accounts for 1.4% of employment in Luxembourg.

People with disabilities
In 2002, there were 19 672 beneficiaries of disabled pensions (12 855 men, 6 817 women).

Women in trafficking and prostitution
The newspaper d'Lëtzebuerger Land estimates that there are about 400 women in prostitution.

Homelessness
According to the Ministry of Employment, there are at least 200 homeless people in Luxembourg (2004).

Domestic violence
Police figures show that between 1 November 2003 and 31 August 2004, there were 239 police interventions for domestic violence, of which 233 concerned people from the same household: 67% were married and 20.4% were cohabiting. In the majority of cases, the aggressor was the partner of the victim.

Population of Luxembourg
No data provided.

Malta

Available national estimates of the size of some of the main disadvantaged groups of women at risk of poverty and social exclusion in Malta

Unemployed women
Employment rates January to March 2005: 79.5% for men, 37.5% for women.

Inactive working-age women
No data provided.

Young women (16 to 24 years)
No data provided.

Older women aged 55+ years
No data provided.

Lone parents
No data provided.

The Roma population
No data provided.

Other disadvantaged ethnic minority groups
No data provided.

Malta (continued)

Migrants
No data provided.

The rural population
No data provided.

People with disabilities
No data provided.

Women in trafficking and prostitution
No data provided.

Homelessness
No data provided.

Domestic violence
No data provided.

Maltese population
No data provided.

The Netherlands

Available national estimates of the size of some of the main disadvantaged groups of women at risk of poverty and social exclusion in the Netherlands

Unemployed women
7.3% of women.

Inactive working-age women
30.8% of the female population in the Netherlands. *Source:* Key indicator 24, quarterly labour force data (QLFD), Eurostat.

Young women (15 to 24 years)
17.6% of the female population in the Netherlands.

Older women aged 55+ years
Aged 65+ years: 1 308 841 women.

Lone parents
5.8% of the female working-age population are lone parents: 1.0% of the male working-age female population are lone parents.

The Roma population
No data provided.

Other disadvantaged ethnic minority groups
No data provided.

Migrants
About 10% of the female working-age population are from disadvantaged ethnic minority groups.

The rural population
No data provided.

People with disabilities
There are almost 1 million disabled people in the Netherlands: 45% of these are women.

Women in trafficking and prostitution
There are no reliable figures on women in trafficking.

In 1997, the number of prostitutes in the Netherlands was estimated to be 25 000; 40 to 60% of these are thought to be of foreign origin. Most of these foreign prostitutes are from countries outside the European Economic Area. It is estimated that the majority of these foreign prostitutes operate illegally.

The Netherlands (continued)

Homelessness

There are no official statistics on the level of homelessness. Based on different surveys, SCP (1998) estimated that there were 25 000 homeless people in the Netherlands; 10 to 15% of these are thought to be women.

Domestic violence

Based on a select sample of 1 005 men and women between 18 and 70 years old, it is estimated that 46% of the women and 43% of the men were once the victim of non-incidental domestic violence.

Dutch population (2004 estimate)

16 258 000. *Source:* Eurostat, first demographic estimates.

Norway

Available national estimates of the size of some of the main disadvantaged groups of women at risk of poverty and social exclusion in Norway

Unemployed women

3.9% of women, 4.9% of men.

Inactive working-age women

23% of women aged 25 to 66 are not in the labour force (labour force survey, 2005).

Young women (16 to 24 years)

2 333 293 **aged 15 to 24** (11.9% of the total female population) (population statistics).

Older women aged 55+ years

No data provided.

Lone parents

77 000 lone mothers, (15% of all mothers with children aged 0 to 15).

The Roma population

No data provided.

Other disadvantaged ethnic minority groups

No data provided.

Migrants

148 600 immigrant women, (6.5% of all women).

The rural population

22% in sparsely populated areas (Statistics Norway).

People with disabilities

14% of women aged 16 to 66 are disabled.

Women in trafficking and prostitution

2 500 women are prostitutes (uncertain estimates).

Homelessness

Estimated 6 200 (*Source*: E. Dyb, *Dagbladet*, 23.12.2002).

Domestic violence

1% of married/cohabiting women report being subjected to violence from family member(s) over the past year (Level of living survey, 1997).

Norwegian population

4 606 000 (1.1.2005).

Poland

Available national estimates of the size of some of the main disadvantaged groups of women at risk of poverty and social exclusion in Poland

Unemployed women

1 568 536

Inactive working-age women

8.684 million (60.5% of inactive people are women).

Young women (16 to 24 years)

2002: 2.014 million in the age group 15 to 24 (53% of women in this age category are inactive).

Older women aged 55+ years

2002: 4.371 million (61.9% of women in this age category are inactive).

Lone parents

2002: 1.798 million lone mothers; 232 000 lone fathers.

The Roma population

2002 census: 12 900. Other source: 20 000. (Both are under 0.5% of the population.)

Other disadvantaged ethnic minority groups

Ethnic and national minorities represent a small percentage of the population (3.3% in 2002). Persons born abroad constitute 2% of Polish society, where the most frequent foreign birth countries are: Ukraine, Belarus, Germany, Latvia, Russia, France and the United States. The most numerous nationalities that emerged from the 2002 national census, are German (over 152 000), Belorusian (over 48 000), Ukrainian (31 000), Silesian (over 173 000) and Roma (nearly 13 000). Minorities may face severe obstacles to full participation in society, although studies and data refer mostly to the Roma.

Migrants

International migration 2004: total immigrants 9 495 persons; 4 800 male, 4 695 female. More people emigrate from Poland than immigrate to the country, resulting in a (negative) net migration of – 9 382 persons.

The rural population

2004: 7.375 million women and 7.315 men lived in rural areas. 12.327 women lived in urban areas.

People with disabilities

2002: 5.457 million disabled people (2.568 million male, 2.888 million female).

Women in trafficking and prostitution

Estimates range from 7 000 to 15 000, approximately 30% of whom are of foreign origin. It is estimated that 60% of foreign female prostitutes in Poland are victims of trafficking. An estimate puts the number of Polish women trafficked out of the country each year at 10 000.

Homelessness

Estimates range from 25 000 to 80 000 people.

Domestic violence

Police statistics 2004: 88 388 female victims, 9 214 male victims.

Polish population

Mid-2004: 38 180 000, of whom 19 702 000 were women.

Portugal

Available national estimates of the size of some of the main disadvantaged groups of women at risk of poverty and social exclusion in Portugal

Unemployed women

3.4% (192 200) of total female population, according to DGEEP (2005).

1.7% (91 000) of women are long-term unemployed, according to DGEEP (2005).

Inactive working-age women

Age group 15 to 44: 650 000 (INE, 2004).

Age group 45 and over: 1 439 200.

Young women (15 to 24 years)

No data provided; 50 000 young unemployed women (0.9%), according to INE (2005).

Older women aged 55+ years

In 2004, there were 676 706 women aged 55 to 64, representing 11.1% of the total female population, according to INE (2005).

In 2001, there were 994 207 women aged 65 and over, representing 18.6% of the total female population, according to the 2001 census (INE). The estimate for 2004 is 1 041 615 (19.2%).

Lone parents

2001: 353 971 lone-parent households (11.5% of all households), 307 801 of which are lone-mother households, corresponding (86.7%).

The Roma population

Estimated at 40 000 for the total Roma population, but no breakdown by gender is available.

Minority groups

No data provided.

The rural population

16% of women in 1994/95 (Carrilho et al. 2002).

People with disabilities

322 240 (5.6% of women) in 2001 (Goncalves, 2003).

Migrants

The immigrant population with a legal status of resident in 2005 was 250 697 (138 046 men, 112 651 women). This figure represents around 2.5% of the total population.

Women in trafficking and prostitution

The most recent study carried out on this subject does not provide any estimate. One of the conclusions derived from the analysis of judiciary sources, press news and interviews with ONG volunteers is that the prostitution market in Portugal is being revitalised by international traffic, from east European countries (since the late 1990s), from Brazil (for the past two or three years) and, to a lesser extent, from Nigeria and Ghana (since 1998).

Homelessness

The study carried out by Dragana Avramov, in the early 1990s, estimated that 3 000 people were homeless on any one day of the year or 4 000 over the course of a year, i.e. 3.4 per 10 000 of the population, the second lowest rate in the EU. However, the proportion of people living in emergency accommodation is estimated to be about 1% (DEPS, 1994; http://www.euro.who.int/document/e62041.pdf). The international aid agency, Eagle Aid, announces in fund-raising advertisements that it gave support to 2 500 homeless people in Portugal. A study carried out in Lisbon points to 1 366 homeless persons, of which 11.9% were female (and 30% of undetermined sex). The authors indicate, however, that the number of women is increasing. The age group 20 to 40 years accounts for 64.5% of them (LNEC, 2001).

Domestic violence

Five women die each week in Portugal as a direct or indirect outcome of domestic violence. This is the most frequently quoted number. In a recent survey on costs of violence against women, 451 (30%) of the 1 503 women

Portugal (continued)

interviewed declared that they had been victim of some kind of violence over the previous 12 months. From those, 180 (40%) had been attacked (physically or psychologically) by their husbands (Lisboa, 2003). The three more quoted socio-occupational groups of the aggressors were industry workers (18.3%), employees in the services sector (10.5%), managers and high professionals (9.4%). This social distribution confirms the transversal nature of the violence against women in Portuguese society.

The population of Portugal

10 529 300 (2004 estimate).

Romania

Available national estimates of the size of some of the main disadvantaged groups of women at risk of poverty and social exclusion in Romania

Unemployed women

231 100 women (41.6% of all unemployed); the unemployment rate was 5.9% for women, 8.2% for men.

Inactive working-age women

No data provided.

Young women (16 to 24 years)

No data provided.

Older women aged 55+ years

No data provided.

Lone parents

No data provided.

The Roma population

2.5% of the population (based on self-identification). Another estimate is 6.7%.

Other disadvantaged ethnic minority groups

Hungarians (6.6% of population).

Migrants

No data provided.

The rural population

Estimated 4 million people in subsistence farming.

People with disabilities

No data provided.

Women in trafficking and prostitution

No data provided.

Homelessness

2004 estimates of rough-sleeping range form 11 000 to 14 000. Homelessness has been a growing phenomenon for the past 15 years.

Domestic violence

No data provided.

Romanian population

No data provided.

Slovakia

Available national estimates of the size of some of the main disadvantaged groups of women at risk of poverty and social exclusion in Slovakia

Unemployed women

In June 2005, 166 833 women were unemployed (51.26% of the total unemployed). In 2004, the total **employment** rate was 56.9% ; the unemployment rate was 18.1%. (NB: the expert report provides data on the characteristics of the unemployed and wage levels.)

Inactive working-age women

2004 economic **activity** rates: 52.5% of females, 68.5% of males.

Young women (16 to 24 years)

443 752 aged 15 to 25.

Older women aged 55+ years

651 119

Lone parents

No data provided.

The Roma population

378 950, of whom 188 750 (49.81%) are women (based on 2001 census and projections to the year 2005).

Other disadvantaged ethnic minority groups

No data provided.

Migrants

No data provided on the total number. In 2004 there were 4 460 immigrants to the Slovak Republic and 1 586 emigrants from the Slovak Republic.

The rural population

No data provided.

People with disabilities

In 2003, disabled persons represented 5.4% of the overall number of registered unemployed.

Women in trafficking and prostitution

No data provided.

Homelessness

No data provided.

Domestic violence

No data provided.

The population of Slovakia

5 379 455, of whom 2 766 940 (51.44%) are female (based on the 2001 census and projections to the year 2005).

Slovenia

Available national estimates of the size of some of the main disadvantaged groups of women at risk of poverty and social exclusion in Slovenia

Unemployed women

2004 unemployment rate: 6.9% of females, 5.9% of males.
End 2004: 418 000 unemployed women (20.9% of the total population).

Inactive working-age women

The female **activity** rate was 62.1% in 2003.
End 2004: 558 538 inactive women (27.9% of the total population).

Slovenia (continued)

Young women (16 to 24 years)
2002 census: 135 109 young women aged 15 to 24 (6.8% of the total population).

Older women aged 55+ years
2002 census: 107 846 women aged 55 to 64 (5.4% of the total population), 181 563 women aged 65 and over (9.2% of the total population).

Lone parents
2002 census: 19% of all families are lone-parent households, 90 000 headed by women, 15 000 by men.

The Roma population
2002 census: the total Roma population was 3 246 (0.17% of the population). The true figure is estimated at 7 000 to 10 000.

Other disadvantaged ethnic minority groups
No data provided.

Migrants
No data provided.

The rural population
2000: 50% of the total population.
2003: 10.3% of all female employment was in agriculture.

People with disabilities
2001: 168 755 people (8.48% of the total population) were legally defined as disabled. No gender disaggregated statistics are available.

Women in trafficking and prostitution
Very few reported crimes in this area. In 2004, the police prosecuted in 14 criminal offences connected to trafficking.

Homelessness
Interview-based estimate: there are around 400 homeless people in Slovenia.

Domestic violence
Approximately 1 300 women annually experience violence at home. Over their life, 20% of women are exposed to domestic violence.

Slovenian population
End 2004: 1 997 590 in total; 1 020 538 (51.09%) females.

Spain

Available national estimates of the size of some of the main disadvantaged groups of women at risk of poverty and social exclusion in Spain

Unemployed women
1 158 000

Inactive working-age women
10 010 000

Young women (15 to 24 years)
2 756 000

Older women aged 55+ years
65+ years: 4 239 027

Spain (continued)

Lone parents

273 200

The Roma population

Estimated to be 90 000 to 1 000 000 people in total.

Minority groups

No data provided

The rural population

16% of women live in rural areas (less than 10 000 residents) and 33% live in intermediate or rural areas (less than 10 000 residents).

People with disabilities

There are 1 475 201 disabled women and 852 379 disabled men in Spain (MTAS, 2004).This means that 63% of disabled persons are women. The proportion of women among the disabled aged less than 65 is 52%. However, the higher life expectancy of women makes this proportion increase with age, so that women make up 69% of the disabled aged 65 and over (1 083 534 women and 483 641 men).

Immigrant population

1 720 547 foreign women are registered as living in Spain, including:
- 656 617 from Europe (139 116 from Romania),
- 200 965 from Africa (148 232 from Morocco),
- 71 031 from Central America,
- 698 675 from South America (245 449 from Ecuador),
- 67 226 from Asia.

Women in trafficking and prostitution

The total number of prostitutes is estimated to be 300 000 to 400 000 (by unofficial sources since there are no official estimations available).

Homelessness

300 000 people living in the streets, 24% of these are women (unofficial estimation).

Domestic violence

In 2004, the legal authorities recorded a total of 57 527 women as victims of actual gender violence (i.e. as a result of judicial sentences). However, this figure is only the tip of the iceberg. In fact, 11.1% of Spanish women could be technically considered as 'suffering from mistreatment', and the percentage goes up to 15.1% for women aged 45 to 64.

Population of Spain

40 847: 20 013 males; 20 834 females, according to the 2001 census.

Sweden

Available national estimates of the size of some of the main disadvantaged groups of women at risk of poverty and social exclusion in Sweden

Unemployed women

3.3% of 16- to 24-year-old women are unemployed.

Inactive working-age women

In 2003, 668 900 women were 'not in the labour force' (23.8%).

Young women (16 to 24 years)

Data for 31 December 2003 show 523 806 women were aged **15 to 24** (11.6%).

Older women aged 55+ years

Date for 31 December 2003 show 1 453 662 women were aged 55+ (28%).

Sweden (continued)

Lone parents
In 2003, 222 494 single women had a youngest child aged 0 to 17, representing a share of 81.8%.

The Roma population
No data provided.

Other disadvantaged ethnic minority groups
No data provided.

Migrants
12% of the whole population in Sweden are foreign born and around 5% are foreign citizens.

The rural population
No data provided.

People with disabilities
No data provided.

Women in trafficking and prostitution
In the most recent survey conducted by the National Board of Health and Welfare in 2003, it was concluded that street prostitution had decreased since the entry into force of the Prohibition of Purchases of Sexual Services Act in 1998. No significant changes were reported since the first survey in 1999 (NAP/inclusion 2005). However, it is not possible to estimate the number of women in trafficking and prostitution.

Homelessness
A 1999 survey estimated that there were about 8 400 homeless persons, of which about one-fifth were women.

Domestic violence
About 22 000 offences classified as physical abuse of women, three-quarters of which were perpetrated by a person known to the victim, were reported in 2003. Overall, reported physical abuse of women has increased by about 20% in the last 10 years. The increase in reported physical abuse of women is probably due both to increased willingness to report crime and to an actual increase in violence (NAP/inclusion, 2005, p. 8).

Population of Sweden
31 December 2003: 8 975 670 total; 4 529 014 (50.5%) females.

United Kingdom

Available national estimates of the size of some of the main disadvantaged groups of women at risk of poverty and social exclusion in the United Kingdom

Unemployed women
573 000 (4.2% of women) *Source:* labour force survey.

Inactive working-age women
4 742 000 (26.7% of women) *Source:* labour force survey.

Young women (16 to 24 years)
3 344 000 (11% of women; 5.6% of the total UK population). *Source:* labour force survey.

Older women aged 55+ years
Aged 55 to 64 years: 3 344 000 (11% of women; 5.6% of the total UK population).
Aged 65+ years: 5 472 000 (18.5% of women; 9.2% of the total population). *Source:* Age Concern, 2004.

Lone parents
1.9 million of a total of 7.3 million (25% of working-age families with dependent children are headed by a lone parent). The majority (89.5%) are women (1.7 million lone mothers and 173 000 lone fathers), and roughly 10% of working-age women are lone parents. The proportion of mothers who are living in lone-parent households is

United Kingdom (continued)

highest among black Caribbean and black African women and lowest among south Asian women. *Source:* labour force survey 2004, Lindley et al., 2004.

The Roma population

An estimated 200 000 to 300 000 Gypsies and Travellers live in the United Kingdom. To put this into some context, this is of a similar order to the size of Britain's Bangladeshi population (280 000), but substantially smaller than the Black Caribbean and Indian ethnic minority groups. *Source:* Commission for Racial Equality, 2004.

Other disadvantaged ethnic minority groups

The ethnic minority population accounted for 8% (4.6 million) of the total population (58.8 million) in 2001. The ethnic minority population in the United Kingdom are younger on average than the white population, and comprise 9% of the working-age population. The extent and form of disadvantage and gender inequalities varies between the different ethnic minority groups. *Source:* Census data, 2001; Women and Equality Unit, 2005a.

Migrants

Migrants represent a significant and growing minority in the United Kingdom. Currently, 3.6 million people of working age are foreign-born, representing about 10% of the working-age population (or 4.8 million people of all ages; about 8% of the total population). Among those of working age about half are women. Migrants are a diverse group from a wide range of countries and the risk of social exclusion varies but is greater for those from poorer countries and whose first language is not English. *Source:* Department for Work and Pensions, 2003.

The rural population

Just over a quarter (28.5%) of the population in the United Kingdom live in rural areas. The rural population encompasses affluent as well as low-income households in the United Kingdom. People at risk in rural areas tend to face different problems. Housing problems are more to do with affordability than quality; rural employment problems relate to the seasonal nature of some jobs and low pay. Other problems include isolation, poor public transport and limited access to key services.

People with disabilities

The incidence of disability is similar by gender. There are an estimated 3.2 million disabled women of working age in the United Kingdom.

Women in trafficking and prostitution

Research for the government's Home Office in 2000 estimated that up to 1 420 women are being trafficked into the United Kingdom for sexual exploitation each year; NGOs believe the scale of the problem has increased dramatically since the research was completed. The Home Office estimates that up to 80 000 people (mainly women, including young women) are involved in prostitution in the United Kingdom.

Homelessness[1]

Local authorities (local government) have a statutory obligation to house certain categories of homeless people: those with children and certain other vulnerable groups are a priority. Black and ethnic minority households are over-represented among the UK's homeless population and account for 20% (over 30 0000) of all households accepted as 'statutory homeless' in 2004.

The number of women who do not qualify as 'statutory homeless' for re-housing by the local government is significant and rising, although the majority of hostel dwellers and homeless persons are men. Around 10 to 25% of homeless people on the street or staying in hostels are women, and women account for a higher proportion of young single homeless persons (20 to 40%). Homeless women are more likely than homeless men to be from minority ethnic groups.

Domestic violence

The Home Office estimates that two women die each week as a result of domestic violence, and one in four women and one in six men suffer domestic violence at some point in their lives. Results from the British Crime Survey[2] show that 4% of women and 2% of men were subjected to domestic violence in the period 2000–01, and that in total there were 12.9 million incidents of domestic violence committed against women and 2.5 million against men.

United Kingdom (continued)

Population of the United Kingdom

Mid-2003 estimates: 59.5 million (30.4 million females and 29.1 million males).

(1) According to Crisis, homeless women fall into three groups. 'Statutory homeless' women have children or are vulnerable and have been accepted by local authorities as homeless and in need of priority housing. Others sleep on the streets or stay in hostels, and are among the single homeless population. The third group of women stay with relatives or friends and are among the hidden homeless population.

(2) The British Crime Survey is a nationally representative household survey. It includes an in-depth study of sexual and domestic violence called 'the inter-personal violence module', which is collected in a confidential way and includes crimes that are not reported to the police. As such, this self-completion questionnaire gives a more detailed picture of the prevalence and incidence of domestic violence in the United Kingdom. Domestic violence is defined by the survey as 'any violence between current or former partners in an intimate relationship, wherever and whenever the violence occurs. The violence may include physical, sexual, emotional or financial abuse.'

Appendix 3. The multi-dimensional exclusion of the Roma – the example of the Czech Republic

In the main body of this report we discuss thematically the different dimensions of social exclusion across the different countries. Here we assemble the indicators for one country case study – the example of the Czech Republic – to emphasise how the different dimensions of social exclusion coexist and compound one another.

A vastly inferior education

- Roma children are 28 times more likely than children from the majority population to be sent to special education schools, and those who do remain in regular primary school are 14 times more likely to fail.

- Half of the Roma population have not completed education beyond primary level.

Employment

- Low qualification levels mean that employment options are limited and largely concentrated in unskilled and physically demanding work and in seasonal/irregular labour, often as part of the informal economy. Women typically hold several jobs and typical activities include cleaning or door-to-door sales. They are also over-represented in prostitution in the capital.

- There is widespread experience of employers' discrimination – one study shows that 61% of Roma stated they had been refused employment because of their ethnic origin.

- There is little motivation to seek employment in the face of widespread discrimination and limited opportunities.

- Unemployment and long-term unemployment rates are high. Unemployment rates are at least four times higher than for the majority population, reaching as high as 90% for the Roma in some regions; 75% of the unemployed Roma are long-term unemployed (more than 12 months) and 30% have been unemployed for more than four years.

Health

- Poverty and poor lifestyle (poor nutrition, strenuous working conditions, problems of alcohol and drug addiction) expose the Roma to higher rates of certain illnesses.

- High fertility rates place physical demands on women.

- There are above average rates of infant mortality (twice the national average according to 1985 data) and child illnesses.

- Life expectancy is lower for Roma men and women compared with the majority (1980 data: 55.3 years for Roma men and 59.6 years for Roma women compared with 66.8 years and 74 years for the majority population).

Family and community life

- There is a high rate of institutionalised care of Roma children who are removed from their parents. Roma children are 15 times more likely to be in institutionalised care than non-Roma children and account for 50 to 60% of all children in institutional facilities. This is associated with the extreme poverty of their parents but determined by the official state assessments that their parents are unable to provide suitable care. This form of intervention does little to break down the Roma's suspicion of the majority population.

- A growing number of Roma mothers have themselves resided in institutional care.

- Youth crime and drug/alcohol/substance abuse are problematic.

- Roma are socially excluded by the majority population (discrimination, rejection, circulation of negative stereotypes).

- There is little civic engagement and few interest groups to provide representation. This stems from the combination of poor education and limited resources, a cultural tradition of hierarchical authority and separatism within the Roma community, and rejection by the majority population.

Source: Křížková 2005, supplemented by European Commission (2004).

European Commission

Gender inequalities in the risks of poverty and social exclusion for disadvantaged groups in thirty European countries

Luxembourg: Office for Official Publications of the European Communities

2006 – 190 pp. – 21 x 29.7 cm

ISBN 92-79-02572-4